Reshaping Supply
Chain Management
Vision and Reality

Reshaping Supply Chain Management
Vision and Reality

A group of specialists in the industry talk about factors that are reshaping the future of supply change management and how to succeed in today's complex environment

Editors: Tig Gilliam, Mark Wilterding, Colin Taylor, Harris Goldstein, James Kalina, and Karen Butner, Editor-in-Chief

PEARSON

Custom
Publishing

IBM Press Program Manager: Tara Woodman, Ellice Uffer
Cover design: IBM Corporation
Published by Pearson plc
Publishing as IBM Press

IBM Press offers excellent discounts on this book when ordered in quantity for bulk purchases or special sales, which may include electronic versions and/or custom covers and content particular to your business, training goals, marketing focus, and branding interests. For more information, please contact:

U.S. Corporate and Government Sales
1-800-382-3419
corpsales@pearsontechgroup.com.

For sales outside the U.S., please contact:
International Sales
international@pearsoned.com.

Printed in the United States of America.

10   9   8   7   6   5   4   3   2   1

ISBN 0-536-28323-0

2006200163

SB

Please visit our web site at *www.pearsoncustom.com*

PEARSON CUSTOM PUBLISHING
75 Arlington Street, Suite 300, Boston, MA 02116
A Pearson Education Company

Dedication

This book is dedicated to our clients who are changing the
way we live by changing the way they work.

Table of Contents

Preface

Anyone looking for a comfortable career with little change would do well to avoid supply chain management. By its very nature of developing, acquiring, converting, delivering and servicing the products and solutions that customers desire, the supply chain is a truly dynamic environment. For well-run integrated supply chains, the pace of change can be even greater as changes in one aspect or function have a ripple effect up and down the supply chain. In addition, continuous improvement requires a never-rest mindset.

As seen in the IBM Global CEO Study 2006: Expanding the Innovation Horizon,[1] today's business leaders continue to rely on supply chain performance improvement to fund investment in top-line growth and even to be the source of operating model innovation that creates market differentiation. This may seem like a tall order, and it is. However, the best-run supply chains have been able to deliver on this expectation. For example, IBM's own Integrated Supply Chain (ISC) transformation has saved more than US$26 billion for the company since 2002 through concentrated efforts to:[2]

- Drive operational excellence in each supply chain function
- Create innovation in the supply chain operating model through collaboration
- Build a truly integrated, end-to-end supply chain capability and mentality.

These three priorities enabled IBM's ISC to increase value for the company, and these same three priorities form the basis for this collection of articles, research, and interviews assembled for integrated supply chain executives and managers to consider in moving forward. Our articles, case examples and interviews address strategy, process design, collaboration, governance and organization, performance management and enabling technologies that can be used to help build, rebuild and continuously improve each supply chain function. Beyond that, you will see why we believe that functional excellence is necessary but not sufficient. End-to-end supply chain integration and optimization are hallmarks of the most well-run supply chains and will increasingly differentiate supply chain performance in the years to come.

This book is presented in four main chapters:

Chapter 1: Executing differentiated supply chain strategies

Chapter 2: Innovation, the perfect product launch and lifecycle management

Chapter 3: The global sourcing phenomenon

Chapter 4: Perspectives on global logistics.

The chapters include articles written by the IBM Global Business Services Supply Chain management team, as well as interviews with and perspectives from industry executives. A list of further recommended reading from the IBM Institute for Business Value appears near the end of the book.

Tig Gilliam
Global Supply Chain Management Leader
IBM Global Business Services

Acknowledgements

Thanks to the many people who contributed their time and ideas to this volume. Chiefly, of course, we owe a debt of gratitude to the authors of the articles that make up the bulk of the pages. Also deserving of special thanks are the executives who generously agreed to be interviewed about the concepts discussed in those articles:

- Christine Breves, Chief Procurement Officer, Alcoa Inc.
- Farryn Melton, Vice President and Chief Procurement Officer of Amgen; Tyson Popp, Associate Director of Manufacturing Materials for Amgen; and Steven DeClercq, Associate Director of Fill & Finish Material and Contract Manufacturing for Amgen
- Dan Kochpatcharin, Director, eBusiness for Chartered Semiconductor Manufacturing
- Ron Schnur, Vice President of Strategic Sourcing, Coors Brewing Company
- Alan Estevez, Assistant Deputy Undersecretary of Defense for Supply Chain Integration, U.S. Department of Defense
- Mark McDaniel, Vice President, Procurement and Logistics for Supply Chain Management, Halliburton's Energy Services Group
- Linda Cantwell, Vice President, Supply Chain Management Operations, IBM Integrated Operations
- Ramin Eivaz, Vice President Strategic Planning and Demand Chain Management, Kimberly-Clark Corporation.

A special thank you to Julia McManus, IBM Senior Marketing Manager, who facilitated the project from inception to publication.

Authors

Marc Bourdé

Karen Butner

Sean Campbell

Frank Crnic

Dietmar Geuder

Tig Gilliam

Harris Goldstein

Charlie Hawker

James Kalina

Udo Kleemann

Peter J. Korsten

Grace Lin

Robert Luby, Jr.

Robert McCarthy, Jr.

Derek Moore

George Pohle

Shanker Ramamurthy

Christian Seider

Stavros Stefanis

Colin Taylor

Simon Terry

Theo Theocharides

Mark Wilterding

Executing differentiated supply chain strategies

Introduction

By Karen Butner

Today's business environment – from globalization and increased price competitiveness to more demanding operational and financial performance – has increased pressures on supply chain management. The stakes are high, the challenges enormous. To remain competitive in this environment, supply chain executives must execute and deliver differentiating supply chain strategies.

Chapter 1, "Executing differentiated supply chain strategies," discusses how today's leading supply chain executives are achieving differentiation, responsiveness and efficiency. They are accomplishing this through:

- Developing a specialized supply chain strategy focused on a distinct set of core competencies, innovative products and services, and strategic value chain partnerships
- Transforming existing supply chains into customer-driven supply chain networks that are specialized, componentized and integrated
- Shifting toward sense-and-respond supply chain strategies to monitor, manage and optimize supply chain performance, event-by-event.

7

We look at how companies are "Scoring high on the supply chain maturity model" through employing leading practices and performance criteria. We also look at trends in performance measurements such as logistics costs, on-time delivery and cash-to-cash cycle time. We draw a parallel between multi-industry benchmarked results and supply chain maturity in four key areas:

- Product introduction and lifecycle management
- Synchronizing supply, conditioning demand
- Global buying power through strategic sourcing
- Logistics excellence for superior customer fulfillment.

Finally, we discuss developing a well-thought-out plan for how to get there – linking the business strategy goals and objectives to supply chain performance results.

Developing a specialized supply chain strategy

By George Pohle, Peter Korsten and Shanker Ramamurthy

The pressing issues facing today's supply chain business executives are well known: from globalization and pricing pressures to a more demanding marketplace and the proliferation of technology. So what are the keys to success in today's complex environment?

According to a recent global study conducted by the IBM Institute of Business Value,[3] when asked to identify the most critical imperatives of success, many executives named differentiation, responsiveness and efficiency. These imperatives mean that:

- Strong, differentiated value propositions are critical for growth and profitability.
- Organizations must be able to sense and respond rapidly to customer and marketplace changes.
- Cost structures and business processes must be adapted in a flexible manner to maintain productivity and reduce risk.

In today's environment, business models must be geared to achieve all three of these imperatives for success simultaneously. In the past, practical limitations forced companies to gear their business models to achieve only one of these attributes, with significant achievement of the others a strong desire but one that was impractical to implement. Competing on price, for example, tended to rule out highly differentiated products or top-notch customer service. Until recently, such tradeoffs were an undisputed reality of doing business. The barriers of time and distance limited the ability of companies to integrate internal and external capabilities.

TRADITIONAL VERSUS PROGRESSIVE BUSINESS MODEL

Strategically, many companies do not yet feel a sense of urgency to change their business and supply chain designs. Instead, they maintain their traditional assumptions about the nature of the firm and what it means to be a successful player in the marketplace. However, these businesses underestimate just how radically the changes of the past few years are impacting the prevailing competitive dynamics in their industries.

On the other hand, more progressive companies view the tools and capabilities that have emerged over the past decade as fundamental to their strategies and operations. These companies are making it an imperative for their organizations to use these tools and capabilities for competitive advantage and, ultimately, to redefine the competitive dynamics in their industries.

Understandably, years of reliance on the same "hard-wired" business functions and technology infrastructures have made it expensive and time-consuming to change a company's business model. Increasing organizational complexity makes efficiency gains difficult to achieve, and attempts to establish best-in-class capabilities across virtually all parts of the business have left many companies with a lack of focus. In addition, persistent business unit silos saddle others with redundant activities across the enterprise.

The organizations that have gone beyond these challenges are redefining their business models by assembling the best capabilities available in the market. For capabilities that confer the greatest competitive position and profit, these organizations are creating pools of specialized capabilities within the structure of their own enterprises. For capabilities that do not provide competitive superiority or critical levers to profitability, they are establishing relationships with external parties, each of which is a specialist in its own right.

We refer to the business model that is developed based on these internal and external specialists as the specialized enterprise. By eliminating the tradeoffs that executives have traditionally been forced to make between differentiation, responsiveness and efficiency, we believe that the specialized enterprise will fundamentally reshape firms and industries for the 21st century.

SPECIALIZATION IN ACTION: DIFFERENTIATION, RESPONSIVENESS AND EFFICIENCY

By driving the organization toward internal and external specialization, firms can deliver simultaneous, step-change improvements in differentiation, responsiveness and efficiency. These improvements can go beyond the scope of traditional business designs. Differentiation through componentization offers a variety of benefits. Differentiated firms command higher revenues through premium product pricing and new markets. Partnering with specialists improves margins and allows companies to exit non-profitable markets. Maintaining few assets in-house enables the reallocation of resources for investment in more strategic components. The focus and expertise required for differentiation and the ability to control performance offered by a component structure serve as powerful risk mitigators. The key is to analyze the firm's positioning within the overall industry environment and only invest in components that are truly differentiating, driving innovation in these key strategic components while pursing the right partnerships to fill out the rest.

Responsiveness is a second advantage of specialized enterprises. Historically, companies have operated a deliberate business model based on forecasted opportunities and perceived threats while forcing customers to accept the predicted value proposition. In effect, these companies are laden with fixed processes and relationships. This inflexibility boosts the lead time required to introduce new business and hampers the ability to partner effectively. In contrast, specialized enterprises are able to sense and respond rapidly to otherwise unpredictable changes in the market environment and the needs of their stakeholders. These specialized enterprises achieve responsiveness through modularization, eliminating nonessential components and leveraging existing specialists.

Specialized enterprises are also far more efficient than companies with traditional business models. Traditional models solidify operations and organizations in silos. These enterprises invest in assets, seek to build scale across the business and pursue in-house development of capabilities.

The specialized enterprise differs in that it is able to adapt cost structures and business processes flexibly to reduce risk and conduct business at higher levels of productivity, cost control, capital efficiency and financial predictability. This is accomplished by investing primarily in strategic components, while external specialists are selected on an optimal price-performance basis.

This focus on differentiation, responsiveness and efficiency helps specialized enterprises provide much greater value to their customers, employees and shareholders. Customers can benefit through increased choice, greater channel options and personalization of services. They also can receive greater value with faster time-to-gratification. Employees can benefit due to clear promotion paths, opportunities for advancement and training and non-commodity skills. In addition, shareholders can reap benefits from greater revenue growth, premium price-to-earning multiples, long-term investment strength and greater predictability. Clearly, using a specialized enterprise business model allows companies the flexibility needed to help achieve the success imperatives critical to navigating today's complex, competitive and ever-changing environment.

Transformation to consumer-driven supply chain networks

By John Nelson, Simon Terry and Charlie Hawker

The growth and financial strength of consumer products companies over the last century have been based on a single principle: Branded goods are the consumer's first choice across virtually all product categories. However, that tenet doesn't hold true any more in today's rapidly changing environment in which consumers often are more concerned with price and product quality than with brand. This is greatly impacting how consumer products companies do business.

Vigorous expansion has produced a new breed of mega-retailer that is asserting ownership of the consumer relationship as well as placing increased demands on suppliers to deliver higher levels of service. More stringent growth objectives and regulatory requirements are compounding the pressures felt by the industry.

Consumer products companies must take bold steps across their value networks to address these challenges. In particular, the supply chain has a key role to play in fueling consumer product companies' growth and profitability. Yet, in many cases, the supply chain has not adequately evolved to meet the demands placed on it by retailers and consumers. As a result, traditional "one-size-fits-all" supply chains can no longer provide an adequate response to the challenges facing consumer products companies today.

PRESSURE FROM ALL SIDES

Consumer products companies are increasingly being squeezed by changing consumer buying patterns, increased retailer demands, more stringent growth objectives and new regulatory pressures. The supply chain plays an essential role in addressing these demands on the business – yet most companies' supply chains are not structured to do so. Without a transformational roadmap that enables consumer products companies to both restructure their supply chain and generate short-term returns, they will struggle for growth in the future.

Consumers polarize toward both low-cost and premium products

Pronounced shifts in demographics and attitudes are changing consumer buying patterns and increasing their complexity. One change in particular has a substantial impact on the way supply chains should be designed: Where consumers were once content to buy a "pretty good product at a decent price", they are now much more selective and their purchasing patterns have polarized. As consumers seek to optimize their own personal value, they are paying premiums for "meaningful" products that respond to their emotional needs while aggressively looking for "good enough" quality at rock-bottom prices for commodity items. So we have shoppers polarized toward both low-cost products on one end of the spectrum and premium products at the other. Unfortunately, traditional supply chains are ill-equipped to deal with either extreme.

Low-cost products require a company to manage massive volume, whereas premium products necessitate flexibility in planning methods and the physical supply network to anticipate unique market demand characteristics. Traditional supply chains are either too complex and cost-laden to distribute low-cost products effectively or too asset-intensive and inflexible to quickly harness and deploy innovation.

Retailer power and expectations grow

Not surprisingly, retailers are demanding more supply chain prowess from consumer products companies. Their objectives are to synchronize inventory flow to the store shelf in anticipation of shifts in shopper demand and, increasingly, to reduce in-store labor and overall retailer supply costs.

Retailer needs may be as simple as how a pallet will be configured, shrink-wrapped and marked or as complex as how that pallet is loaded on a truck, radio frequency identification (RFID)-tagged and date-sequenced. They also may extend to how product and demand data will be shared and used for analysis and planning. Account-specific requirements often mean that standardization and automation are difficult. Meeting these demands can be complicated and time-consuming, and consumer products companies have less and less ability to resist them.

Consolidation, geographic expansion and an increase in goods sold on promotion are strengthening the relationship that retailers have with consumers and reducing the influence and importance of consumer products companies. When out-of-stock levels on retail shelves are high, particularly when a product is on promotion, consumers often choose other brands. This points to a need for improved service levels or consumers will choose other brands at other stores.

Growth requires handling more volume at even lower cost

As consumer products companies respond to stakeholder demand for growth, they must address two key pressure points. First, companies need to determine how to provide more service and volume in their supply chains at a lower cost. Second, they must address the organizational issues that stem from lack of sufficient resources to support virtually all growth initiatives in the supply chain. Companies need to make choices on where to focus and where to partner.

Over the last few years, consumer products companies have reduced supply chain costs as a percentage of revenue to improve profits in a flat-growth market. Now, to maintain margins while driving growth in demand, companies must reduce supply chain costs further to free funds for new sales and marketing efforts. The pressure on supply chains to "do more with less" becomes even more intense as the traditional approaches to cost-cutting are exhausted.

Regulatory pressures mount

In addition to the general competitive and consumer changes outlined above, compliance (and, in particular, traceability) is becoming more important. There is now tremendous momentum in the industry to react to a wide range of regulatory and political pressures:

- New regulations such as Sarbanes-Oxley create a greater onus to make accurate public disclosures.
- Corporate ethics are becoming increasingly scrutinized by consumers.
- Tariffs and import restrictions are more stringent than ever.
- Restrictions on the use of genetically modified organisms (GMOs) have been tightened.
- The threat of bio-terrorism may lead to new product safety regulations.
- Traceability of raw materials is being demanded by government regulatory bodies in response to public health issues.
- Consumer privacy safeguards are increasingly required by governments and consumers themselves.

The consequences of noncompliance can be significant. Noncompliant consumer products companies could see brands damaged by negative publicity or a major product recall. Retailers could "delist" products, and banks or analysts might view some companies as too high of an investment risk. Finally, noncompliant companies might be hit with significant regulatory penalties, which could lead to increased legal costs and higher insurance premiums. In virtually all of these cases, the key challenge is not simply to comply but to make the required changes in supply chain operations at the lowest possible cost to the organization.

BUILDING CONSUMER-DRIVEN SUPPLY CHAIN NETWORKS

With product development and marketing costs rising constantly, the supply chain must become more dynamic, flexible and cost-efficient. Companies need to tailor their supply networks to increase responsiveness to changing consumer tastes and buying patterns and to deliver greater efficiency and value for commodity products. To accomplish this, companies need to transform traditional supply chains into consumer-driven supply chain networks.

While most consumer products companies have pursued piecemeal initiatives to take costs out of the supply chain, the potential of these ad-hoc initiatives has largely been exhausted. It is critical now to make radical changes to the supply chain to deliver step changes in performance.

The traditional supply chain exists within the "four walls" of an enterprise, where material and information flow linearly along fixed routes starting with the receipt of raw material through to shipment of the customer order. Some supply chains have been extended to share information with trading partners, although these relationships are generally limited to long-established, trusted customers and suppliers.

The consumer-driven supply chain network is best thought of as a dynamic construct of organizations and supply chains that come together, at a given point in time, to provide a seamless pipeline for products and information from source suppliers through to end consumers. This union may be temporary – perhaps for a single transaction – or an enduring alliance. It will consist of multiple partners, each with a role to play: from brand owners, product designers and contract manufacturers to co-packers and other service providers, all of whom, when combined, act as a single entity to deliver the overall business value sought by retail customers and consumers.

KEY CAPABILITIES OF A WORLD-CLASS, CONSUMER-DRIVEN SUPPLY CHAIN NETWORK:

- Close and deep collaboration with customers, suppliers and service providers
- A single consistent set of information (for example, inventories, committed orders and forward production schedules) visible across the whole "supply network"
- Realtime information, blurring the distinction between planning and execution systems
- The ability to make future commitments, not only "available to promise" but also "capable to promise", with online availability, configuration and pricing that take into account all parties within the network
- Elimination of the traditional gaps among supply chain management, customer relationship management and supplier relationship management
- Web-enabled applications to facilitate speed and ease of connectivity
- Automated and intelligent exception-based decision-making and process management
- Focus on profit optimization while maintaining continuity of supply.

To respond to polarizing consumer tastes, companies need to differentiate and focus. To remain relevant and attractive to retailers, companies need to offer higher service levels in a greater range of areas. The leading companies will operate comfortably in a more fluid and complex environment where the line between raw materials supplier, manufacturer and retailer is blurred. To better reach consumers, they will increase the number of channels to market and work efficiently with fragmented distribution volumes. To respond to the incessant drive for innovation, they will shorten product lifecycles and cope effectively with many more product launches. New processes, partnerships and technologies will be instrumental to enabling greater focus, responsiveness and flexibility in the supply chain of the future.

Leaders will rely on data to build insights and drive efficiency, and they will develop a governance structure where the traditional barriers among geographies, divisions and functions are eliminated. And (as if that weren't enough) they will do virtually all of this at lower costs than ever before to maintain margins while investing in growth initiatives or reducing prices. Tackling these challenges is not an option – it is essential for success in the hyper-competitive, increasingly complex and globally integrated marketplace that will emerge over the next few years.

To position themselves effectively, consumer products companies must have a clear view of what to prioritize and where to partner. Therefore, to build a consumer-driven supply chain network, we recommend that companies concentrate on six key areas.

1. *Build "fit-for-purpose"* supply chain networks, which means configuring supply networks in a tailored fashion to deliver innovation and responsiveness for premium brands and high efficiency for mass value products.

2. *Accelerate innovation processes* so new products and promotions can be introduced into stores more cheaply and quickly.

3. *Reinvent the value chain business model* by reconfiguring operations to radically cut costs and proactively meet consumer demands.

4. *Comply with new regulatory requirements* to increase product performance and quality (or face the consequences).

5. *Innovate* and achieve more effective collaboration with retail partners across various process areas.

6. *Exploit technology* in innovative ways to unlock performance improvements across the supply chain.

Transformation to a consumer-driven supply chain network does not happen overnight. It may take years to transform a static, inflexible supply chain into a dynamic consumer-driven supply chain network. But to drive profitability well into the future, this process of change must begin now.

Build "fit-for-purpose" supply chain networks

In a market where consumer shopping patterns polarize into low-cost and premium extremes, consumer products companies need to more precisely align their supply chain capabilities with the specific characteristics of each part of their business, which may vary by product, channel and geography.

A few companies may have it comparatively easy: those with a single brand, a few customers in a few countries, or a very focused portfolio with a homogeneous customer base and the same market position across a number of countries. For such competitors, a single focused supply chain may be all that is needed.

But for the vast majority of consumer products companies – those with multiple brands, customers and markets – the challenge is more difficult. Today's "one-size-fits-all" supply chain cannot accommodate the varied needs both cost-effectively and efficiently. At the same time, operating and managing many different supply chains tailored to each product-customer-market combination is not a viable option since a separate supply chain for each product would clearly be cost-prohibitive and unmanageable.

Consumer products companies need to find a middle ground that leverages common supply chain elements as much as possible while distinguishing those few elements where differentiation is needed. Such an approach allows companies to innovate and helps ensure the quality of premium products while providing the lowest cost operations for price-driven lines. For virtually any given business unit, companies can thus establish a fit-for-purpose, differentiated supply chain that offers the right combination of flexibility, efficiency and cost-effectiveness.

Assess the relevant capabilities

Companies must first assess which capabilities are most relevant to their target market segments. Broadly, supply chain requirements fall into two categories (see Figure 1):

- The "mass value" supply chain caters to the value-driven segment and operates on a low-cost basis. It is designed for low-priced commodity products that are predominantly sold at high volume through major retailers. These products typically do not enjoy strong consumer loyalty, with shoppers purchasing alternative brands if a particular brand is not available on the shelf, thus placing the risk of supply chain problems predominantly on the consumer products company. The primary concern is to provide greater levels of service to the retail customer to support consistent availability of the product on the shelf.

- In contrast, a "sense-and-respond" supply chain is needed to support high-margin, premium brands. It optimizes value, innovation and responsiveness for consumer brands and provides a high level of service for a premium. Production and distribution are tuned to satisfy fluctuating consumer demand levels, and products are often sold through a wide range of channels. Supply chain risk is borne by both retailers and suppliers. Consumers specifically seek out these products and will delay purchases or shop elsewhere if the product is not available, thus requiring consumer products companies and retailers to work together closely.

Figure 1. The consumer marketplace is polarized to opposite ends of the spectrum.

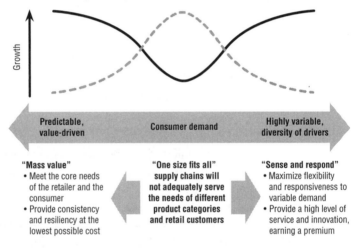

Source: IBM Global Business Services analysis, 2006.

Componentize the supply chain

Next, companies should reassess their existing supply chain capabilities. Because traditional process-oriented analytical techniques reinforce the rigid, linear nature of existing supply chains, a new approach is needed.

Component business modeling (CBM) is a new tool for analyzing a company in terms of its basic activities. A "business component" is a discrete set of business activities that has the potential to operate as a distinct entity. It has a unique purpose and includes the resources, people, technology and know-how necessary to accomplish that purpose. By breaking down current supply chains into business components, consumer products companies will be better able to identify which parts effectively meet market needs and which need to change. To find the best tradeoff between differentiated product availability, economies of scale and manageability, consumer products companies will need to identify those components that need to be differentiated and those that can be common across geographies, product groups and channels.

After determining what supply chain capabilities are required for a given business unit and which components are common or differentiated, the last step is to evaluate the best way to manage each component to optimize operational efficiency and flexibility. The decision on how to best manage a business component is a critical one. Companies have four options when deciding what to do with each component:

- *Achieve superiority* – Invest to gain competitive advantage in areas that are strategic differentiators for the business and where it is essential for the company to become best-in-class.

- *Consolidate* – For activities that are not differentiating to the business but are specialized in the way they are performed at a company level, consolidate these activities within the business to optimize efficiency and consistency.

- *Outsource* – For activities that are generic to the industry and provide little competitive advantage to the business, seek explicit service-level and variable pricing agreements with service providers to benefit from the economies of scale they offer.

- *Leverage specialists* – Where internal capabilities are not unique and best-in-class service providers exist, seek tightly integrated, exclusive relationships with partners.

Accelerate innovation processes

A key facet of consumer-driven supply chain networks is the ability to accelerate innovation and drive greater responsiveness to new market needs. As historical evidence demonstrates, highly innovative companies that have larger proportions of turnover from new products and services tend to grow revenues faster. Given the difficulty of improving the hit rate for new products, to increase the possibility of success, consumer products companies need to drive a higher volume of new introductions. The key is to innovate and renovate more often (see Figure 2).

Figure 2. Accelerating the innovation process.

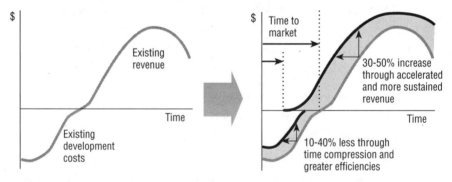

Source: IBM Global Business Services analysis, 2006.

The supply chain is critical to successful and speedy innovation and can help deliver substantial benefits to a company. To help achieve this, supply chain improvements should focus on four key elements:

- *Time to market* – Consumer products companies need a supply chain that enables them to get new products to the store shelves faster than their competitors. The goals should be earlier revenue generation and first-to-market advantage, in terms of both time to "first market" and time to "full market." Leading innovators are using project portals, stage gate processes and technology to enable high-speed development at reduced cost.

- *Internal integration* – Integrated planning and execution among the disparate divisions of a consumer products company can help cut through the red tape that inhibits creativity and innovation. Early involvement of procurement, manufacturing, logistics, customer service and planning from the start will reduce inefficiencies and optimize revenues. Whether it is innovation or renovation, the ability to capture, distribute and reuse knowledge, information and content enterprisewide will prove invaluable. Greater levels of integration – including consistent cross-business metrics – will help deliver project-wide visibility and synchronization across functions and divisions.

- *Collaboration* – Wider collaboration with suppliers, distributors and retailers will be key to achieving new levels of cost and service efficiency. Retailers, in particular, need to be involved early in the new product development process; their cooperation and advice on timing can help determine the success of a new product introduction. It is about more than just virtual teamwork. Companies must consider new ways of working together across functions. They can achieve this by drawing on expertise from suppliers, creative partners and trading alliances and pursuing joint ventures for both idea generation and the execution of innovative strategies.

- *IT enablement* – New technologies enable companies to involve suppliers and partners in idea generation and to execute innovation across the new product development and introduction process. Collaborative applications and business integration middleware are reaching sufficient levels of maturity; however, there is no single solution that meets all requirements. Competitors who seek to build competitive advantage will need to adopt best-of-breed solutions to fill selected gaps, integrating them with legacy systems to enable end-to-end processes and provide global visibility of the innovation "pipeline".

Companies that focus on these four elements can use their supply chain to accelerate innovation to help improve market responsiveness.

Reinvent the value chain business model

Traditional value chains hamper the development of consumer-driven supply chain networks, limiting enterprise flexibility and responsiveness in the face of specific retailer and consumer demands. Thus, companies must redefine the end-to-end value chain and identify more efficient ways of managing the supply chain both to cut costs and to achieve substantial service improvements.

Cost reduction

With traditional cost reduction methods largely exhausted, consumer products companies need to think and act more radically. They need to consider a broader range of activities for cost-cutting opportunities, including those that take place beyond the organization's four walls. There are still sources of untapped potential if companies examine the end-to-end supply chain, exploit new technologies such as RFID, and include suppliers, retailers and the outsourcing of business processes in their assessment.

Service improvement

Even when taking into account all the work that has been done over the last 20 years to synchronize the supply chain, massive amounts of out-of-stocks still occur in the market, representing multibillion dollar opportunities for improvement. While beneficial, the Efficient Consumer Response (ECR) and Quick Response movements, followed by the creation of trade exchanges and the development of Collaborative Planning, Forecasting and Replenishment (CPFR), have not come close to solving the problem.

This issue encompasses out-of-stocks for both newly introduced products and existing products. Predicting new product sales is more art than science, but, at the least, improvement can be made by receiving demand signals early in the product launch and finding ways to quickly integrate those signals into demand planning. For existing products, even more improvement is possible by revamping forecasting and demand planning into a common, new framework.

Opportunities remain for consumer products companies to improve sales by lowering out-of-stocks. The consumer-driven supply chain network enables even better synchronization of supply to improve on-shelf position.

Comply with new regulatory requirements

Consumer-driven supply chain networks must be able to respond quickly to the compliance demands and regulatory pressures generated by consumers, retailers and government. A common and key capability that companies need to develop to meet various compliance requirements is traceability – the ability to identify the location of a finished product after it has entered the distribution network, trace backward to identify the source of its constituent raw materials and track the route of raw materials through the conversion process. Companies may also need to identify other finished products that may have shared a raw material or conversion process.

Most consumer products companies today have some capability to manage traceability issues, although the systems they rely upon generally are manual and paper-based. But while companies can answer some traceability questions, they do not capture enough detail to be able to answer them all, and they certainly cannot answer them quickly.

This issue must be addressed on several fronts. Companies need both the applications to capture the information and an IT infrastructure that can store, cross-link and make the information easily accessible. New capabilities that companies should consider include:

- Manufacturing execution systems to provide improved tracking and lot traceability
- Laboratory information management systems to streamline the capture of lab and R&D data
- RFID-enabled systems to help trace both inbound material and outbound product flow.

The substantial amounts of data that a comprehensive compliance system generates need to be managed effectively. The success of virtually any compliance program will rest on its ability to deliver the necessary requirements at the lowest possible cost. Companies will need to standardize business processes and equipment to reduce deployment time and simplify their rollout. Applying a common approach across the whole organization, with a preference for low-cost, scalable and repeatable application integration, also will help reduce the cost of compliance.

Innovate

A fundamental success factor for the development of consumer-driven supply chain networks is finding new ways of driving innovation, managing the end-to-end value chain and complying with market demands. To help accomplish this, consumer products companies need to develop stronger relationships with trading partners to improve process management and responsiveness to the end consumer.

Many consumer products companies have not wholeheartedly embraced collaborative initiatives and processes. But now it is time for industry executives to think "outside the box" to prepare their organizations to work with retail customers in new ways. By exploiting new capabilities, they can deliver higher value to trading partners and, thus, greater sales and profits for themselves.

SEVEN STEPS TO EFFECTIVE COLLABORATION:

1. Develop alliance management as a core capability, including development of a mechanism to share savings and opportunities between partners.

2. Interact easily and efficiently with partners via broad adoption of industry-wide data standards and data synchronization.

3. Present "one version of the truth" across multiple systems through application and process integration and coordination.

4. Develop end-to-end visibility through realtime, event-driven processing and RFID.

5. Design easy-to-use, scalable solutions (such as workflow, process choreography and portals).

6. Implement internal processes (such as alerts and contingency planning) that can respond to unforeseen events.

7. Create an adaptive organizational structure that can align with individual customers' needs.

Exploit technology

Technology is the underpinning of virtually all the other elements of a consumer-driven supply chain network. However, resources for new technology investment are scarce in consumer products companies today since most IT departments are busy stabilizing current projects and operations. Therefore, they may have little capacity for new development. Nevertheless, it is important that companies find creative ways of reallocating resources to invest in the supply chain technology infrastructure necessary to compete effectively in the future. Specifically, consumer products companies need to address the following three key areas:

- *Fix the current IT architecture* – Consumer product companies' technology architectures are often characterized by disparate business operating models resulting from merger and acquisition activity, complex application and information architectures, large multifaceted projects to support business change and short-term activities that do not lead to benefits realization. Consumer products companies need to clean up their information systems and consider new technology investments such as service-oriented architecture to help facilitate the process.

- *Integrate applications internally and externally* – Consumer products companies need to exploit technologies that give them full visibility across their extended supply chain networks. They must seamlessly integrate internal applications and link to external partners' applications. Doing so will enable them to better respond to both consumer and customer demands as well as provide them with visibility to anticipate changes in market conditions.

- *Link the digital and physical worlds* – Consumer products companies' online planning and execution systems must link to the physical world to sense what is happening to the companies' products. For dynamic response to real-world issues, companies need technologies such as satellite tracking and RFID as well as analytical systems to identify critical problems in service to be able to resolve them rapidly, if possible, or prioritize and escalate them if not.

In the next five to ten years, the consumer marketplace is likely to undergo rapid and extensive change, driven by shifts in consumer patterns, retailer demands and regulatory requirements. Consumer products companies need to radically re-engineer their supply chain into "consumer-driven supply chain networks" just to keep up with these developments and maintain competitiveness. Furthermore, they need to start now, as these changes will take time to implement, and the future will not wait.

CONCLUSION

To be able to achieve their business objectives in today's complex environment, consumer products companies need to accelerate innovation, restructure their end-to-end value chain business model and develop collaborative capabilities to be able to comply with mounting global pressures. Essential foundational elements include developing collaborative trade relationships and investing in a flexible, integrated technology infrastructure. Consumer products companies must prioritize these efforts according to their unique business needs to be able to achieve significant cost reductions, provide optimal customer service and optimize return on investment (ROI).

Each step that consumer products companies take must move them closer to the overall objective of having the capability to respond quickly and efficiently to increasing and rapidly changing demands from both retailers and consumers. By building consumer-driven supply chain networks, they will be well-positioned to respond to today's marketplace challenges and those that are sure to arise in the future.

Sense-and-respond supply chains for optimized performance

By Karen Butner

Successful companies are responsive. They adapt to market changes quickly, remaining nimble in the face of continual economic evolution. Supply chains, too, must be responsive. Yet supply chains – once relatively simple product and information pipelines – are becoming more global and complex. The result is executives face ever-increasing challenges in managing supply and demand as customer needs continually shift.

These challenges span the entire supply or value chain process. In the planning stage, fragmented information hinders synchronization of supply and demand. Ever-shifting global sourcing patterns make it difficult to find low-cost goods. Companies may be forced to build inventory at virtually every stage of the supply chain process due to poor or nonexistent integration with suppliers and contract manufacturers. There is also a lack of global visibility into products in transit and in the pipeline, which interferes with the ability to meet customer service levels. Finally, there's no ability to effectively up-sell or cross-sell across business units and actually condition market demand.

CEOS SEEK INNOVATION TO SUSTAIN GROWTH

When IBM conducted the IBM Global CEO Study 2006 to discover the greatest concerns of CEOs across various industries, top-line growth and profitability topped the list. The study also revealed that CEOs are looking to innovation to drive fundamental change that enables sustainable growth (see Figure 1).[4]

Figure 1. Most common operations innovations.

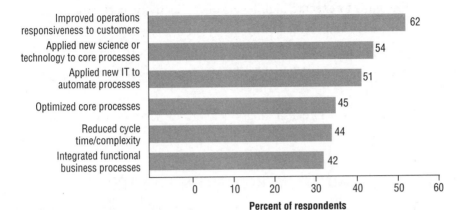

Note: This question was asked of operations innovators only.
Source: IBM Global CEO Study, 2006.

However, few CEOs believe that their organizations are able to react with sufficient speed and agility to changing market conditions and supply chain events. Many rated their organizations as being "less than capable" of responding adequately. CEOs recognize that their organizations need to sense, analyze and respond much more effectively and quickly to market fluctuations if their companies are to remain competitive.

Executives recognize the need to establish effective and proactive real-time responses to evolving market conditions and daily supply-and-demand shifts. To do so and to achieve their business objectives, they're focusing on supply chain responsiveness initiatives. Specifically, they are adopting advanced practices in four focus areas:

1. *Responsive end-to-end supply chains* – The ability to sense and respond with flexibility and speed to virtually any customer demand, market opportunity or external threat.

2. *Variable cost aligned with revenues* – A variable cost structure designed to execute high levels of productivity, cost control, capital efficiency and predictability.

3. *Realtime information* – Gaining realtime access to transactional information to be able to quickly identify exceptions and alert supply chain constituents.

4. *Shared risk* – Orchestrating a network of partners and sharing risks across the network.

SENSE-AND-RESPOND SUPPLY CHAINS FOR IMPROVED RESPONSIVENESS

Some companies are shifting toward sense-and-respond supply chain strategies because sense-and-respond supply chains can monitor, manage and optimize business exceptions – anomalous events that occur within supply chains – with a limited need for human intervention. They can provide event assessment and optimize supply chain performance between planning and execution, based on realtime information. Ultimately, they allow businesses to remain nimble and responsive to shifting demand. And in a proactive business environment, sense-and-respond supply chains can be used to influence market demand.

Sense-and-respond supply chains align strategies and imperatives with ongoing daily activities and decisions. They proactively monitor and observe ongoing supply chain issues, enabling companies to respond quickly to market shifts and proactively pursue potential market opportunities.

A feature of sense-and-respond supply chains is realtime visibility into virtually all transactional event information, allowing companies to quickly identify the root causes of issues. They can sense potential problems and respond with flexibility and speed to infrequent or sudden demands. Sense-and-respond supply chains can dynamically adapt to supply chain shocks through end-to-end visibility and proactive exception management. They can detect company-defined exceptions and alert those affected, which leads to faster resolution. By identifying situations that are designated as out of tolerance, they can determine and execute the appropriate action.

These types of supply chains are characterized by optimized performance and metrics, supply chain visibility, collaborative decision processes, exception management, a variable business structure and knowledge retention. These features are discussed below.

Optimized performance and metrics

The end-to-end supply chain consistently and continuously measures performance. Dashboards report across the entire chain, and those measurements are shared with all the partners and service providers. Daily report cards and alerts provide information regarding exception events. These measurements are then used to gauge supply chain performance on a regular basis with all constituents. Supply chain partners can also use them to monitor key events or groups of events that may miss business expectations. They can proactively measure on-time delivery performance to customers. Sense-and-respond capabilities can also monitor discrete events, make decisions based on business rules and recommend responses; some of those responses can be automated transactional changes.

Supply chain visibility

Sense-and-respond supply chains allow constituents to see virtually all transactional event and performance information. Both executive and operational dashboards aggregate and synchronize information and support collaboration. Integrated workflows model where critical decision points reside and help determine targets and thresholds for event notification. The information available as a result of end-to-end visibility supports exception management decisions and adaptive planning and execution.

Collaborative decision processes

Collaborative decision processes help resolve problems and execute processes when cross-functional supply chain teams – such as suppliers and service providers – are involved. Events are mapped to key decision points within the supply chain processes, and user profiles define who receives action items. The escalation process helps ensure that the appropriate parties are notified to take collaborative corrective action. Dynamic, cross-functional teams monitor performance and analyze event exceptions and trends to determine which changes to make to improve planning and execution.

Exception management

Sense-and-respond supply chains drive problem resolution by proactively detecting exceptions and alerting affected parties. Alert messaging warns decision-makers when an action should be taken in response to an event or if a trend is emerging. When an exception is detected, the system analyzes the event to determine its implications on other parts of the supply chain, such as inventory or service levels. After assessing the implications, the system uses detailed analytics and optimization logic to determine the most effective way to remedy that exception.

Variable business structure

A variable business structure is an organizational construct that focuses on core competencies and supports an open and integrated operating environment. This supports and promotes collaboration with suppliers, service providers and customers by providing virtually all supply chain constituents with current data. Performance and event information is shared on a timely basis so mutual or collaborative decisions can be made quickly. Business processes are low latency – keeping products moving expediently through the supply chain – and are dynamically aligned with core process components and capabilities. Management governance is adaptive; it can change as needs evolve. Those accountable for outcomes perform governance on the basis of context.

Knowledge retention

Cross-enterprise knowledge sharing and knowledge bases support decision-making and identify performance trends and recurring issues. Collaborative knowledge bases provide the foundation for analyzing performance trends and identifying root causes – and how often problems occur – to assist teams in determining corrective action.

CONDITIONING MARKET DEMAND WITH SENSE-AND-RESPOND SUPPLY CHAINS

When companies can move away from reacting to market conditions and take a more proactive stance, they can gain competitive edge. Sense-and-respond supply chains can enable market conditioning through trend analysis and supply-and-demand information. For example, a major high technology firm uses order trends and actual demand to provide early warnings of constraints and excesses. These early warnings result in the company's ability to position itself to condition demand for existing and planned supply.

The sense-and-respond system identifies forecasting events and order events. This provides early warning for demand conditioning. It can correlate and analyze the information and detect early insight into supply constraints and excesses. It will then alert the appropriate parties of exceptions and recommend actions. Based on this information, sales teams adjust selling tactics and supply teams rebalance supplies. The core team is collaborative, composed of members from marketing, operations, procurement, finance and development. They identify supply imbalances, create a conditioning plan in partnership with the geography sales organizations and manage the plan's execution.

GAINING VISIBILITY AND MANAGING EVENTS FOR ADVERTISED CAMPAIGNS

Many retail companies find it challenging to proactively manage advertised campaigns. To help ensure product availability, they must closely monitor:

- Rejected purchase orders or those not confirmed by suppliers
- Products shipped beyond the time frame necessary for store allocation or delivery
- Products shipped to the wrong store
- Advanced shipping notice (ASN) quantities that do not match ordered quantities
- When suppliers cannot meet purchased quantity commitments
- When suppliers indicate a shipment date beyond the required date.

The supplier sends purchase order acknowledgements, inventory status and capacity plans to the retailer. The sense-and-respond system validates the supplier information against business rules and thresholds to determine if the event is critical for the upcoming campaign. If virtually any situation is out of tolerance, the system sends a proactive notification to the merchandise planner. In some cases, the system generates an automatic transaction and sends it to the appropriate supply chain constituent. For example, a late shipment may initiate a shipping request to another logistics service provider, or a purchase order quantity discrepancy may automatically generate a reorder of merchandise from another supplier.

An open and services-based technology architecture incorporates realtime information, data integration, business rules and analytics to optimize supply chain performance (see Figure 2). Intelligent agents detect signals and send responsive transactions, often without manual intervention. The intelligent agents assist in analyzing event exceptions and, through dashboards, allow employees to view exceptions. In some cases, the agents anticipate an event and notify the appropriate party when the event has not occurred; for example, if delivery notification is not received. They support the ability to make either automated or better-informed decisions based on what the exceptions are.

Figure 2. Supply chain sense-and-respond components.

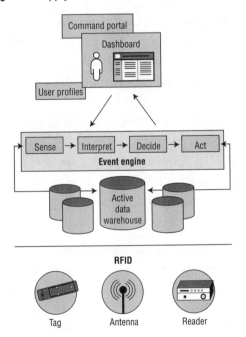

Management dashboards
Portal view to display supply chain performance measurements and alert notifications. Provides access to "drill-down" views of supporting information

Event engine
Tool which provides the foundation for supply chain visibility. Constantly monitors supply chain transaction data. Contains rules required to identify and build event notifications, profiles of notifications and user interaction rules, and thresholds for performance alerts

Active data warehouse
Primary data repository of supply chain integrated information for event engine processing. Updated in realtime as events occur

Product tracking
Technologies, such as RFID, to provide realtime data collection and detection of product in the pipeline. Sends automated messages to the event engine

Source: IBM Global Business Services analysis, 2006.

Analytics detect business trends and support root cause analysis. Optimization components support the planning of actions in reaction to trends and situations. These may include:

- Notification to key business managers
- Changes to operational parameters or business rules
- Reallocation of resources
- Invocation of exception processes or transactions.

These elements serve to optimize supply chain performance.

CONCLUSION

Sense-and-respond strategies and capabilities offer many benefits that can generate both quantitative and qualitative value. For example, constituents can see integrated information and processes, allowing for rapid decision-making and corrective action before problems escalate. This end-to-end visibility also provides the opportunity to proactively identify and resolve problems like inventory gaps and possible out-of-stock issues. Bottlenecks and interruptions – such as a supplier's inability to fill an order prior to a cancellation date – can also be identified and resolved. In addition, because it's easy to see current stock positions, in-transit stock and on-order status, the inventory in the pipeline can be reduced.

Sense-and-respond supply chains can provide continuous performance improvement through measurement, accountability and event notification of pending problems. When performance measures and targets are standardized and aligned, performance excellence confined to isolated silos can be eliminated, and overarching supply chain objectives of synchronous excellence can be met. But the ultimate value of the sense-and-respond approach is supply chain responsiveness – the ability to quickly and effectively adapt to impending threats and opportunities, making companies more nimble and better able to meet the demands of an ever-evolving marketplace.

Scoring high on the supply chain maturity model: Leading practices and benchmarks

By Karen Butner and Dietmar Geuder

Top-performing supply chains have a common trait: the ability to respond quickly to shifts in demand with innovative products and services. To do this, they employ a variety of business strategies and models coupled with leading management practices. They also consistently measure their performance based on such key indicators as:

- Perfect order attainment
- Demand management accuracy
- Time to value
- Cash-to-cash cycle time
- Supply chain cost.

These indicators of supply chain performance are the gauges used to monitor the efficiency of the business.

Leading companies have evolved and transformed their supply chains. They have moved from seeking operational excellence in static and isolated silos to seeking operational excellence across the value chain network to achieving horizontal integration within the company to external collaboration with partners and, eventually, to on demand performance.

According to IBM's 2006 Value Chain Study,[5] supply chain executives' top three objectives remain:

1. Increased profitability
2. Reduced costs
3. Improved responsiveness.

To meet these objectives, the leaders understand that supply chain effectiveness is about more than efficiency and low cost. They understand that revenue growth and profitability are best achieved by creating an integrated value chain with the ability to condition demand and respond to supply chain shifts with innovative products and services.

Many companies are progressing toward the vision of an on demand, customer-driven supply chain – one that is integrated end-to-end across the business and with key customers, partners, suppliers and service providers. The top-performing supply chains are actively transforming their strategies and adopting leading management practices including:

- Coordinating business functions across the supply chain
- Developing mutually beneficial ways to strengthen supply chain relationships
- Synchronizing supply and demand through planning and forecasting
- Managing supply chain cycles
- Developing variable cost structures
- Sharing risks with partners
- Using realtime information to create responsive, customer-driven processes.

SNAPSHOT OF THE FOUR KEY AREAS OF SUPPLY CHAIN MATURITY AND TOP-PERFORMING SUPPLY CHAIN PRACTICES

Let's look now at multi-industry benchmarked results and supply chain maturity in the following four key areas:

- Product introduction and lifecycle management
- Synchronizing supply and conditioning demand
- Global buying power through strategic sourcing
- Logistics excellence for superior customer fulfillment.

We will present survey findings, discuss what leaders are doing to achieve success and include success tips for each of these key areas.

Product introduction and lifecycle management

A key driver of revenue growth is innovation and being able to bring innovative products to the marketplace quickly. This requires a coordinated product launch by multiple functional areas (e.g., product design, procurement, planning and manufacturing/process, sales and marketing) within a company working together. Furthermore, as companies expand their supply, manufacturing and logistics capabilities globally, this requires them to work together in a collaborative manner to deliver these innovative products through virtual networks. Therefore, organizations need to integrate internally as well as externally with suppliers and customers. Thus they can create end-to-end supply chain processes and capabilities with responses better mapped to customer requirements.

Key survey findings

Bringing innovative products and services that meet customer wants and needs to market is the top goal for new product development. The primary strategy for new product development is collaboration with customers to understand their requirements, followed by customer product configuration and specifications for design. Most supply chain executives in the study (97 percent and 90 percent, respectively) consider these practices within their company to be extremely effective.[6]

Identifying and meeting customer requirements is the primary challenge for remaining competitive. Over 56 percent of respondents indicated that the correct identification of customer needs is their most significant management challenge in new product development.[7] To design for customer requirements while maintaining cost control objectives, many manufacturers are incorporating product commonality and reuse techniques with standardization of components. Reusing existing designs and other knowledge assets can help streamline the product development process and, at the same time, significantly improve product quality by standardizing and reusing proven components and assemblies. A formal program of commonality and reuse can also help reduce direct materials procurement costs, speed time to market and improve product quality.

There has been little change in the past three years in developing new products/service innovations (see Figure 1). Growth has primarily been in new customer markets and extensions to existing products. IBM's study shows that new product variations increased 16 percent from 2003, plus average time to market is decreasing for new product variations.[8]

Figure 1. Average time to market for new product variations versus three years ago.

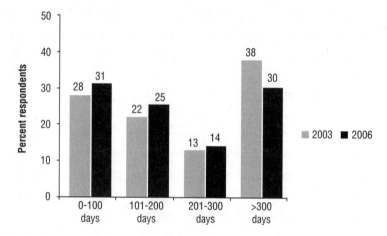

Source: IBM Institute for Business Value 2006 Value Chain Study.

Historically, new product development efforts have concentrated on achieving on-time and on-budget targets. However, IBM's study reveals that a significant proportion of respondents miss their product development schedule targets, and it's getting worse. Likewise, a significant proportion of respondents miss their product development budget targets, and, here as well, performance is falling.

What the leaders are doing to achieve product launch success

As companies evolve up the supply chain maturity model toward an on demand supply chain, they realize that business performance is directly related to their ability to bring superior products and services to market in a cost effective manner. Many of the leaders are implementing the following practices:

- Collaborating with customers to explicitly define requirements
- Including logistics and "get-to-market" requirements in product/ service design
- Integrating with suppliers and supply chain service providers during design, development, production and service
- Using componentization and standards to develop variations on products at lower costs
- Outsourcing design and development activities for non-core products and/or components.

SUCCESS TIP:

Achieve product launch success through the integration of product/ service lifecycle management activities with customers, suppliers and service providers, superior products/services innovation and effective cost management.

Synchronizing supply and conditioning demand

When companies move away from reacting to market conditions toward a more proactive stance, they create a sharp competitive edge. Responsive supply chains can help enable market conditioning through trend analysis and supply-and-demand information. They can achieve this by using order trends and actual demand to provide early warnings of constraints and excesses, identifying key forecasting events and order events. This activity provides advanced insight for demand conditioning. The processes and systems can correlate and analyze the information and detect likely supply constraints and excesses, then alert the appropriate parties of exceptions and recommend actions. These early warnings allow the company to position itself to condition demand for existing and planned supply.

Demand-driven synchronization of supply chain planning and execution activities, in collaboration with suppliers and partners, enables companies to balance demand and supply and to optimize customer service and inventory levels by continuously planning, in real time, across organizational boundaries. The result is a feasible, synchronized plan.

Key survey findings

Political/economic uncertainty is affecting costs and lead times (see Figure 2). Trending indicates that these influences are affecting sales less, but they are continuing to impact supply chain effectiveness.

Figure 2. Impacts of political/economic uncertainty on supply chain efforts over the past three years.

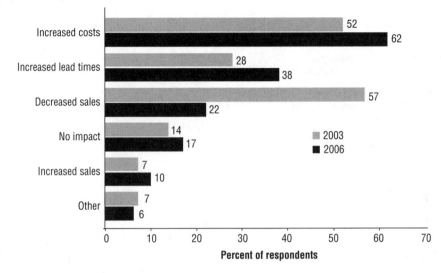

Source: IBM Institute for Business Value 2006 Value Chain Study.

Companies are employing customer-focused practices to synchronize customer demands for product delivery (e.g., the "perfect order") while balancing the costs associated with excessive inventory in the pipeline. Many companies are using continuous replenishment programs to maintain customer-specified levels of products on the shelf and direct material inventories in supply. As shown in Figure 3, they are finding these programs to be extremely effective.

Inventory planning and deployment are primarily based on customer sales (78 percent) and volume, followed by product grouping, region or geography and, lastly, margin or market share. Few respondents (only 15 percent) use customer profitability as a determinant for inventory deployment even though profitability is the number one objective.[9]

Figure 3. Effectiveness of customer practices implemented.

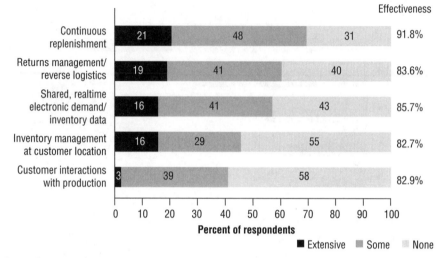

Source: IBM Institute for Business Value 2006 Value Chain Study.

A majority of the respondents are effectively using realtime, shared electronic demand and inventory data to gain visibility into customer demand and to collaborate on forecasts. In a totally integrated supply chain, customer point-of-sale or demand information is used within the organization to better plan and adapt production and other schedules in accordance with demand requirements. To further synchronize supply with demand, the customer forecast information is fed back to key suppliers. When demand spikes, the company can then shift production back and forth between suppliers.

Most respondents said that they are "rapidly" responsive to changing market conditions (70 percent) and have realtime visibility inside and outside the enterprise (60 percent). Yet when asked about collaborative planning initiatives, only 31 percent said they are implementing collaborative approaches with suppliers and only 25 percent with customers. Likewise, few (31 percent) said they are sharing visibility into inventory and demand with suppliers.[10]

As organizations seek to get closer to their customers and "pull" demand through their supply chains, an accurate reflection of product demand is critical to increasing sales revenue and customer satisfaction while reducing inventories and order cycle times. Demand planning and inventory planning and replenishment applications are being used more extensively than they were three years ago. Since 2003, the use of these applications has grown by 9 percent. Most respondents are using vendor packages, and some (an average of 29 percent) are using internally developed software.[11] Demand/supply planning is becoming much more organizationally integrated, with sales and marketing, finance, supply chain operations, information technology and even key partners involved in the sales and operations planning processes.

Effective demand management can significantly impact not only new product introductions but the decision to retire an existing product as well. Key issues that businesses must consider every day when attempting to forecast demand include pricing, product mix, promotions and other factors that impact the delivery of products and services.

Respondents indicated that they measure forecast accuracy primarily by stock keeping unit (SKU), product family or grouping, and customer segmentation. Thirty-three percent said they measure forecast accuracy at the market level.[12]

As shown in Figure 4, demand/supply planning and synchronization result in quantifiable supply chain performance improvement. Companies employing advanced demand planning techniques typically carry less inventory, are more likely to meet customer requirements for perfect order attainment and generally are more profitable. Our study shows that customer lead-time improved significantly from 2003, with over 60 percent delivering products in 7 days or less. Inventory turn rates for finished goods are higher, and the cost of quality has improved from 2003. Cash-to-cash cycle time has made a leap, with 71 percent achieving less than 60 days and 41 percent with cash-to-cash cycles of less than 30 days. In addition, on-time delivery has improved, with over 54 percent of the respondents achieving levels of 95 percent and above versus only 48 percent in 2003.[13]

Figure 4. Key supply chain performance indicators.

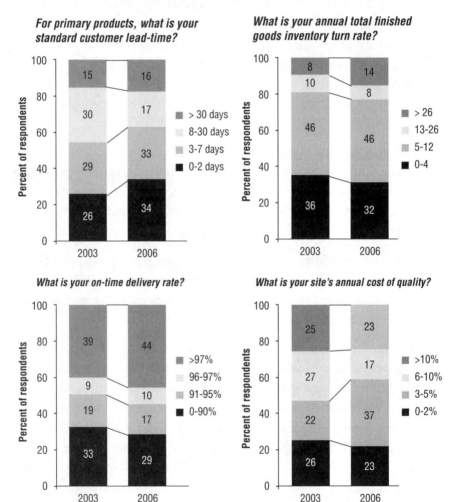

Source: IBM Institute for Business Value 2006 Value Chain Study.

What the leaders are doing to achieve supply and demand synchronization

As companies evolve up the supply chain maturity model toward an on demand supply chain, they are developing demand-driven extended supply chain networks. Many of the leaders are implementing the following practices:

- Collaborative demand planning and forecasting with customers and suppliers
- Customer inventory planning and deployment programs including continuous replenishment and shared management of inventory
- Integrated sales and operations planning among functions within the organization and the extended supply chain network
- Bundled pricing of products and services.

SUCCESS TIP:

Achieve profitability objectives by synchronizing demand and supply. Implement collaborative planning processes integrated organizationally (for example, across sales and marketing, supply chain operations, finance, IT) with key customers, suppliers and service providers. Use real demand to replace forecasts.

Global buying power through strategic sourcing

Global sourcing patterns continue to shift dynamically in search of lower cost sources. In addition, companies continue to rationalize and harmonize their own global value chain resources in search of more efficient and effective means of meeting global customer demands. Fast, flexible, efficient and transparent response to changing end-customer demands and supply shocks remains a strategic mission for supply chain management and will be essential to remaining competitive.

To effectively analyze and manage total procurement spend, companies need basic as well as comprehensive information and visibility into purchasing spend and consumer patterns. Enterprises need operational and supplier performance measurements to effectively manage supplier relationships. Shifting to customer-driven supply networks can be accomplished by integrating sourcing, procurement, operations and logistics with partners to better manage global strategic sourcing and spending and to achieve reduced procurement costs, enhanced profitability and cash flow.

Key survey findings

Profitability (77 percent) and cost containment (65 percent) continue to be the major objectives for procurement and supplier management functions, followed by improved quality and increased customer responsiveness.[14] Collaboration with suppliers and global sourcing of direct material are viewed as the key factors to achieving profitability and reduced costs (see Figure 5).

Collaborative design and development, where companies engage suppliers and exchange knowledge during the entire product lifecycle, can help reduce costs and time to market and, at the same time, maintain quality standards. Working in isolation and making assumptions about supplier capabilities may undermine sourcing strategies because of higher costs and may fail to leverage supplier knowledge for componentization and reuse.

Figure 5. Key initiatives underway to achieve company objectives.

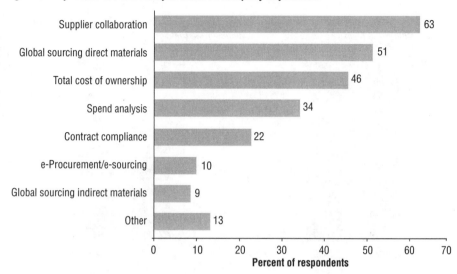

Source: IBM Institute for Business Value 2006 Value Chain Study.

Global sourcing of direct materials is definitely on the rise. Sourcing within North America has remained relatively stagnant since 2003; however, direct material sourced from Europe, South America and China/India is increasing (see Figure 6). Global sourcing is posing some difficult performance challenges for many industries – longer lead times, slower inventory turns and unpredictable delivery – often compounded by cultural issues.

Figure 6. Global sourcing by region.

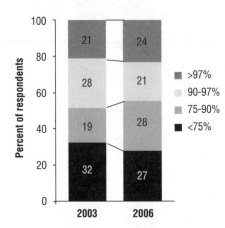

What percentage of your site's direct materials are sourced from North America?

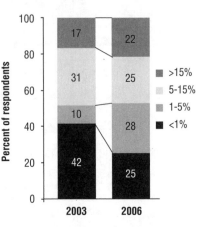

What percentage of your site's direct materials are sourced from China and India?

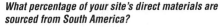

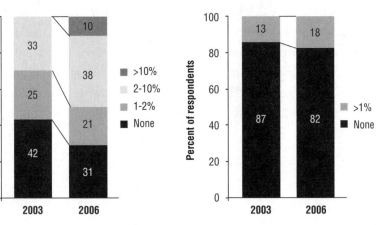

What percentage of your site's direct materials are sourced from Europe?

What percentage of your site's direct materials are sourced from South America?

Source: IBM Institute for Business Value 2006 Value Chain Study.

As companies continue to seek qualified global sources to fulfill supply, many are beginning initiatives where the total cost of ownership (TCO) is a key driver of strategic sourcing. TCO involves the analysis and inclusion of virtually all process costs, actual procurement costs, and even operations and maintenance costs, if applicable. Fifty-nine percent of the survey respondents use total cost as the key performance criteria in evaluating suppliers, followed by price, quality and delivery.

Many companies struggle to capture accurate, timely data that could give them insight into enterprisewide spend patterns, such as maverick spend rates, contract compliance and price optimization opportunities. Most respondents do not plan to invest in procurement applications, but the demand for supply chain integration technology and electronic payment systems appears solid. Respondents are making supplier management and procurement technology investments in the following areas:

- Electronic payment: 67 percent
- Internal supply chain integration: 60 percent
- Web-enabled e-Procurement and e-Sourcing: 59 percent
- Spend analysis: 54 percent.[15]

Establishing global buying power through strategic sourcing involves creating supply relationships that help optimize potential value contribution by accurately matching demand requirements with supply market capabilities. There is continued emphasis on overall supply chain performance and profitability, as evidenced by the results of the key sourcing and procurement measurements shown in Figure 7 and described below.

Supplier lead times have improved, with 74 percent reporting stable or decreasing lead times over the past three years. Study results from 2005 show a significant improvement in supplier on-time delivery, with 63 percent reporting delivery of at least 85 percent of supplier orders by the date originally requested. There has been a slight improvement in purchase order processing cycle time, but inventory turn rates have remained relatively stagnant.[16]

Figure 7. Supplier management and procurement performance.

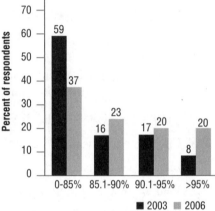
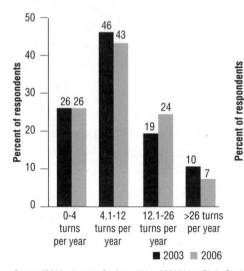
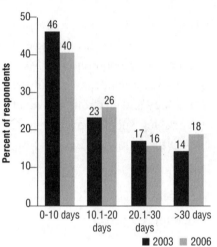
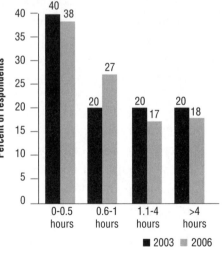

Source: IBM Institute for Business Value 2006 Value Chain Study.

What the leaders are doing to achieve global buying power

As companies evolve up the supply chain maturity model toward an on demand supply chain, they are increasing their buying power through strategic global sourcing while creating virtual supplier networks. Many of the leaders are implementing the following practices:

- Global sources of supply for direct and indirect materials
- Collaborative supplier relationship management programs with mutual objectives and performance criteria
- Increased attention and information on spend analysis and total cost of ownership
- Outsourced basic procurement, payment and audit functions
- Consolidation of supplier management and sourcing organizations.

SUCCESS TIP:

Achieve profitability objectives by increasing your global buying power through an integrated high-performance network of suppliers and service providers.

Logistics excellence for superior customer fulfillment

Today's decentralized supply chain models and tighter trading partner collaborations demand expanded logistics capabilities – more stocking locations, more frequent ordering, smaller order sizes, more costly modes of transportation, multichannel distribution, configure-to-order capabilities, personalization and distributed responsibility. With improved visibility and fulfillment tools, the logistics function has become a key component of supply chain operations, helping to combat inefficiencies in warehouse labor, transportation and space utilization, and inaccuracies in inventories and customer shipments. Implementing expanded yet cost-effective strategies for supply chain logistics has become a mission-critical objective.

Key survey findings

As virtually any shipper of products knows, transportation costs are out of control. Transportation cost increases, driven primarily by fuel prices in the past several years, combined with a capacity shortfall have led to a significant rise in logistics costs (see Figure 8).

Figure 8. Site total logistics cost as a percentage of sales.

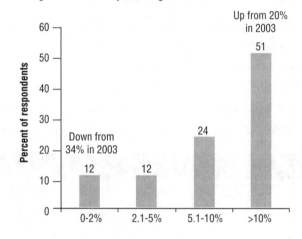

Source: IBM Institute for Business Value 2006 Value Chain Study.

Formal distribution strategies are being implemented as companies look for ways to balance the global sourcing of material with increasing transportation and distribution costs and, as usual, rising customer service requirements (see Figure 9). Many are considering the placement and deployment of inventories in their networks to counter-balance the recent sky-rocketing increases in transportation costs. Some companies are even reestablishing distribution facilities closer to the customer to combat transportation capacity and costs issues. Another tactic is implementing differentiated logistics services for particular customer segments and markets, which over 73 percent of the respondents are embracing.[17]

As companies strive to develop an integrated and informed logistics network, many are implementing collaborative processes, including supply chain visibility and exception management, with logistics service providers. Many are seeking improvements in collaborative order fulfillment and visibility – designing and implementing processes and Internet-based technologies to provide visibility and realtime management of distributed order fulfillment across today's complex, highly outsourced supply chains. Companies are finding that these practices are effective (80 percent and above) in meeting their objectives for increased profitability, cost containment and increased customer responsiveness/service.[18]

Figure 9. Implementation of logistics practices at companies.

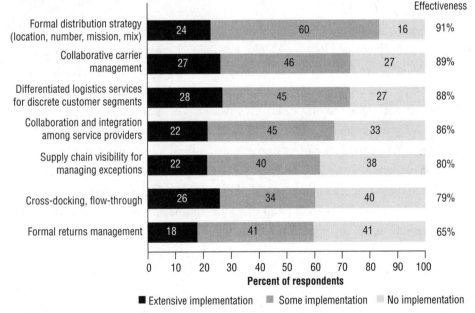

Source: IBM Institute for Business Value 2006 Value Chain Study.

More and more companies are developing a variable global logistics network of service providers to better manage end-to-end logistics costs while providing greater levels of on-time delivery, fill rate and other customer performance expectations. They are accomplishing this by outsourcing components of their overall logistics capabilities to transportation and distribution service providers. Transportation (inbound and outbound) continues to be the highest ranking outsourced function (57 percent), with customs/export, warehousing and/or distribution centers and transportation management services (TMS) following. Overwhelmingly, the respondents indicated that those outsourced functions are effective in meeting their desired objectives (transportation 93 percent, customs/export 87 percent, warehousing/distribution centers 88 percent and TMS 75 percent).[19]

Superior customer fulfillment requires keeping a careful eye on logistics performance and key indicators. For the last three years, customer order cycle times have been improving (see Figure 10). For more than 75 percent of the respondents, cycle times are below 10 days. Seventy-five percent are achieving order fill rates above 90 percent, which is relatively consistent with the 2003 data. On-time delivery (OTD) remains the major indicator of customer satisfaction and logistics performance excellence, along with other perfect order components (e.g., complete, in the right place, undamaged). Eighty percent of the respondents achieve OTD rates of 90 percent and greater.[20] In this survey, OTD was defined as scheduled delivery time versus the customer's original request date.

Figure 10. Customer fulfillment performance measurements.

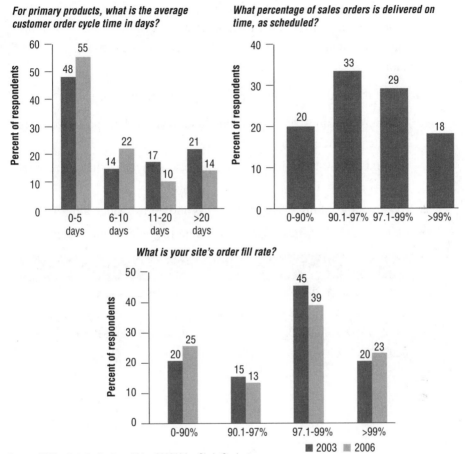

For primary products, what is the average customer order cycle time in days?

What percentage of sales orders is delivered on time, as scheduled?

What is your site's order fill rate?

■ 2003 ■ 2006

Source: IBM Institute for Business Value 2006 Value Chain Study.

What the leaders are doing to achieve logistics excellence

Companies continue to strive to improve their logistics execution and performance to meet profitability and cost containment objectives and, much more importantly, to deliver "the perfect order" and meet customer requirements for the right product at the right time for the right price.

As companies evolve up the supply chain maturity model toward an on demand supply chain, they develop robust, global logistics capabilities that are variable in structure and cost – logistics networks that are highly integrated and can fluctuate to accommodate varying customer demand.

Many of the leaders are implementing the following practices:

- Outsourcing non-core logistical functions to leading third-party logistics providers
- Integrating end-to-end processes with key service providers and other supply chain partners
- Keeping a watchful eye on key events and performance criteria
- Managing the logistics network by monitoring events and exceptions.

SUCCESS TIP:

Achieve superior customer fulfillment (e.g., the perfect order) by restructuring logistics processes from end-to-end to develop a variable network of partners and cost structure that are responsive to customer service requirements.

CONCLUSION

The role of the supply chain is changing as it moves from a static, cost-centric approach to an evolving, integrated model. Organizations are focusing on the supply chain to help transform their businesses by:

- Altering the way they think, organize and execute
- Looking at business processes horizontally rather than vertically
- Integrating processes within and beyond the enterprise.

Companies are moving toward a dynamic, realtime supply chain model. This type of on demand supply chain is supported by applications that enable realtime information visibility both inside and outside the enterprise. It can respond to changes in market conditions faster than traditional supply chains can, and it uses information to sense shifts and redirect resources. An on demand supply chain is adaptable and can help companies respond rapidly to market opportunities based on actual demand and market conditions. And responsiveness is the name of staying in the game.

Building a roadmap to the innovative supply chain strategic vision

By Karen Butner

Transformation to an innovative supply chain is a journey and requires a roadmap, or structured approach, on how to get there. The journey should begin with a diagnostic assessment of your company's current supply chain performance in regard to the various attributes and characteristics of the desired vision, or end state.

The assessment should also determine how your company is positioned according to the maturity model of leading practices. As a company matures through the various stages – functional optimization, horizontal process integration, external collaboration, on demand supply chain – certain characteristics are evident. A diagnostic assessment will help you determine where you are on the supply chain maturity model and help you prioritize initiatives that will have the greatest impact on shareholder value and return on investment (ROI). Your diagnostic assessment might include the questions shown in Figure 1.

Figure 1. Questions to ask for a diagnostic assessment of your supply chain performance.

Stages and questions to address				
Analyze situation	**Define capability gaps**	**Develop vision**	**Define solution and roadmap**	**Transform performance**
• What are our strategic goals and objectives? • What is the performance baseline? • How satisfied are our major customers? • What drives our total delivered cost and margin? • What are the supply chain challenges and opportunities?	• What are our supply chain capability gaps? • Is our organization structured to best practices? • Do we collaborate effectively? • What are the expected benefits? • Do we have the right infrastructure to deliver expected or desired results?	• What are the trends in our industry? • What are our competitors doing? • How should we integrate demand and supply management in the future? • What vision will guide all of our activities? • Where should we focus our activity? • What initiatives may we need to invest in?	• Which initiatives contribute the most value? • What is the business case for change? • How ready is the organization for change? • How long will it take and how will we measure progress? • What requirements will determine fit of potential solutions?	• What is the final solution? • How can we best implement to reduce risk while optimizing value? • How will we manage the change program? • How do we avoid operational disruption? • How do we help ensure business ownership? • How do we integrate our partners?
Analysis complete	*Capability gaps defined*	*Vision complete*	*Roadmap developed*	*Transformation executed*

Source: IBM Global Business Services analysis, 2006.

Based on this assessment of your supply chain maturity in regard to processes, organizational aptitude and enabling technologies, you can begin to formulate a supply chain vision and strategy. This strategy should include the following key steps:

- Identify the company's core supply chain differentiators and capabilities, and assess current performance.

- Determine which functions could be better performed by a partner, and begin to identify these partners.

- Define the supply chain process components and the needs for organizational reconstruction.

- Define the measurement framework, which is aligned with business objectives and goals. Set targets and thresholds for the key supply chain performance indicators.

- Evaluate the financial and operational value to be achieved in terms of financial performance and operational performance characteristics such as cycle time, quality and service level attainment. Use modeling tools to simulate end-state financial statements and operational performance criteria.

- Define the realtime information and connectivity vision, including an open and services-based technology architecture, required to support the strategic vision.

- Prioritize which initiatives will have the greatest impact on growth, operational excellence, ROI and shareholder value.

Figure 2. Steps to formulating a supply chain vision and strategy.

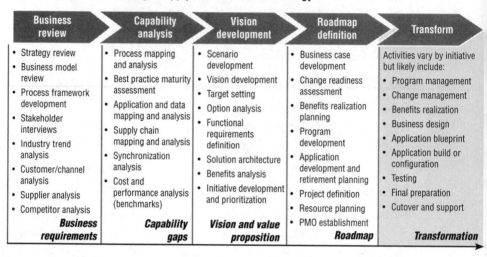

Business review	Capability analysis	Vision development	Roadmap definition	Transform
• Strategy review • Business model review • Process framework development • Stakeholder interviews • Industry trend analysis • Customer/channel analysis • Supplier analysis • Competitor analysis	• Process mapping and analysis • Best practice maturity assessment • Application and data mapping and analysis • Supply chain mapping and analysis • Synchronization analysis • Cost and performance analysis (benchmarks)	• Scenario development • Vision development • Target setting • Option analysis • Functional requirements definition • Solution architecture • Benefits analysis • Initiative development and prioritization	• Business case development • Change readiness assessment • Benefits realization planning • Program development • Application development and retirement planning • Project definition • Resource planning • PMO establishment	Activities vary by initiative but likely include: • Program management • Change management • Benefits realization • Business design • Application blueprint • Application build or configuration • Testing • Final preparation • Cutover and support
Business requirements	*Capability gaps*	*Vision and value proposition*	*Roadmap*	*Transformation*

Source: IBM Global Business Services analysis, 2006.

Transformation requires a roadmap that establishes the steps required to achieve the vision. Each supply chain component has associated performance criteria – both financial (i.e., costs, revenue influence) and operational (i.e., cycle time, quality, service level attainment). The initiatives with the greatest business impact, both financially and operationally, can be prioritized and implemented with speed to bring value to the organization. A transformation portfolio should be created which focuses on the prioritized initiatives that will have the greatest business impact the fastest.

In addition, a new mindset is required for implementing the strategy. The old model of fixed strategy and long implementation timescales is dead. In its place, companies are demanding either rapid ROI or ROI that is self-funding, with a modular approach to implementation, often involving pilots followed by scale-up. More scrutiny is also being placed on benefits delivery and tracking, helping to ensure that benefits flow through to the bottom line and that multiple supply chain initiatives do not double (or worse) account for benefits and overstate the business case, especially in inventory and process cost reductions. On demand implementation approaches (e.g., gain sharing, pay-as-you-use) can provide the impetus to kick-start major transformation programs and generate the change momentum required to build a longer term vision.

Meeting the challenge of today's tough market conditions requires companies to treat their supply chains as a competitive weapon. In doing so, breakthrough business models must be designed and implemented. Supply chains must become connected and integrated end-to-end with suppliers, partners and customers – realtime in constant collaboration. The supply chain must be able to respond rapidly in a variable and resilient manner to virtually any opportunities or threats.

Such a supply chain cannot be built overnight but can be developed as the industry and technology evolve. The transformation has already begun in several distinct process areas (e.g., leveraged procurement, demand-supply synchronization) for many companies, and early adopters are already realizing the benefits.

HOW IBM TRANSFORMED ITS SUPPLY CHAIN INTO A COMPETITIVE WEAPON[21]

A few months after he took office as IBM's CEO in 1993, Lou Gerstner set about transforming IBM's supply chain. At the time, IBM had 30 different supply chains and spent nearly US$45 billion on them yearly. Instead of maintaining the traditional view of the supply chain as just a cost of doing business – the unglamorous work of negotiating contracts, procuring parts, getting them to the people who make the products, then shipping the products to clients – he wanted to turn the supply chain into a front-line competitive weapon that would be better able to respond to market fluctuations and add value to the company.

To accomplish this, IBM had to not only dramatically improve operations but also make its supply chain accountable to the business by applying a fundamentally different set of expectations of the benefits it can deliver. The goal was to revolutionize the very concept of a supply chain.

While parts of the transformation began in procurement in 1994, it wasn't until January 2002 that IBM officially launched its Integrated Supply Chain division with 19,000 employees in 56 countries. This division combined the 30 supply chains into one globally integrated function that continues to evolve.

IBM's supply chain transformation required a radical re-engineering of our processes and systems across the company. The first step required us to create a common framework for configuring solutions and to enforce it through a governance model. The idea was to have the Integrated Supply Chain touch every part of IBM and play an active role in aligning and integrating the company horizontally.

IBM formed three diverse teams to manage issues cross-functionally in the areas of operations, strategy and talent development. Our management approach is helping us make better decisions faster and fostering collaboration across the supply chain. And we're reinforcing it with changes we have made to our performance measurement system, adding new metrics that tie the entire supply chain together with common goals and objectives, such as improvements in customer service or cash generated. Thanks to the adjustments we have made to both our management and measurement systems, we are gaining more visibility into exactly how the supply chain is operating and how IBM is responding to client needs.

By now, there is no doubt that a supply chain like the one we are building is, and will continue to be, a driving force in the business, and we have the proof:

- IBM's Integrated Supply Chain has improved productivity by US$3-$5 billion a year every year for the last five years.

- At the end of 2004, the Integrated Supply Chain reduced IBM's inventory to its lowest levels in 30 years (in 2003 it reached the lowest level in 20 years).

- The 4Q2005 was the best quarterly turns performance in over five years.

- By speeding inventory turns and improving client collections and supplier payment terms, IBM's supply chain efforts generated millions in cash to the bottom line in 2005.

- IBM's supply chain transformation efforts have reduced the amount of time the sales force spends on activities like checking order status, proposal generation and contracts by 25 percent. As a result, they are spending 38 percent more time with clients.

- We have cut the time to process a purchase order from a month to less than a day, which has resulted in significant savings. And thanks to ongoing automation, 99 percent of purchase orders are now processed electronically.

- In 2005, IBM's Integrated Supply Chain improved overall client satisfaction by 1 percent on delivery satisfaction, which potentially equates to millions of dollars of revenue in future sales.

Our supply chain transformation is not complete yet, but we have laid a solid foundation that is continuing to evolve as IBM moves from a hardware-based business to a services-based business. We also decided to share our supply chain transformation experience externally, so in June 2005 we formed the world's first Supply Chain Business Transformation Outsourcing Services business, with 8,000 consultants and 15,000 Integrated Supply Chain employees. Initial offerings focus on procurement, logistics outsourcing and supply chain optimization. Today, IBM is successfully managing outsourcing and/or logistics for several large companies and government organizations.

Executive interview

Ramin Eivaz, Vice President of Strategic Planning and Demand Chain Management, Kimberly-Clark Corporation

Kimberly-Clark and its well-known global brands are an indispensable part of life for people in more than 150 countries. Every day, 1.3 billion people-nearly a quarter of the world's population-trust Kimberly-Clark brands and the solutions they provide to enhance their health, hygiene and well-being. With brands such as Kleenex, Scott, Huggies, Pull-Ups, Kotex and Depend, Kimberly-Clark holds the No. 1 or No. 2 share position in more than 80 countries. [1]

This interview with Ramin Eivaz, Vice President of Strategic Planning and Demand Chain Management, Kimberly-Clark Corporation spotlights the company's supply chain strategy and how they are addressing challenges such as integration and globalization.

IBM: *What has been the biggest challenge in crafting Kimberly-Clark's supply chain strategy?*

Ramin Eivaz: I think for us it was changing our mindset from a "push" supply chain model to one that is truly demand based and very customer responsive. Historically, everything from our manufacturing footprint and equipment design to our key performance indicators and score-cards was designed with a cost/capacity utilization mentality. We made the most out of manufacturing and manufacturing efficiency and then optimized our distribution network. We are now making a 180-degree turn to create a supply network that is customer focused and demand responsive.

---

[1] http://www.kimberly-clark.com.

"Now we feel there is an even bigger opportunity for us to differentiate ourselves by delivering better customer services and value-added capabilities through our supply network."

IBM: *What specifically prompted this shift in thinking?*

Ramin Eivaz: We realized that although we were cost-competitive and deemed a strong supplier, we were not being viewed by our customers as an indispensable partner. Although, our customers viewed us as a good supplier, it was clear that there was an opportunity to be more innovative and flexible. Consequently, we took a hard look at ourselves, talked with our customers, internal teams and suppliers and conducted a lot of external benchmarking in order to identify strategic areas of opportunity.

As we developed our broader strategies to drive our company forward, we concluded that our supply chain was critical to supporting our vision while creating and sustaining an advantaged status. We believe our supply chain has historically given us an advantage in collaborating and engaging with customers in certain areas but not in all the fundamental areas. When the fundamentals of supply chains are not working, it's hard to have any meaningful engagement with customers.

Now we feel there is an even bigger opportunity for us to differentiate ourselves by delivering better customer services and value-added capabilities through our supply network. If we start from the shelf and work our way back to our suppliers, I believe that not only can we improve our current level of efficiency but also enhance current service levels well beyond anything we have achieved to date.

IBM: *So for you, supply chain is about more than just efficiency.*

Ramin Eivaz: Absolutely. Efficiency is simply the entrance fee. So you are efficient, so what? Many organizations out there are efficient. Efficiency is not what will differentiate us from our competition – it is everything else about our supply chain that will distinguish us.

Our senior management remains focused on efficiency but is placing greater attention on making sure we deliver against our customer's expectations. We truly appreciate and value supply chain's role in enabling growth and enhancing our relationship with our retail customers. If the basics are in place, we can move on to more productive discussions on key growth opportunities.

A lot of our work with customers requires supply chain innovation even if it's just to change the configuration of the delivery, pallet or package. Instead of leaving supply chain out of the equation, we are taking advantage of it heavily with our customers – and as our customers recognize our abilities in supply chain, it creates a halo effect for us. Supply chain is clearly a component of our differentiation strategy.

IBM: *Can you give us an example of how you're using supply chain as a differentiator?*

Ramin Eivaz: We're seeing our customers becoming increasingly sensitive to the level of capital investments and inventory. We have customers whose business model is designed around maintaining inventory and service levels and others that are focused on managing high velocity flow. We're looking at ways we can adapt our supply chain so that we generate better flow through our manufacturing process and to our customers' shelves and reduce working capital.

At the same time, we're able to be much more responsive to changing needs or unique customer demands. We recognize that our customers have different expectations of our supply chain that invalidate a "one-size-fits-all" supply chain strategy. We must be different things to

"We're looking at ways we can adapt our supply chain so that we generate better flow through our manufacturing process and to our customers' shelves and reduce working capital."

different customers, and our supply chain plays a critical role in achieving this differentiation. Additionally, diversity of product portfolio is also increasing the need to develop a hybrid supply chain network.

IBM: *Can you tell us more about your vision of a hybrid supply chain network?*

Ramin Eivaz: Everything that happens at the consumer and customer level has a ripple effect throughout the supply chain. As consumers and customers are changing and fragmenting in their needs and preferences, we must also be changing our product portfolio and offerings to meet those needs.

While we've been innovating and streamlining our current supply chain model, we've also been expanding our portfolio to include products and channels with different characteristics (e.g., smaller form factors, broader product portfolio) which might require a different type of supply chain to handle them. Having products with very different manufacturing and handling characteristics amplifies the need for a hybrid approach to a supply network as opposed to a traditional, single-dimensional model. And if you're trying to maintain a leadership position or to get your supply chain to the next level, a hybrid strategy and approach will be key.

IBM: *What are the greatest challenges you see in developing hybrid supply network?*

Ramin Eivaz: If you're going to use your supply chain as a differentiator, you need to create and share information and performance metrics to a much higher degree. This means your systems and infrastructure must be able to accommodate that. Not everybody will want to have the same set of metrics or targets.

In order to do this effectively you need to collaborate with your retail partners to understand their unique needs and be able to integrate and/or harmonize your network and systems with theirs. Making sure systems are integrated and capable of managing a diverse set of capabilities and metrics is one of the key challenges that must be addressed. Additionally, your footprint, equipment capability, suppliers and distribution network need to be able to respond to that information in a way that creates value and not only meets but *anticipates* customer and consumer needs.

IBM: *So synchronization of information is a critical factor?*

Ramin Eivaz: Yes, it is a very critical factor, although I call it "transparency of information" across the supply chain. It includes both the accuracy of basic data through data synchronization and visibility of the activities that are taking place.

We've learned that it is critical for the transparency of information to extend beyond our four walls all the way down to the shelf. We have done a lot of work on data synchronization and data integration with retailers over the last five years and are one of the leaders in this area.

When you start thinking about all of this data, whether it's POS (Point of Sale) data or RFID (Radio Frequency Identification), it plays a major role in developing our supply chain network. Good data is critical if we are going to make sure our systems are transparent and synchronized and don't have artificial barriers or time lag.

> *"We've learned that it is critical for the transparency of information to extend beyond our four walls all the way down to the shelf."*

IBM: *And how is this integration progressing?*

Ramin Eivaz: Our industry is still a ways away from true integration of trading partners. Right now, you still have handoffs; at best you have linkages and connections but not true integration. Whether you're talking about demand planning, inventory management or any other area, you still have multiple systems with point-to-point connections making multiple handoffs.

This raises a series of challenges around data standards and systems standards. While a lot of the manufacturers have integrated their enterprise systems on SAP platforms, they have customized them to such a degree that the data architecture isn't the same. From a retail standpoint, it is still a very fragmented environment.

IBM: *Any thoughts on what can be done to accelerate the efforts?*

Ramin Eivaz: Part of the challenge is that while supply chain can be a differentiator, many key components of it do not need to be customized. Standardization from a data exchange standpoint is far more important and advantageous than having proprietary data or a proprietary system architecture. In many cases, the benefits of standardization outweigh the benefits of differentiation.

With data in particular, the structure becomes complex very quickly if standards are not followed. As an industry, we just are not there yet. As for accelerating the integration efforts, unfortunately, the exchanges have been slow in delivering against the vision that was set forth.

IBM: *Finally, what are your thoughts on globalization and how it affects Kimberly-Clark from a supplier and retailer point of view?*

Ramin Eivaz: I see globalization as much more of a factor on the sourcing and manufacturing side of the supply chain today. As you look at how the supply chain is evolving, it's fascinating to see it transform on one end to become so globalized, while on the other end it is getting more localized. This reflects the world of extremes that we are operating in. As retailers become truly global and expect the same service and services throughout the world, we recognize that Kimberly-Clark must have consistent supply chain capabilities in each region we do business in to meet those expectations.

Executive interview

Linda Cantwell, Vice President, Supply Chain Management Operations, IBM Integrated Operations

The IBM Integrated Supply Chain (ISC) comprises 19,000 employees in 56 countries. These employees are responsible for building a very advanced and cost-effective on demand supply chain to enable IBM to gain market share, grow revenue and profit, improve cash flow, and enhance customer satisfaction. In 2005, the ISC generated US$580 million in cash for the IBM Corporation, while it reduced costs by US$6 billion and improved sales productivity by 25 percent.[B]

Linda Cantwell, Vice President, Supply Chain Management Operations, IBM Integrated Operations, talks about the strategic direction and challenges facing the ISC.

IBM: *Have you witnessed any increase in boardroom involvement with respect to supply chain issues?*

Linda Cantwell: Yes. When we formed the integrated supply chain back in 2002, one of the first real proof points that we were coming together as an organization more than in name only was specifically "having a seat at the table." It was truly the first time from an IBM perspective that supply chain was elevated to discussion at the chairman's level.

Initially, what we did was to join the organization together and centralize it; but it truly became real when we had to bring forward our business results as a consolidated, integrated supply chain organization. Having to report metrics that were meaningful and relevant to the overall company's operations was a new way of thinking for us.

[1] IBM Global Business Services analysis, 2006.

Making these measurements visible had two effects. Number one was that it forced us to come together as a team, because we were bringing our metrics forward into one integrated report card. The second impact was more of a corporate cultural one. IBM Chairman & CEO Sam Palmisano was now talking about how supply chain management affected the prior quarter's results. He also started making comments publicly about how supply chain was helping our company's performance, which is something that we as supply chain professionals had never heard stated at that level nor in that way before.

IBM: *Who is really involved in developing the supply chain strategy?*

Linda Cantwell: When we first started we had an innovative twist on supply chain strategy because, while the initial development was done at the senior leadership level, the deployment was done quite differently. The strategy initially was defined by Bob Moffat, IBM Senior Vice President, and his direct reports along with a few other leaders who pulled it all together and packaged it as a comprehensive report. But Bob realized that he somehow had to make it real – make it resonate with our employees at all levels. We didn't need another "white paper." What we needed was 19,000 people operating as one team.

So we embarked on an ISC strategy "champions" project. We received nominations from the worldwide leadership team of key employees from around the world who were considered top talent and future leaders. We joined them together as a team of champions and brought them in to review, challenge and influence the strategy document. We motivated them to understand it fully by telling them that they would be the leaders driving the deployment and education. They then led a global rollout, setting up and leading education sessions that were very well received because the strategy was real – not a document, not a Webcast, but truly a set of principles supported by strategic initiatives. Our people understood the strategic direction and their place in our future. Since that

"We continually ask ourselves, 'What's the next improvement leap now that we've got this supply chain running very effectively as an integrated on demand operation?'"

time there is a disciplined strategic planning process driven by a senior leader with cross-functional participation that updates the strategy and supporting initiatives annually.

IBM: *Do you look to any other companies or organizations for best practices in supply chain?*

Linda Cantwell: We're constantly monitoring other companies' practices. In earlier years, each functional unit determined whether to benchmark others formally and to what extent. Recently, we became more serious about benchmarking more consistently across all of our functional areas.

IBM: *What would you say is the company's biggest success with regard to improving the supply chain?*

Linda Cantwell: I would say it has been our ability to drive to the on demand supply chain – to really put ourselves in the position where the supply chain responds in a more cohesive and consistent way to market conditions. In our early days of being an integrated organization, we saw improvements in collaboration and partnering across the supply chain functions when reacting to some type of pressure, such as unplanned orders or extreme weather conditions. There are great stories about our "quarter-end heroics" – brute force and lots of manual intervention. As we became more sophisticated and really put the on demand agenda in play, we positioned ourselves to be much more predictive in our responses to late information or natural events. We communicate through technology and manage complex situations more seamlessly.

Each advance brings the challenge of how we take our supply chain to the next level. We continually ask ourselves, "What's the next improvement leap now that we've got this supply chain running very effectively as an integrated, on demand operation?"

IBM: *Would you say cost control is still the primary supply chain concern, or do you think other issues like profitability or customer responsiveness may be more dominant?*

Linda Cantwell: The latter. I think that cost control is the price of entry and is fundamental for the supply chain. But in our business now, our supply chain priorities are focused on driving sustained business improvement in the areas that are most important, such as client satisfaction and shareholder value.

IBM: *How has collaboration of your supply chain with your suppliers, partners and customers impacted your business?*

Linda Cantwell: We've had to become nearly totally reliant on the collaborative side of the supply chain relationship model, as we have chosen to drive a variable supply chain. In moving ourselves to the on demand model, we had to lessen our dependency on the physical asset-based infrastructure that we had worldwide. So, by definition, we put ourselves in the position where we had a huge dependency on partners.

For example, once we decided it no longer made any sense to have our own warehouses, distribution facilities and our own local ways of moving products around, we had to go out and secure the best global partners we could find and then put high trust and reliance on them. While you wouldn't want to place total control in your partners' hands, you do need to figure out where that balance point is. The supplier consolidation activities we performed were part of making a deliberate choice to have a set of trusted partners. We did experience some initial missteps, as we sometimes gave away too much control or didn't set up

"We have to operate as a globally integrated company since we have supply chain relationships in virtually every country in the world."

the right kind of metrics. At this point in our on demand journey, I would say that we have the supplier collaboration model right, and we depend on it every day.

We decided a long time ago to be very open with our suppliers and to share critical supply chain information. We are honest with each other and know what our common goals are. It may sound simple, but there's a lot of corporate culture change that's required to make that happen. We find that our suppliers are looking to prove that they have the capabilities to step up and do even more to bring value to IBM. It's a very good lesson – what we have learned from our suppliers makes us a better supplier ourselves.

IBM: *To what extent has globalization affected your supply chain? For example, are you sourcing materials globally in particular regions, or are you doing any manufacturing in low-cost jurisdictions?*

Linda Cantwell: We've embraced IBM's global footprint in a big way. We approach the world as our global market, and it's not just about low-cost labor. Where many people look at globalization and offshoring as the same thing, we see them as entirely different business models. We have to operate as a globally integrated company since we have supply chain relationships in virtually every country in the world.

For example, where in the world is the best talent? Where in the world are the most effective manufacturing capabilities? As a global company and a sophisticated supply chain operation, we study the marketplace and decide for IBM where we're going to operate for optimum effectiveness.

We very much try to factor in the implications of, say, moving manufacturing operations to another region and look at all of the complexities, such as what it does to your cycle times, customs operations and logistics model. We must be able to evaluate the different factors and assess the total cost of available alternatives.

In fact, we are now applying these supply chain lessons to other parts of the IBM organization – thinking about things like shared services models and centrally operated global business centers. We are choosing to invest in countries with emerging economies and big appetites for the solutions that IBM has to offer. Gaining market access in parts of the world that have been traditionally out of our reach is part of the decision criteria of choosing where we operate.

IBM: *What supply chain issues and challenges do you foresee either coming on board or continuing over the next three to five years?*

Linda Cantwell: One issue, unfortunately, is the continued focus on unplanned global events, such as terrorism or natural disasters, and what those have done to change the dynamic of the supply chain. Supply chain security is something that we as an industry paid little attention to not too long ago, and it is now core and central for the business. We have had to step up and build more sophistication into what we're doing about issues like pandemic planning, where our company is trying to approach the challenge in one organized multifaceted way so we're ready to address those types of crises should they come upon us.

There are also issues like port congestion and insufficient infrastructure, realities of the global marketplace. It's interesting to me that in some cases, we're basically contributing to new problems as we're addressing others.

"...our supply chain success has largely been driven by a corporate cultural transformation."

Another ongoing challenge is talent. The traditional supply chain talent that served us well for a long, long time was built around manufacturing – professionals doing a great job, from development through reverse logistics. However, it's not just the product supply chain that we're operating anymore – we are now a solutions and services supply chain.

One of the biggest components of our supply chain is labor. How are we positioning our supply chain professionals of the future with more training and skills and enabling them with new technology that the traditional supply chain professional of the past didn't have to worry about? This problem statement leads us to the partnerships that we've struck with universities worldwide in trying to get that win/win – our getting their best supply chain talent and influencing their curriculum development on new supply chain challenges.

If we're still teaching students that supply chain is about factories and parts, warehouses and trailers, then we're short-changing them and only telling them half the story. The supply chain that they're going to enter post-graduation looks a little bit like that but a whole lot more like something else – a complicated global business enabled by sophisticated technologies.

IBM: *Do you feel there is a company that you think is doing something really innovative in their supply chain?*

Linda Cantwell: Cisco stands out to me. At IBM, we have a multifaceted relationship with Cisco – as an alliance partner, a supplier and a customer. In terms of looking at where we might help them in supply chain challenges, we've found them very sophisticated in their own right, and they have some lessons to teach us about aspects of their supply chain that they're operating particularly well.

IBM: *Any closing comments?*

Linda Cantwell: The main message I'd like to drive home is that our supply chain success has largely been driven by a corporate cultural transformation. Without corporate culture change, the rest of it doesn't really matter – it won't be sustainable. We are focused on making our people truly proud to be supply chain professionals. We're trying to drive a strong supply chain community which is, of course, an ongoing journey.

Innovation, the perfect product launch and lifecycle management

Introduction

By Mark Wilterding

> *"Innovation is the application of invention and fusion of new developments and new approaches."*
> – Nick Donofrio, IBM Senior Vice President of Innovation

Chapter 2, "Innovation, the perfect product launch and lifecycle management," explores the emerging trends, key components and case studies of the perfect product launch and lifecycle management. Each article and case study in this chapter illustrate why the era of innovation is expanding the definition of the perfect product launch and some of its key process components like design commonality and component reuse. We hope that these topics become the impetus for publishing and sharing new examples and insights to help everyone who is engaged in the business of innovation, to innovate more effectively.

As a leading global high technology engineering and manufacturing company, IBM has concluded that corporate activities associated with product innovation are the sum total of the work performed by an ever-changing and virtual collaborative network. This network includes companies, research institutions and individuals who work together to produce and launch virtually any line of business product and offering, ranging from servers to software to services.

Put in the context of the era of innovation, the perfect product launch and lifecycle management are becoming viewed in a different and expanded way. Traditionally, determination of a successful product launch revolved around proving whether the best integrated product design (IPD) or the integrated supply chain management (ISCM) should take credit. Michael Burkett of AMR Research wrote in his article, "Perfect Product Launch": "Supply chain professional and design engineers have clashed for years over the challenge of delivering innovative products in sufficient volumes – and at a price and lead time that the market will accept."[22] Furthermore, success of these product launches was based on traditional measurements such as return on investment (ROI), Key Performance Indicators (KPI) yield, time to market and market share.

With the advent of the era of innovation, the definition and measurements of success are changing from the chicken-egg argument of the relative contribution of the engineering (Engineering Bill of Materials) or supply chain (Manufacturing Bill of Materials) domains. Up until 2005, only a very small number of companies had begun to integrate IPD with ISCM. Even a smaller number of companies, such as IBM, have experienced and measured the results of launching an integrated product plan and supply chain management product plan through an innovative collaborative network of partners. What is emerging is that the new redefined measures of success must take into account three primary component drivers of the era of innovation:

1. Leadership and culture

2. Collaboration and partnering

3. Integration of business and technology.

This chapter provides examples and proof points of the perfect product launch. In the coming years, as integrated efforts through collaborative networks become more common, we expect there will be hundreds upon hundreds of examples of perfect product launches from virtually every industry and geography.

The perfect product launch: Innovation drives growth in the consumer products industry

By Karen Butner and Mark Wilterding

You know the story: Consumer products manufacturers are under increased pressure to grow revenues and improve operating efficiency. Challenges in meeting growth targets include changes in consumer demographics, increased competition in a mature market, increased spending on services, the rise of private labels and the low success rate of new brands.

THE ERA OF INNOVATION

Enter the era of innovation. It is pervasive. It is influencing the way companies think about virtually every aspect of research, marketing product development, supplier and materials management, manufacturing, distribution, warranty and defect management, maintenance repair and overhaul, and product end-of-life and disposal.

Innovation is global. Innovation knows no boundaries. Its growth is being nurtured by active investments, grants and tax incentive policies of both established, industrialized nations and emerging economies. Placed in the context of the era of innovation, the "perfect product launch" and lifecycle management are now viewed in a different and expanded way.

Innovation in products, services and markets commands top attention from CEOs, who recognize that sustainable growth requires several different types of innovation. According to the IBM Global CEO Study 2006: Expanding the Innovation Horizon, CEOs are allocating their innovation emphasis accordingly:

- Products/services/markets: 42 percent
- Operations: 30 percent
- Business models: 28 percent.[23]

One of the greatest opportunities for revenue growth is through new products and services, new markets and customer intimacy. According to the CEO study, products/services/markets innovators maintain a 1.2 percent higher operating margin than their competitors. Outperforming products/services/markets innovators exploit current offerings and use electronic channels to improve reach and penetrate new markets.[24]

The perfect product launch involves managing the development and support of complex products and services throughout the entire lifecycle from product design to product build to post-sale service. It includes the integration of traditional new product introduction (product innovation, design and collaboration) with sourcing and procurement, supply chain planning and execution, and service.

Benefits of being first to market

The importance of being first to market is discussed extensively in various sources. In addition to the instinctive idea that it is best to be first, other measurable benefits are possible for those who get to the market sooner with innovative products and services (see Figure 1). These benefits include:

- *Increased sales through longer sales life* – The earlier the product reaches the market relative to the competition, the longer its life can be.
- *Increased margins* – The more innovative the product (that is, the longer it remains on the market with little or no competition), the longer consumers will pay a premium purchase price.
- *Increased product loyalty* – Getting the first opportunity to attract customers, especially early adopters, offers an advantage in terms of customer loyalty; customers will most likely upgrade, customize or purchase companion products.
- *More resale opportunities* – For components, commodities or products that other companies can private-label, being first to market can often help ensure sales in other channels.

- *Greater market responsiveness* – The faster that companies can bring products that satisfy new or changing customer needs to market, the greater the opportunity to capitalize on those products for margin lift and to increase brand recognition.

- *A sustained leadership position* – Unlike best-selling, fastest or other superlative market positions, first is the only market position a competitor cannot claim – only one company can be first. And repeated firsts establish companies as innovators and leaders in the market.

Figure 1. The value of time-to-market.

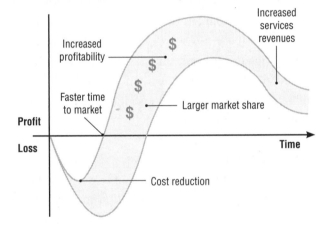

Source: IBM Global Business Services analysis, 2006.

Clearly, quick product introduction is a competitive differentiator. Accelerating time to market supports achievement of almost every primary design, sales and marketing goal a company has (or should have) in today's increasingly competitive, increasingly global marketplace. The challenge facing virtually every manufacturing organization today is to continually accelerate time to market while reducing development costs.

Product introduction is the only source of long-term competitive advantage. Companies with fast and efficient product introduction processes who provide customers with the products and services they demand will win over competitors who are slow to react to market changes and advances in product and process technology.

High-performing companies – those that generated annual total shareholder return in excess of 37 percent and have also experienced consistent revenue growth over the last 5 years – averaged 61 percent of their sales from successful launches of new products and services. Furthermore, companies that generated 80 percent of their revenue growth from new products typically doubled their market capitalization in a 5-year period.[25] We believe these positive results will continue to be realized when traditional leadership and cultural styles are replaced by new leaders who foster a culture of networked professionals who share the objective of realizing the combined and individual positive return on their participation in the product launch.

New product innovation success rates down

Ironically, as companies rely increasingly on new products and services to meet growth targets, new product innovation success rates have been historically low. A significant proportion of companies miss product launch schedules; according to IBM's 2006 Value Chain Study, on-time rates are down 8 percent from 2003, and on-budget rates are down 7 percent over the same time period.[26]

One of the primary reasons for product launch failure is poorly defined customer needs. Another is the lack of a clear business strategy linked to supply chain objectives and initiatives for go-to-market product launch and customer service. Insufficient resources – both human and monetary – and lack of executive-level support are additional reasons for product launch failures.

THE IBM GLOBAL CEO STUDY 2006 EXPOSED SEVERAL MYTHS ABOUT THE PURSUIT OF INNOVATION:

Myth: Innovation is the responsibility of brand and product managers.

Reality: Innovation must be orchestrated from the top.

Myth: Innovation happens from within – most often generated by product developers and research groups.

Reality: External collaboration is indispensable.

Myth: Innovation means coming up with new or better products and services.

Reality: Business model and operations innovation matter.

REVENUE GROWTH NOT NECESSARILY FLOWING TO BOTTOM LINE

Consumer products companies are facing another challenge: variability in business growth. One of the reasons for this has been the variation in consumer per-capita spending. The economic downturn of the late 1990s slowed growth in consumer spending, although there are now signs of a more healthy turn, with retail trade sales up 6.7 percent above last year.[27]

Another reason for variable business growth is the change in consumer spending patterns. On one hand, consumers are demanding lower prices for basic goods, and, on the other hand, they are willing to pay premium prices for products that hold individual value for them. This results in mega-retailers and premium luxury brands enjoying growth on both sides of the competitive spectrum while companies in the middle of the spectrum are facing growth challenges.

The rise in mega-retailer private labels has also contributed to slower growth for some consumer products companies. Private labels have been growing twice as fast as consumer products brands, with some variation across categories, and they currently represent the leading brand in most product categories.[28] As a result, private labels often offer cheaper prices to consumers and greater margins to retailers, leading to an increase in their market share.[29]

The revenue index for consumer products manufacturers is up 4.4 percent compared to the previous quarter, and it's even higher (up 7.9 percent) compared to the same period in 2004 (see Figure 2).[30] Growth can be attributed to product innovations, improved product mix, strategic pricing, customer segmentation and increased sales in emerging markets.

Figure 2. Consumer products manufacturing industry revenue index.

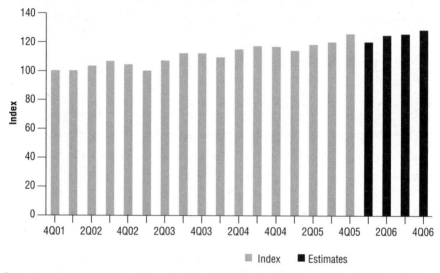

Source: Witty, Michael, Jay Holman and Jason Spaulding. "CPG Manufacturing Industry Update, 1Q06." Manufacturing Insights, an IDC company. Document #M1201026. March 2006.

Consumer products manufacturers are increasingly being pressured to increase revenues and improve operating efficiency and margins. Average net profit margins were 8.2 percent – nearly flat compared with the previous quarter and same period in 2004.[31] Meeting revenue growth and profitability targets has become more difficult due to higher commodity and energy prices, increased competition in mature markets, the rise of private labels and the low success rate of new brands.

SUCCESSFUL INNOVATION: THE PERFECT PRODUCT LAUNCH

Successful innovation has become a key driver for revenue growth, competitive margins and, in some cases, even survival. The ability to bring this innovation to market quickly, efficiently and ahead of the competition is becoming increasingly important.

An efficient product launch requires integration and coordination among multiple functional areas, including product design, procurement, planning, manufacturing/process, and sales and marketing. In addition, as organizations increasingly leverage core capabilities of other companies, this innovation has to be delivered through virtual networks, working with partners in a collaborative environment to bring product and services to market faster, smarter and cheaper. Consequently, organizations now need to integrate not only internally but externally as well with suppliers and customers. This creates end-to-end supply chain processes and capabilities that differentiate on product and customer requirements.

Strategies for success

Launching products and services that best fit customer requirements is clearly the top strategy for new product development. Lower introduction costs and first-to-market strategies pale in comparison to bringing to market innovative products that meet customer wants and needs (see Figure 3).

Figure 3. What is the primary strategy for your site's new product development efforts?

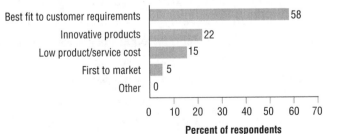

Source: IBM Institute for Business Value 2006 Value Chain Study.

In accordance with the primary strategy, over half of the consumer products company respondents reported "Correct identification of customer needs" to be the most significant challenge for new product development efforts, followed by "Remaining competitive" (see Figure 4).

Figure 4. Most significant management challenges for new product development efforts.

Source: IBM Institute for Business Value 2006 Value Chain Study.

It's all about collaboration

The participants in a new product launch can be members of centralized or decentralized organizations. They can be employees of multinational corporations; tier one, two or three suppliers; university departments; or independent contract engineers. An innovative work product is the result of the successful design and integration of ever-changing and evolving professional and technical disciplines. The concepts, specifications, designs, materials, components, software and processes are sourced from a variety of interdepartmental, intracompany, interregional, inter-dependent and collaborative networked relationships.

And it all begins, as it should, with the customer. Study respondents reported that their most widely implemented practice is "Collaboration with customers to achieve customer requirements for product specifi-cations" (99 percent), followed by "Customer product configuration and specifications for design" (94 percent), as shown in Figure 5. Most respondents consider these practices effective (100 percent and 91 percent, respectively), and 43 percent even claim collaboration to be *extremely* effective.[32]

Figure 5. To what extent have the following customer practices been implemented?

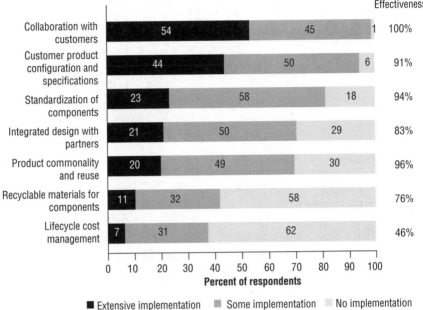

Source: IBM Institute for Business Value 2006 Value Chain Study.

Collaboration with customers, suppliers, and other value chain partners is viewed as having the most significant impact on time-to-market performance (see Figure 6). Also related to performance, CEOs who participated in the IBM Global CEO Study 2006 described a broad spectrum of benefits from collaboration and partnering to achieve innovation. Collaboration and partnering reduces costs, increases customer satisfaction, increases revenue and provides access to skills and products (see Figure 7).

Figure 6. Most significant impact on reducing product development time-to-market.

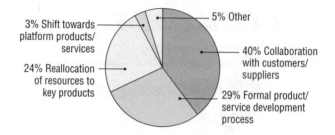

Source: IBM Institute for Business Value 2006 Value Chain Study.

Figure 7. Collaboration and partnering benefits cited by CEOs.

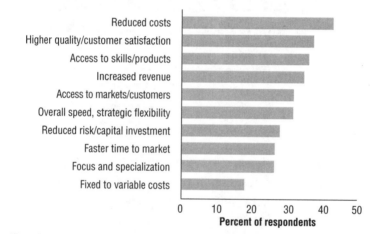

Source: "Expanding the Innovation Horizon: The Global CEO Study 2006."
IBM Corporation. March 2006.

Balancing the three success factors: time, cost, lifecycle

Managing costs in product design, development, launch and service is always top-of-mind with executives. First-to-market strategies are also critical and often become the competitive differentiator in generating growth and profit.

Eighty-five percent of the consumer products participants in the IBM 2006 Value Chain Study identified "Sales or profit contribution" as the primary measure of success for new product development projects. An increasing reliance on new products for growth means that more products are needed in the pipeline, and new products need to be launched more frequently. As a result, the new product development process is becoming critical to business success. The IBM 2006 Value Chain Study also supports this argument by showing that nearly a third of consumer products companies had more than 20 percent of their annual sales generated by new products launched within the previous year (see Figure 8).[33]

Figure 8. Percentage of sales generated from products launched in the past year.

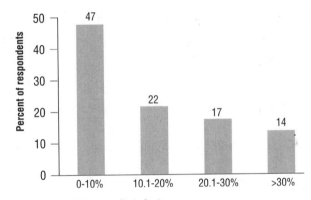

Source: IBM Institute for Business Value 2006 Value Chain Study.

However, delivery adherence-to-plan measures, such as on-time launch and on-budget launch, indicate room for improvement as a significant proportion of respondents miss their product development schedule targets. Similarly, a significant proportion of respondents miss their product development budget targets (see Figure 9). In both cases, the trend, based on a comparison to studies in prior years, is toward even more misses.

Figure 9. What percentage of new products is launched to market on time/on budget?

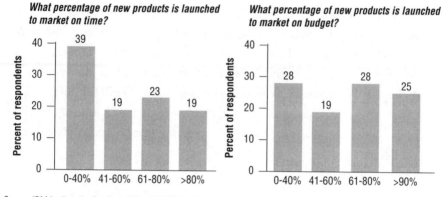

What percentage of new products is launched to market on time?

What percentage of new products is launched to market on budget?

Source: IBM Institute for Business Value 2006 Value Chain Study.

For new product *variations*, there has been a significant improvement in time-to-market performance. In the past 3 years, consumer products companies have improved time-to-market by 7 to 8 percent, with 41 percent of new product variations reaching the shelf within 100 days.[34]

Time to market and the total cost of the product including design, development and execution, and launch into the market are certainly two important criteria. But there's a third, frequently overlooked, success factor for the perfect product launch: lifecycle management (see Figure 10).

Figure 10. The three success factors for a perfect product launch.

Time-to-market

Total product cost

Lifecycle management

Source: IBM Institute for Business Value analysis, 2006.

It is important to take a holistic view of product/service lifecycle management, which includes:

- Quality programs
- Customer service requirements
- Global supply readiness
- Scalability into new markets
- Returns programs and spare parts planning for repairs
- Designs and plans for product variations for subsequent launches.

All of these elements must be integrated within the context of the overall supply chain processes, from planning to reverse logistics, and among all significant constituents.

Consumer products companies must reinvent their business models and processes based on innovation, integration and collaboration to bring profitable products and services to market on time and on budget. As one CEO in the IBM Global CEO Study 2006 remarked, "A good business model, good products and market, and superior operations supplement each other to form a continuous cycle." [35]

"A good business model, good products and market, and superior operations supplement each other to form a continuous cycle."

– Consumer products company CEO, IBM Global CEO Study 2006

CONCLUSION

Consumer products executives realize that business performance and growth are directly related to their ability to bring superior products and services to market in a cost-effective manner. In this discussion, we have shown that:

1. High levels of competition, shorter product lifecycles and changing market conditions intensify pressures on consumer products companies' growth.

2. To meet their business targets, consumer products companies need new ways to deliver value to their customers.

3. Innovation depends on introducing new products and services to existing markets while expanding into new market channels and geographies.

4. Reducing time to market is a key success factor.

5. Consumer products companies have not yet significantly improved their time-to-market and on-budget performance.

6. To help shorten time to market while reducing development costs, companies should adopt a holistic view of the development process and involve stakeholders from outside the immediate scope of the process, such as contract manufacturers, suppliers and other service providers.

7. Implementation of point solutions aimed at reducing time to market may achieve only local improvements and may not provide widespread business benefits. New product development objectives and initiatives must be tied to corporate strategies.

8. One of the most critical strategic initiatives in new product introduction is acquiring an explicit definition of customers' requirements in collaboration and communication with customers – not in an R&D vacuum.

9. Use of componentization and standards to develop variations on products can help companies achieve "faster-to-market" objectives at lower costs.

The message is clear. The perfect product launch can support business growth initiatives. It can support innovation for superior products and services. It can support effective cost management through the integration of product/service lifecycle management activities with customers, suppliers and service providers. And, for any organization in any industry that wants to achieve sustainable growth, the time to achieve the perfect product launch is *now*.

Cost-effective supply chains: Optimizing product development through integrated design and sourcing

By Robert McCarthy, Jr.

In today's global economy, industrial manufacturers face complex challenges such as fluctuating market conditions, aggressive competition, pricing pressures and rising costs for raw materials. Against this backdrop, they must continue to bring new, highly differentiated products to market – cost-effectively and within compressed timeframes. What can manufacturers do to optimize the product development process?

COLLABORATION, REUSE AND STANDARDIZATION

To solve these challenges, leading manufacturing companies are deploying next-generation digital design initiatives to reduce product development costs, improve product quality and speed time to market. Indeed, digital design technologies and techniques can help design engineers fully exploit existing investments in knowledge assets and integrate key suppliers into the product development process – essential in today's hyper-competitive marketplace. Best-in-class industrial firms are embracing core design principles that focus on collaboration, reuse and standardization to reduce costs and improve performance.

Platform commonality, standardization and design reuse

Reusing existing designs and other knowledge assets can help streamline the product development process and, at the same time, significantly improve product quality by standardizing and reusing proven components and assemblies. A formal program of commonality and reuse can also help reduce direct materials procurement costs, speed time to market and improve product quality.

To achieve the full benefits of commonality,
an integrated tools environment must support
business processes.

To further accelerate product development and improve product quality, it is critical that industrial firms access and leverage the specialized skills and knowledge available through their strategic suppliers. Managing this process effectively requires a tight integration between the manufacturer and the supplier through a collaborative design process and tight linkage between the design and sourcing processes. This gives manufacturers the capability to manage product cost and target profitability over the product design lifecycle.

Integrated design tools environment

Today's mechanical design, electronic design and supply chain processes typically operate independently, with their own isolated silos of information. To achieve the full benefits of commonality, an integrated tools environment must support business processes. By extending access to the product data management environment, firms can share design and cost information across business units and collaborate with strategic suppliers to accelerate design and sourcing processes across and beyond the enterprise.

Design commonality and component standardiza-
tion begin at the product platform architecture
level.

DEFINING COMMONALITY AND REUSE INITIATIVES THROUGH THE PRODUCT PLATFORM ARCHITECTURE

Design commonality and component standardization begin at the product platform architecture level. The product platform architecture should specify the hierarchy of functional components, defining an allowable set of product options and facilitating innovation and change within a particular product feature while protecting the integrity of the platform design. An architecture defined as a hierarchy of building blocks can help manufacturers simplify creation of the engineering bill of materials (BOM) and facilitate component standardization and reuse.

Cost information can be integrated into the product hierarchy, giving design engineers early lifecycle visibility into the total designed cost and letting them determine whether the product can be built within market-place cost and time constraints. Indeed, design engineers can evaluate the impact of design changes on direct materials costs, engineering design costs and manufacturing costs by allocating target costs to major building block components. This knowledge provides the incentive to implement standardization and reuse, which can have a significant impact on improving product cost and quality.

Standardizing steel grades and thickness has significantly reduced costs for steel.

JOHN DEERE: THE BUSINESS IMPACT OF STANDARDIZING STEEL

In 2003, John Deere and Company launched an initiative to standardize the steel used in its product lines. Standardization of steel grades and thickness has significantly reduced costs for steel. Standardization also helped Deere avoid production shutdowns in the face of dramatic demand increases for specialty steel in 2004.

To achieve the benefits of design standardization and reuse, consider the following principles when defining the product architecture:

- Create a product structure that anticipates change and localizes the impact of change.
- Leverage product data management tools and decision support tools to identify standardization and reuse opportunities across component designs, design processes, tooling and supplier expertise in the design of purchased components.
- Align engineers according to functional product areas to create centers of excellence in a specific design discipline.
- Leverage common tools and design processes to improve engineering efficiency and effectiveness.
- Create governance processes and metrics and deploy tools to identify and measure the downstream impacts of asset reuse, component standard-ization and commonality on cost, quality and time to market.

The most efficient way to launch a comprehensive program of commonality and reuse is to start with commodity components.

EXECUTING A COMPREHENSIVE PROGRAM OF COMMONALITY AND REUSE

Once commonality and reuse initiatives have been defined from the top down – at the architectural level – industrial firms must implement this strategy from the bottom up. The most efficient way to launch a comprehensive program of commonality and reuse is to start with commodity components.

Standardizing the design specifications for common components such as sheet metal, fasteners and electrical and electronic parts can help firms capture substantial cost savings and set the stage to standardize and reuse more complex components. Standardization also spurs successive, associated benefits such as:

- Standardization and reuse create opportunities to aggregate spend with a smaller number of suppliers
- Increased spend volume provides greater leverage with suppliers
- Higher purchase volumes allow buyers to negotiate lower prices and achieve greater assurance that critical components will be available in the quantities required.

Similar benefits can be achieved for design components, purchased assemblies, and tooling, plant and equipment.

Similar benefits can be achieved for designed components, purchased assemblies, and tooling, plant and equipment. A consistent product architecture – supported by common design processes and metrics – provides the foundation for "design anywhere, build anywhere" capabilities and facilitates global sourcing. By creating better visibility into component design requirements, the product platform architecture and current business needs, industrial firms can optimize aggregated component and equipment purchasing requirements and negotiate cost reductions for strategic components and assemblies, and other asset classes.

These assets can include:

- Production assets such as plant automation, machine tools, jigs and fixtures, material handling equipment and test equipment as well as intangible assets such as manufacturing processes, training materials and quality programs
- Purchased components including assemblies, engineered components, electronics and embedded software, raw materials and commodity components
- Processes spanning product development, product verification and testing, and after-sale service and support processes
- Knowledge assets including computer-aided design (CAD) information about products and components as well as the core knowledge of how to design, manufacture and sell products and how to manage the supplier population.

IBM has developed deep expertise in planning and deploying commonality and reuse initiatives.

KEY ENABLERS: STRATEGY AND PROCESS

Although most executives have an intuitive understanding that commonality and reuse strategies are critical to business effectiveness, creating a comprehensive program to drive product commonality, standardization and asset reuse can be a daunting task. Our experience with large industrial customers and our own internal computer design practice has led IBM to develop deep expertise in planning and deploying commonality and reuse initiatives. Indeed, we have identified a set of key business processes that must be deployed to create a comprehensive program for platform commonality and reuse. These processes include portfolio planning, design for commonality and reuse, integrated design and sourcing tools, closed loop product design and sourcing, and total cost management.

Portfolio planning

Through portfolio planning, a company can acquire a detailed understanding of its customers' wants and needs. It can then translate this understanding into a set of high-level design requirements for product platforms and for the development of product models from the product platform. As part of the portfolio planning process, it is important to define and organize the product architecture into a hierarchy of "common building blocks" (see Figure 1). This enables simplified "as designed" and "as built" BOM structures and creates downstream opportunities for component standardization and asset reuse. The output from the portfolio planning process should be a precise definition of the target market and customer requirements, the platform architecture and product model specifications, the product financial targets and a product development roadmap.

Figure 1. The portfolio planning process.

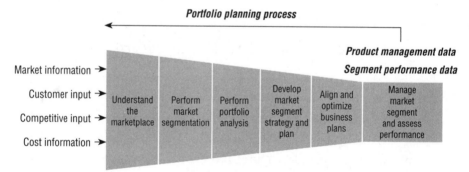

Source: IBM Global Business Services analysis, 2006.

The portfolio planning process defines the product architecture and creates design parameters and targets for the product set.

Design for commonality and reuse

The portfolio planning process defines the product architecture and creates design parameters and targets for the product set. The design process translates these requirements into an engineering BOM and product design specifications. The engineering BOM is then converted into a set of manufacturing BOMs that specify how the product will be built at each individual manufacturing site. By leveraging design and sourcing tools and motivating design engineers to reuse assets, the business can significantly improve the efficiency and effectiveness of the product development process and achieve structural product cost reductions. While it takes time to deploy tools and processes that enable commonality and reuse and to stimulate design engineers to reuse existing assets, the anticipated net result is a leaner and more effective product development process that enables manufacturers to "design anywhere, build anywhere" within the enterprise.

Integrated design and sourcing tools

An effective program of commonality and reuse cannot be achieved without an integrated design tools environment that links design, procurement and manufacturing. IBM is working closely with IBM Business Partners to create the data standards and functional requirements that will result in a flexible, interoperable design tools environment. IBM has created a Product Development Component Reference Model that leverages IBM middleware and the Websphere® Integration Framework to enable the integration of software tools from multiple vendors in the following areas:

- Mechanical CAD tools
- Electronic CAD tools
- Software design tools
- Computer aided manufacturing design tools
- Knowledge management tools
- Configuration management tools
- Design analytics
- Cost management tools.

It is critical that design tools portfolio and supplier management tools become more tightly integrated.

Closed loop product design and sourcing

The newest generation of design tools makes it possible to design products and identify opportunities for component standardization and reuse. However, while design tools are becoming more effective at identifying components that could be reused, they have not yet evolved to provide decision support capabilities that will empower design engineers to determine if component designs should be reused. This decision depends on an understanding of component costs, an assessment of whether performance must be enhanced to meet customer requirements and a determination as to whether the component can properly address safety, quality or regulatory requirements.

It is critical, then, that design tools portfolio and supplier management tools become more tightly integrated. Integrating design information and product cost information into a wholly aligned design collaboration and sourcing environment creates a closed loop product design and sourcing environment. This allows design engineers to evaluate the cost and feasibility of alternate design strategies and makes it possible to monitor the product's actual cost versus target cost so program managers can modify component design specifications to achieve cost, quality and customer value targets set during the portfolio planning process.

A closed loop design and sourcing environment can serve as the foundation for managing the product development lifecycle against target costs.

Total cost management

A closed loop design and sourcing environment can serve as the foundation for managing the product development lifecycle against target costs. On a more granular level, a system of total cost management allows design engineers and executives to extract product costs from the product selling price and required gross margins in order to calculate the financial impact of design alternatives (see Figure 2). Indeed, cost modeling can help manufacturers accurately predict total landed product costs, design costs and manufacturing-related costs. Then they can set appropriate cost targets and optimize product content at each stage of the product design cycle.

THE COMMON BUILDING BLOCK PROCESS: INSIDE IBM

In response to a highly dynamic IT marketplace, IBM has defined a reference architecture for each of its product lines, categorized by major market segments. At the highest level, this architecture defines the target market, the competition, and the life span of the product platform as well as the value of price versus computing capacity. On a more granular level, the plan defines functional capabilities of the models within the product line and traces the upgrade path. At the design stage, engineers carefully isolate product functionality and define standard interfaces among subsystems – demonstrating the ability to enhance performance and capacity without comprehensive component replacement. IBM maintains a library of reusable product design templates and a searchable catalog of components designed within the guidelines of the common reference architecture. IBM also supports an up-to-date catalog of available components from approved vendors.

Figure 2. Sample hierarchical product structure.

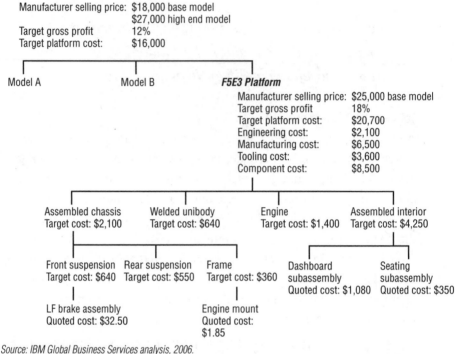

Source: IBM Global Business Services analysis, 2006.
Note: Figures are in U.S. dollars.

To be successful in the global economy, products must be tailored to meet local customer preferences, but it is often too costly to create unique products for each marketplace.

THE NEXT WAVE: DESIGN FOR REUSE IN A GLOBAL ECONOMY

The newest generation of design tools integrates sourcing with design to create a closed loop design and sourcing environment and enables alignment of the participants in the product development lifecycle into a seamless, extended enterprise development team. Tools, common processes, and governance and metrics strategies give design engineers the information and motivation to leverage existing designs and reusable assets to create better products more efficiently and effectively.

This capability has become the new imperative for industrial companies focusing aggressively on global marketplaces. To be successful in the global economy, products must be tailored to meet local customer preferences, but it is often too costly to create unique products for each marketplace. To meet this challenge, design engineers must understand local preferences and then leverage existing product platforms and available resources to design products that will be profitable within each geography. By providing visibility into local customer requirements at each stage of the product design process – from portfolio planning to manufacturing design and build – engineers can create local variants with a cost structure and product features that are designed to allow the products to be successful in each target market.

The anticipated net result is greater flexibility in facing new markets – a quality that can provide a distinct competitive advantage.

The same strategies for commonality, standardization and reuse that can be used to improve the efficiency and effectiveness of the design and manufacturing process can provide an even greater competitive advantage in foreign markets. Closed loop product design and sourcing, total cost management tools, and integrated design and sourcing are designed to make it much easier to understand the impact of changes mandated by local content rules. They also are designed to make it easier to integrate local suppliers into the design and manufacturing processes and to assess the impact of local preferences and requirements on the product architecture. The anticipated net result is greater flexibility in facing new markets – a quality that can provide a distinct competitive advantage.

Product commonality and reuse

By Stavros Stefanis

Digital technology and embedded computing have become more pervasive, leading product design requirements to become more complex. Thus, managing the new product development process has become more complex than ever before.

It is not enough for industrial products companies to create reliable mechanical designs for new products. Digital design technology is now a critical element of virtually every complex industrial product. Embedded computing is a prerequisite for achieving optimal product performance across the range of operating conditions that the product will encounter over its service lifetime. At the same time, product design constraints imposed by external factors such as product safety requirements and emission control standards make the design challenges even more difficult. Product designers and suppliers must meet all of these challenges and design constraints – while at the same time completing the new product development process at lower cost and in shorter timeframes.

BEST PRACTICES, NEW DESIGN TOOLS, GOVERNANCE STRATEGIES AND PERFORMANCE METRICS

In this perspective, we present an integrated approach to product development that leading companies have utilized to reduce the overall cost of new product development and direct materials sourcing and procurement. We describe how processes, tools, organization and management strategies can be applied to optimize cost, quality and cycle time across the product development lifecycle and how to partition design responsibilities so a design team comprised of design engineers in multiple geographies can collaborate on the product design.

We also examine the key features of a new generation of design tools that go beyond the design discipline-specific focus of the current generation of CAD design tools. This next generation of design tools creates a closed loop design and sourcing environment that can seamlessly integrate all participants in the product development lifecycle into an extended enterprise development team. In addition, we describe the governance strategies and performance metrics that are required to motivate design engineers to leverage the processes, tools and organization strategies to create better products at lower cost and in shorter timeframes.

BENEFITS OF PRODUCT COMMONALITY AND REUSE

Conceptually, the impact of product commonality and component and design reuse on product cost is easy to understand. By standardizing the design of key components within a product family, those components can be reused in future designs. This reduces complexity and takes cost out of the product development process by reducing design work and creating opportunities to obtain improved component pricing from suppliers based on increased purchasing volumes for existing components.

A commonality and reuse strategy creates other downstream benefits. The greater use of proven designs and components with a known reliability history will improve overall product quality and reduce the likelihood of component failures due to design issues that are more likely to go unrecognized in new component designs. Greater consistency in the design process and greater reuse of standardized components and subassemblies reduce the number of hours required to design the product and provide time to consider issues such as design for manufacturing and for design collaboration with suppliers.

When supported by knowledge management tools that can capture the impact of design decisions on cost, quality and manufacturing efficiency, design engineers can create product and component designs that create opportunities to reuse existing plant and equipment. This leads to improvements in manufacturing efficiency and product quality and ultimately results in lower capital expenses, increased flexibility in the manufacturing process, and reduced cost and time required for model changeover.

Although it is easy to understand how benefits can be achieved through commonality and reuse, it is not nearly as simple to create the process and tools environment that makes it easier to recognize opportunities for component and design reuse and then to provide design engineers with the ability to predict the impact of individual design decisions on product cost, quality and time to market. This requires processes, tools and governance strategies that create an environment where replicability in the product design process becomes a required best practice and mandates a tight integration between the design and sourcing processes and those of the tier one and tier two supplier population.

DEFINING A STANDARD ARCHITECTURE

Product commonality is typically described in the context of a product "platform." A product platform defines a standard architecture for a product family and specifies the core components that will be shared across all of the models defined for the product family.

The basic product platform is extended to appeal to additional customer market segments by adding additional features and functions that improve perceived value to the customer. These enhanced features and functions are grouped together to form models within the product family. The cost of new model development is reduced because the core functional components of the product remain unchanged. By designing a product architecture that allows for evolution of the product design in response to consumer preferences and technology changes, new models can be developed more quickly and at lower total cost since styling changes and performance improvements can be made without impacting other areas of the product.

Best-in-class firms, such as Toyota and Airbus, have made product commonality and reuse a core design strategy that extends across the entire product line and across all of the business processes in the product development lifecycle. Toyota has the lowest vehicle assembly costs in the industry because all Toyota vehicles are designed so they can be assembled on the same assembly lines with significantly reduced setup time between models. Greater flexibility in manufacturing means that Toyota can easily adjust production capacity to build more hot-selling models and reduce the production volumes for slower-selling models without constraints in the production and assembly processes.

Airbus uses the same cockpit, avionics and flight controls across all of its aircraft models. The commonality in the aircraft flight systems makes it possible for pilots trained on one Airbus model to be flight certified on all of the other Airbus models. This saves millions of dollars annually in training costs for airlines and makes it much easier for airlines to change equipment on routes as traffic patterns change without being constrained by a lack of pilots qualified to fly the new equipment.

The experiences of Toyota and Airbus are typical of the kinds of compelling results that can be achieved through product commonality and asset reuse. However, many firms have found it difficult to drive reuse below the level of the major subassemblies within a product family, and few firms have been able to extend the concept of commonality and asset reuse to other asset categories used in the design and production processes of the enterprise.

As Figure 1 illustrates, there are other asset classes in addition to components that can be reused during the product development process. Intangible assets such as manufacturing "know-how," knowledge of the customer and expert knowledge of the product development process are all assets that are critical to bringing new products to market quickly and at low cost. A characteristic found in best-in-class companies is the ability to reuse knowledge assets such as common processes, common tools and knowledge capital across the product lifecycle to achieve greater efficiency and shorter cycle times across the enterprise. This is important as considering reuse and commonality from a more global perspective is key to achieving sustained performance improvements for the business.

Figure 1. Reusable assets classes.

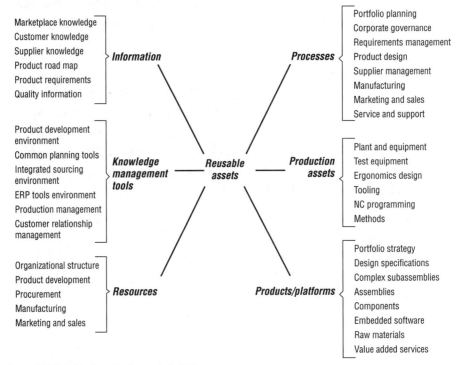

Source: IBM Global Business Services analysis, 2006.

Products and platforms

Most of the commonality and reuse initiatives for large manufacturing companies have focused on the physical assets associated with products and platforms. It is standard business practice to mandate reuse of major subassemblies such as engines, power transmission components and frame components for all models in an automotive product line. At a discrete component level, many firms have also deployed tools and processes that mandate reuse of standard commodity components such as fasteners, connectors and electronics parts. Reuse of commodity components is relatively easy to achieve because commodity components conform to existing industry standards, are easy to describe and catalog, and produce quick-hit savings. Managing commonality and reuse for complex components is more difficult and requires process, tools and governance strategies that create an environment that reduces complexity and establishes commonality and reuse as a key objective for the product design process.

Production assets

Production assets are assets that are used to support the production processes of the enterprise. These assets include physical assets such as assembly lines, tooling, manufacturing cells and test equipment as well as intangible assets used to support the production processes such as node control programming, production control processes and quality control processes. A disciplined program of product commonality and design reuse will help create flexible manufacturing environments that can accommodate a range of products and product models using existing plants and equipment.

Processes

Processes are enablers of commonality rather than an outcome of product commonality. Common processes and process discipline provide the foundation for achieving quality improvements and cost savings. Governance, performance metrics and product portfolio planning processes form the foundation for programs that enable product commonality and design reuse.

Knowledge management tools

Knowledge management tools are required to organize and manage asset information used by the firm's commonality and reuse initiatives. Information technology tools play a vital role in synchronizing product lifecycle development processes and making reusable assets visible to the participants in the product development processes. Knowledge management tools need accurate and timely information about the state of the assets used in the product development processes. A comprehensive program of commonality and reuse needs accurate information about product design requirements, design constraints, asset cost and the status of the reusable assets in order to assist design engineers and sourcing specialists in making optimal decisions about what assets can and should be reused.

Organization

Organization goals and skills need to be aligned and the participants in the product development lifecycle must be motivated to identify opportunities for reuse and then design new products and components to leverage reuse. A comprehensive program of commonality and reuse requires a high level of process discipline and tight synchronization between business processes and organizational entities that are involved in each stage of the product development lifecycle.

PORTFOLIO PLANNING PROVIDES THE FOUNDATION FOR COMMONALITY AND REUSE

The capacity to reuse parts needs to be addressed early in the product design – it cannot be added on later. The framework for product commonality is created at the product portfolio planning phase of the product development lifecycle.

Portfolio planning requirements are translated into a series of design decisions about the product's functional capabilities and a definition of the product's high level architecture. This architecture defines the major subassemblies within the product structure and then refines the architecture down to the performance criteria for components that will be used across all of the models in the product family. A second iteration defines what feature set variations will be applied to the product platform to define the models in the product family.

Inputs to the portfolio planning process include information about: the competitive environment, customer needs and wants, the market opportunity and the current product and component costs, all of which serve as the basis for estimating product development costs. These inputs are used to understand the needs of the marketplace and each of the market segments within the marketplace. This understanding of the marketplace is used to analyze the current product portfolio. Then a determination can be made as to how the product portfolio needs to be enhanced to meet future customer needs.

The portfolio planning process interacts with the concept phase of the product development lifecycle process to translate these requirements into a conceptual design for the product family and the definition of the feature set for the models within the product family.

The portfolio planning process provides the definition of the product and includes:

- Target pricing
- Gross profit
- Target cost
- Required product features and functions
- Channel strategies
- Service lifetime
- Reliability and serviceability requirements
- Product support strategy.

On an ongoing basis, the portfolio planning process includes monitoring the performance against plan for the individual product lines and continuously adjusting the product roadmap for the business to help ensure that the product mix continues to meet the demands of the marketplace. This also will help ensure that new products are developed at the right price, at the right time and with features that can continue to capture market share and grow profitability.

Product commonality in the design process

Portfolio planning defines features and functions of the product set and sets the financial and quality targets that must be achieved to meet profitability and market share goals. Portfolio planning is performed by a cross-organizational team drawn from the senior leadership team, Sales and Marketing, Design, and Manufacturing in order to capture the voice of the customer and then translate this understanding of customer wants and needs into a product that will achieve its financial and market share objectives.

Figure 2 illustrates the linkage between the portfolio planning and product development process. The later stages of the portfolio planning process are executed in parallel with the initial Concept phase of the product development lifecycle. During the Concept phase, the product functional requirements developed during the portfolio planning process are translated by the Product Engineering group into a set of high-level design specifications, first for the product platform and then for each of the models within the product family. The proposed product architecture is reviewed by management to validate the design assumptions and to verify that the product can be designed and built within the cost, quality and time-to-market parameters defined at the outset during the portfolio planning process

Figure 2. Portfolio planning and product development process linkage.

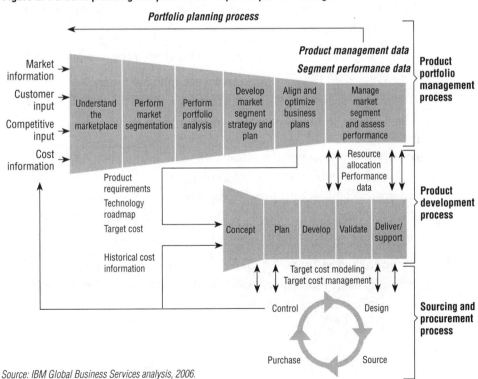

Source: IBM Global Business Services analysis, 2006.

During the Plan phase, the engineering design team creates a hierarchical product structure map that defines the major functional components and systems for the product family and maps the product technical features and performance requirements against the proposed product structure. Using decision support tools, the product designers map the portfolio of existing components and subassemblies from current products to the proposed product structure. Then they execute an iterative process of evaluating the performance, cost and quality history of these components against the required performance characteristics for the new product set.

Where performance gaps exist, the design team identifies what improvements will be required. Then they start the design collaboration process with the key suppliers to determine the cost and time required to develop the components and to determine whether the requested enhancements are technically feasible.

At this stage, the product design is continuously reviewed and reevaluated against not only the primary dimensions of cost, quality and time to market but also against the dimensions of manufacturability, serviceability, reliability and the need to create a platform that can support a clear upgrade path for customers. System boundaries and interfaces need to be carefully structured to localize areas in the product structure likely to experience a high level of technology-driven change. For example, environmental concerns may require lower emissions or a reduction in the use of hazardous materials, so competition would accelerate the need for improved product performance and value.

At the product and model design level, the process becomes one of translating the functional requirements and conceptual design for the product into detailed designs for each of the models within the product family.

This must be done within the constraints imposed by the reference architecture; within the cost, quality and time-to-market constraints defined by the portfolio planning process; and within the goals for manufacturability, serviceability, reliability and other goals and constraints defined for the product line. Component and design reuse is a key enabler of this process because it provides a starting set of designs and components that have already met these criteria and for which both the OEM and its suppliers have experience in designing and manufacturing these components.

In the Develop phase of the product development lifecycle, the proposed design has been validated, and management is confident that the product can be taken to market within the constraints defined during the portfolio planning process and the Concept and Plan phases. In the Develop phase, design engineers create the detailed designs for the major subassemblies and product design features and collaborate with suppliers to design and build key product components. This involves an iterative cycle of design and cost quotes to converge on the design and manufacturing cost of key components.

The concept of total cost management is a key success factor. It allows product design teams to target cost and maintain control over product costs since participants in the design process have the greatest degree of control over design decisions that have the greatest impact on product cost and profitability.

This top-down approach to product design utilizing a formally defined reference architecture for the product simplifies the design process, reduces the impact of future design changes on the overall product, and makes commonality and reuse the foundation of the entire product development process. Design engineers use existing proven designs as the starting point and then work within the reference architecture to design new products that meet the customer requirements captured and validated during the portfolio planning process.

This creates a compelling need for accurate and timely information about the cost, quality and reliability of the components that could be reused in the design process. It requires tools to organize the data and make it available to the design engineers during product development. It also requires processes, governance and metrics to motivate design engineers to use the available information to design new products more efficiently.

While it is relatively easy to create a library of components and designs that could be reused, it does not answer the question as to whether they *should* be reused. To answer this question, the design engineer needs to understand whether it is less expensive to modify an existing component or subassembly design, or whether an entirely new component design should be created. This requires an ability to analyze the cost tradeoffs involved in the design versus reuse decision.

The next section focuses on how management can leverage product commonality and asset reuse to transform the enterprise to create product development and manufacturing efficiencies. These efficiencies can, in turn, help achieve significant reductions in cost and cycle time while improving product quality and reliability.

DESIGN CONSIDERATIONS

Many industrial firms address new product development on a project-by-project basis. When a decision is made to develop a new product, a project team made up of design engineers and other staff within the organization is formed and headed by a chief engineer. Their task is to create a new model with specific features using an existing platform. The chief engineer and his or her team are assigned responsibility for the way the project is planned and executed. Typically the team is motivated to hit specific targets via performance bonuses tied to completing the product design at or ahead of schedule and at or under target cost.

However, if the design team only exists for the duration of the product, there will be little opportunity to detect product quality problems. And if the team is strongly motivated to reduce costs and cycle time, then the team may place undue pressure on suppliers to reduce costs and shorten design cycles.

Since few firms have implemented technology tools that incorporate the capability to leverage existing designs with a known quality history, the logical outcome would be a higher than expected level of quality problems after product launch. If the design team does not have long-term responsibility for product quality, manufacturability or service-ability, there are no personal disincentives to designing in poor product quality.

In industries with low product volumes and high unit costs, such as the aerospace and heavy equipment industries, there is no consistent defini-tion of a product platform. Each iteration of the design cycle results in a host of design changes to accommodate specific customer requests and to correct design defects. Design modifications proliferate across the product design due to the number of interrelated systems. This increases the product cost and impacts the reliability and maintainability of the product because of the number of components that are unique to the product. Under these circumstances, the reference platform is effec-tively the last version built. This leads to part proliferation issues and manufacturing, quality and maintenance problems because all of the products are essentially unique.

Unfortunately, design engineers are accustomed to this method of designing products, and there are no disincentives in place to discourage them from continuing to design products in this fashion. Management has typically been very hesitant to make changes to the product devel-opment processes because they are critical to the future success of the firm. In addition, there typically is strong resistance from the product development community to changing the basic process.

Lacking strong incentives to change and a strategy and proven design methodology that are clearly superior to the existing ad hoc approach to product design, management has left the product development process unchanged. Other than push for the adoption of technology tools to create greater efficiency in the design process, management has largely maintained the status quo.

A convergence of independent events are now creating a reason for change in most industries. These events, which will combine to push companies toward greater replicability in the product development process and a more disciplined approach to knowledge reuse, include the following:

1. The marketplace has changed in most industries. Customers have more choice and are buying products from firms that can deliver high quality products, provide more features at the same or comparable prices, and have a lower total cost of ownership. Firms that cannot meet these expectations quickly lose market share and find their product margins under extreme pressure.

2. Leading edge companies in each industry have found that increased discipline in the product development process and greater leverage of existing knowledge assets lead to higher quality products and faster cycle times. Firms have also discovered that a strong reputation for quality allows them to charge higher prices for their product and achieve greater profitability. It also provides a buffer during economic downturns. Reinforcing this cycle creates competitive advantages that persist over a long period of time.

3. Greater discipline and replicability in the design process make it possible to move design work to low-cost countries and to address new emerging markets in Asia and Eastern Europe. The ability to leverage existing design assets and knowledge capital is essential to quickly establish a market presence and to design products that meet the unique requirements and supplier capabilities in emerging markets.

The best-in-class firms in each industry have discovered the power of commonality and asset reuse in establishing design processes that can reduce cost and cycle time and improve product quality. Because the design process utilizes knowledge assets, common design processes and reusable assets, it becomes much easier to divide design tasks between onshore and offshore resources. It also makes it much easier to design products that are tailored to the buying preferences of consumers in other countries and that can be built locally with components that are within the capabilities of suppliers in these global markets.

Component Councils and Design Review Boards

In most organizations, the reporting lines for product development, manufacturing, procurement and information technology typically come together only at the highest levels of the business. Often, these groups have different performance metrics that can lead to the sub-optimization of one organization's metrics to the detriment of other aspects of the product performance.

For example, procurement often has cost reduction targets to achieve in its negotiations with suppliers. If component cost is the only metric on which procurement is measured, to the exclusion of product quality and performance metrics, procurement may attempt to negotiate the lowest possible cost for virtually all components to optimize performance against its target metric. This can lead to downstream product quality problems that can result in increased warranty claims and support costs and manufacturing and assembly problems. It can also lead to expensive product recalls and redesign efforts to correct product defects. These effects can easily exceed any cost savings achieved by forcing suppliers to design and manufacture low-quality components that satisfy cost constraints imposed by procurement.

To address these problems, all of the internal groups that participate in the product development process as well as the firm's key suppliers need to participate in the definition of balanced metrics and have a stake in execution of the total cost management and commonality initiatives. An important tool for achieving this objective is to create Component Councils and Design Review Boards.

The role of Component Councils and Design Review Boards is to represent the needs of the different constituencies within the business so the product design meets the needs of the customer, and the final delivered product achieves a balance between cost, quality and cycle time. These groups are tasked with setting the strategic direction for the business area and reviewing the work products at each stage of the product development lifecycle. They are also tasked with controlling critical processes that affect commonality and reuse.

The Component Council is a group that is responsible for establishing and managing strategic relationships with the key partners in the firm's supplier community. The Component Council fulfills five key roles:

- Works with suppliers to understand the direction and evolution of new technology and product functionality for each major class of components for which the council is responsible
- Sets supplier qualification guidelines and defines supplier performance metrics
- Defines and documents the sourcing and design roadmap for the component classes for which the council is responsible
- Manages the accuracy and quality of the content of the component catalog used by the business
- Controls the new part introduction process by approving or denying requests to introduce new part numbers.

Component Councils do not replace the commodity teams within the procurement organization of the firm. Component Councils set strategy, define performance metrics and define the sourcing guidelines for the procurement teams to follow in negotiating with the firm's suppliers. They are tasked to help ensure that design groups share knowledge across the business, help ensure that best practices are applied, and help ensure that the business achieves the lowest total product cost and highest quality for the firm's product lines.

The Design Review Board plays a similar role in the product lifecycle development process. The Design Review Board plays a central role in defining product development strategy and sets guidelines for design reuse and product commonality. The Design Review Board defines performance metrics and governance strategies for the product design groups and defines the strategic direction for the product platform strategy of the firm. Finally, the Design Review Board plays a role in the stage gate review process by reviewing the work products against the existing criteria and making decisions about whether to cancel new product development projects that do not seem capable of achieving the profitability and revenue targets.

The Design Review Board has five key roles:

- Reviews the results of the portfolio planning process and determines when to initiate the development cycle for new products
- Sets commonality and reuse guidelines, publishes best practices guidelines, and helps ensure that the product development organization follows the design guidelines during the product development lifecycle stages
- Sets performance metrics and monitors and publishes performance results across all of the firm's development projects
- Reviews and approves the work products produced at each stage of the product development stage gate design process and authorizes the project teams to advance to the next stage in the development cycle

- Controls the product development tools environment and helps ensure that the accuracy and quality of the content in the reusable design catalog are sufficient to meet the needs of the business.

To help ensure that the organizations that are most directly impacted by the design of new products are adequately represented on the Design Review Board and the Component Councils, participants on the councils are drawn from across the business areas in the enterprise. There are representatives from the sales organization, the product development organization, the procurement organization, manufacturing, and the sales and distribution organization. The goal is to create an organization that will be able to balance cost, quality and time to market to create an entire portfolio of products that optimize overall profitability and market share.

Supplier collaboration

To reduce costs and improve flexibility, most large industrial OEMs are moving responsibility for much of the design and manufacturing processes to their tier one suppliers. While this has substantial benefits, it also increases complexity and introduces additional risk into the product development process.

The way the partnering strategy should be structured depends on the past relationship with the supplier, the role of the supplier in the product development process, and the nature of the component to be designed and sourced. For simple commodity components such as fasteners and steel, the type of relationship that an OEM will need to establish with suppliers depends on market supply versus demand. At times when supply is expected to exceed demand, commodity prices would be expected to fall, and the OEM can buy commodity components on the spot market at market prices. At times when demand is expected to exceed supply, the OEM will negotiate pricing and supply agreements with a fixed price agreement with a single supplier or a small group of suppliers to obtain delivery commitments on larger quantities of commodities at the lowest price.

For make-to-order components, such as castings or instrument clusters, where there are multiple qualified suppliers, the OEM can provide drawings and design specifications and then initiate a competitive bid process to obtain pricing and supply commitments from the key suppliers. These types of components are typically procured through an open or closed RFI/RFQ process or through a multi-round bid process.

Complex sub-assemblies and highly engineered products that have a high level of engineering design content, such as automobile trans- missions or jet engine fan blades, are best managed through a collab- orative design and sourcing cycle between the OEM and the supplier. Typically, a limited number of suppliers have the specialized design skills and manufacturing expertise to qualify as approved suppliers for these types of components. Therefore, design specifications and the logical and physical design of the product are developed and refined through a collaborative design effort between the design engineers for the OEM and the design engineers from the supplier. A best estimate of the component cost is developed at the outset of the design process and then updated through a change order process.

Costing for complex sub-assemblies and engineered components can be very complex with suppliers quoting separate line item costs for design services, testing and verification, tooling and production start-up costs. Product costing quotes also tend to be very complex. Suppliers typically quote pricing for complex components at different tiered prices depending on the production volumes within a specific time period. OEMs often add to the complexity of the pricing process for compo- nents by requesting that the supplier buy sub-components sourced by the supplier at lower cost than the supplier could obtain independently or by supplying OEM-manufactured parts.

At the other extreme is a sourcing and design scenario where the supplier is given primary responsibility for the design and manufacturing of complete products or major subassemblies. In this scenario, the supplier will be provided with design requirements and product specifications, and the supplier will design the product or will use designs from a third party contract design shop. This approach is commonly used for low margin, commodity products such as low-end inkjet printers and PCs in the electronics marketplace or branded garments made for large retail dry-goods chains. It is typical for OEMs who outsource full responsibility for the design and manufacturing of products to take on full responsibility for component sourcing. The OEM typically integrates the supplier into the design, supply chain planning and firm's financial systems to provide visibility into sales planning and production requirements.

CONCLUSION

The ability to introduce new products quickly and efficiently is critical to the health of virtually any business. Industrial products companies design in an environment where the products themselves are becoming more complex, where responsibility for design is moving outbound to key suppliers and offshore design centers, and where externally mandated design constraints are making the design process much more complex. Therefore, in summary, it is increasingly important for industrial products companies to:

- Apply key design strategies such as common building-block design, commonality and reuse, and total cost management to improve the efficiency and effectiveness of the product lifecycle development process.
- Create a set of end-to-end integrated product development and supplier management processes that can significantly reduce the cost and cycle time required to develop new products.
- Apply the tools and techniques of total cost management to monitor and control the product development process across the extended enterprise.
- Leverage technology to reduce costs and improve time to market through product commonality and reuse strategies.

Leading companies have taken this integrated approach to product development and are reaping the benefits.

Executive Interview

Dan Kochpatcharin, Director, eBusiness for Chartered Semiconductor Manufacturing

Chartered Semiconductor Manufacturing, one of the world's top dedicated semiconductor foundries, offers leading-edge technologies down to 90 nanometers (nm), enabling today's system-on-chip designs. The company further serves the needs of customers through its collaborative, joint development approach on a technology roadmap that extends to 45 nm. Chartered's strategy is based on open and comprehensive design enablement solutions, manufacturing enhancement methodologies and a commitment to flexible sourcing. In Singapore, the company operates a 300 mm fabrication facility and four 200 mm facilities.[1]

In 2003, IBM and Chartered established a collaborative partnership which helped change market perceptions of Chartered as just another semiconductor foundry into a provider of leading-edge systems-on-chip technology. The partnership offered both IBM and Chartered customers flexibility in manufacturing locations, as well as cost and time-to-market advantages.

Dan Kochpatcharin, Director, eBusiness for Chartered Semiconductor Manufacturing shares his perspectives on product lifecycle management and the perfect product launch.

---

[1] http://www.charteredsemi.com

"Perfect product launch means a complete product package, customers who are excited about the product and the readiness for production."

IBM: *What are the biggest challenges your company is experiencing with product lifecycle management?*

Dan Kochpatcharin: The biggest challenge, for any company, I believe, is often business process re-engineering. Moving to a more uniform way of tracking and managing product lifecycles requires the company to adapt quickly and allow for the product to be managed by product lifecycle management tools. Also determining the level of product granularity to track using product lifecycle management tools is a challenging task.

At Chartered, the management and staff keep abreast of the market and are always ready to adapt to the changes required of us by the customers and the environment, thereby ensuring that our products meet both the needs and high-quality demanded by the market.

IBM: *How does your organization approach portfolio planning?*

Dan Kochpatcharin: We actively and constantly seek feedback from the market, our partners and customers. This allows us to enhance areas we do well in and perfect areas we can improve on.

IBM: *In the product development process, do you collaborate with suppliers and partners?*

Dan Kochpatcharin: We certainly do. By collaborating with both suppliers and partners and maintaining constant communications with them, we ensure that we understand the market's and our customers' needs and demands.

IBM: *Are customers involved in the design of new products or services?*

Dan Kochpatcharin: Definitely! Involving our customers in every stage of product development enables us to constantly meet their needs and exceed their expectations.

IBM: *To what level has your organization been able to implement commonality, standardization and design reuse for its product development?*

Dan Kochpatcharin: With our commitment to constantly engage our customers and collaborate with our partners, we have implemented the use of shared community space and knowledge databases which facilitate commonality, standardization and design reuse.

IBM: *What does the term "perfect product launch" mean to you?*

Dan Kochpatcharin: Perfect product launch means a complete product package, customers who are excited about the product and the readiness for production.

Basically as we maintain close communications with our suppliers, partners and customers, we understand what they need and customize our products to suit them. In doing so, we are always prepared to manufacture according to their demands, creating a win-win situation for all.

3

The global sourcing phenomenon

Introduction

By Harris Goldstein and James Kalina

Procurement performance is in the spotlight. Increasingly, CEOs and boards are counting on procurement initiatives to keep their companies favorably positioned in today's intensely competitive marketplace. To better understand what is separating the leaders from the laggards, IBM Global Business Services conducted the IBM Chief Procurement Officer Study.[36] This study highlighted several strategic imperatives that, taken collectively, are fundamentally altering the role of procurement – not only what is expected in terms of outcomes and performance but also the type of organization and individuals that excel in this new procurement environment.

One very topical imperative is sourcing from low-cost jurisdictions. As companies shift more production to locations where manufacturing is cheaper, global sourcing, procurement and logistics have become a growing challenge. An integrated, global approach to sourcing is now critical to the success and optimized performance of most global businesses. Supplier networks and relationships have grown exponentially to support new global sourcing and other growth initiatives.

Multinational sourcing decisions have become more significant to business performance but are more and more difficult to make due to volume growth, fragmented information, process complexities and the need to integrate along the entire supply chain.

In this chapter we discuss how:

- CPOs (Chief Procurement Officers) are dealing with globalization and other supplier management and sourcing decisions.

- Sourcing in low-cost countries helps companies improve their competitiveness.

- Procurement savings can significantly influence bottom-line results.

- Sourcing in low-cost countries becomes the starting point for a company to achieve market growth in emerging regions.

- Risks associated with low-cost country sourcing can be addressed and managed in a comprehensive way.

As these concepts converge, it should become apparent that sourcing and procurement decisions and capabilities can influence the performance of the entire supply chain.

Procurement takes center stage: The IBM Chief Procurement Officer Study

By Charlie Hawker, Theo Theocharides, and Marc Bourdé

Ready or not, procurement is moving to center stage, with top billing on the corporate agenda. At companies around the world, CEOs and boards are counting on procurement initiatives to keep their businesses favorably positioned in today's intensely competitive marketplace.

To better understand current procurement performance and future expectations, IBM Global Business Services conducted the IBM Chief Procurement Officer Study. IBM consultants spoke at length with 45 Chief Procurement Officers (CPOs) from 14 different industries about current performance and their views on critical procurement topics. IBM also conducted an online survey that encompassed 64 different countries and a wide variety of industries. The 50 CPOs and 250 other C-level executives that responded electronically voiced similar perspectives in almost every instance.[37] We will look at significant findings from the survey and discuss five key areas of change that CPOs should focus on to help boost their company's competitive edge.

Spotlight on procurement performance

For businesses worldwide, the steady beat of market pressures continues. Budget cuts are common. Deregulation and globalization are upsetting the competitive equilibrium. Companies are feeling the squeeze from rising materials costs and yet find it difficult to raise prices in a "zero inflation" world.

Meanwhile, the fundamental structure of the corporation is changing. Companies are spending more with third parties and, at the same time, are outsourcing many more functions that historically were performed in-house. Across the enterprise, the increased contribution of suppliers is adding more value – and more risk.

Collectively, these factors have elevated the importance of procurement. Today, perhaps more than ever, procurement has a broad and direct impact on corporate performance. Consequently, procurement performance is prominently positioned on boardroom agendas worldwide.

Our survey results suggest that CPOs are beginning to feel the heat of the spotlight. The majority of those surveyed reported procurement savings to be much more important in the near term (see Figure 1). And many of the respondents who reported procurement savings to be only equally or slightly more important in the near term reasoned that procurement savings were already extremely important to their organizations.

Figure 1. Importance of procurement savings over the next three years.

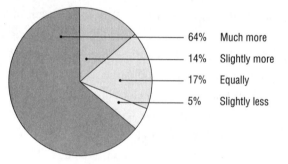

64%   Much more
14%   Slightly more
17%   Equally
5%   Slightly less

Source: IBM Institute for Business Value Chief Procurement Officer Study.

But cost savings are only part of what procurement contributes to the bottom line. CPOs are beginning to wrestle with bigger, more strategic questions: How can procurement become a stronger competitive weapon? How can procurement contribute to increased shareholder value?

> *"We've gone as far as we can in leveraging price. Now we have to find other ways of meeting our targets."*
> *– Industrial products CPO*

FIVE FOCAL AREAS FOR CPOS WHO WANT TO BOOST THEIR COMPANY'S COMPETITIVE EDGE

According to the CPOs surveyed, basic strategic sourcing competencies are relatively mature (see Figure 2). As business strategies evolve, procurement organizations are looking for ways to create additional value.

Figure 2. CPOs rank procurement effectiveness higher in historical focus areas.

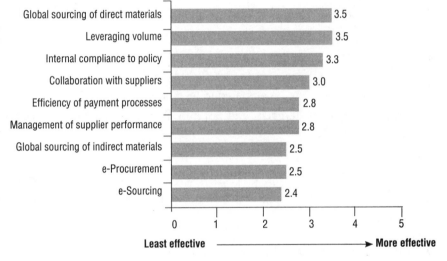

Source: IBM Institute for Business Value Chief Procurement Officer Study.

"Having a customer service mindset and being able to manage change are essential parts of the new role."

– Technology industry CPO

Based on our analysis of the study results, we identified ways that CPOs can potentially increase their company's competitive edge and add value to the bottom line. Specifically, we recommend that CPOs focus on the following five key areas of change:

- *Become business partners, not just buyers* – CPOs must overcome a pervasive buyer mentality and position procurement to identify and respond proactively to broader business goals.

- *Explore new value frontiers: It's not just about price* – CPOs need to reorient organizations that are historically biased toward buying raw materials and supplies and convert their thinking and actions to fit the very different demands of capability sourcing.

- *Make suppliers part of your team: The best value chain wins* – Procurement organizations need to champion the full contribution potential of strategic suppliers, taking proactive steps to seek out value beyond the supply chain.

- *Pursue low-cost sources: A world worth exploring* – Procurement organizations have to be prepared to leap hurdles imposed by borders and geographic differences and tap into more cost-effective sources around the globe.

- *Conduct the ultimate talent search* – CPOs must equip their teams with the necessary skills and expertise to address all of these challenges – and, perhaps more importantly, they must do so in record time.

As procurement influence grows, performance in these key areas will dictate the position of industry leaders and laggards. Too often, procurement organizations focus on one aspect of their role while ignoring others. For instance, it is common for procurement organizations to concentrate so intently on supplier management that they neglect stakeholder management. As a result, companies frequently end up with tremendous supply-side value that rarely gets realized because their internal customers decide not to leverage it.

To make the most of the limelight, procurement organizations need to address each of these five key areas in a synchronized manner – and use their superior procurement performance to distance their companies from the competition. Now let's take a closer look at each of the five focus areas.

Become business partners, not just buyers

To break out of the buyer mindset, procurement organizations have to focus on a bigger picture: the overall objectives of the business and how they can help their internal customers meet these objectives. Procurement strategies need to be shaped by business strategies and need to be flexible to be able to adapt as those business strategies change.

Stakeholder engagement remains a constant challenge for procurement. The value that procurement provides to the corporation is contingent upon the degree of buy-in from its internal customers throughout the organization. Misalignment between sourcing strategies and business needs leads to maverick buying, causing companies to forfeit the value that procurement worked so hard to deliver.

Becoming a business partner involves a mindset shift for procurement – from price to value, products to solutions, inputs to outcomes. To make this transition, CPOs need to invert their traditional models, focusing more on relationship and category management, where the opportunity for strategic impact is high (see Figure 3). Procurement organizations must serve as the conduit for converting supply-side potential into broad, business value contributions. Shifting to such a model is not simple; procurement organizations will need deeper relationship management and customer service expertise – attributes that are not necessarily intuitive among existing procurement staff.

Figure 3. Model better suited to future procurement demands.

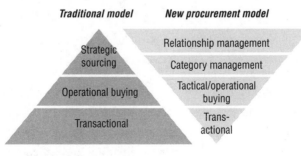

Source: IBM Global Business Services analysis, 2006.

To stay focused on what matters, procurement organizations also need the right measurements. However, among the companies surveyed, comprehensive, balanced scorecards were the exception, not the rule. Performance measures were heavily skewed toward traditional external results – the price and quality that buyers could negotiate – largely ignoring how the procurement organization itself was performing or how well it was serving internal customers. To produce superior results, procurement organizations have to balance both, identifying effectiveness and efficiency measures that are critical to their constituency and putting practices in place to track results.

> *"It is a real challenge to have sourcing skills related to services."*
> – *Industrial products CPO*

Explore new value frontiers: It's not just about price

Capability sourcing is totally different from traditional procurement, and it is a game that CPOs feel inadequately equipped to play. Instead of simply negotiating the price of a particular transaction, procurement personnel must understand the nuances of the capability in question and have the ability to assess a broader variety of factors. With capability sourcing, the focus turns to overall business outcomes, total cost of ownership (TCO) and the potential for long-term value creation.

> *"We have no real history of managing outsourcing."*
> – *Financial services CPO*

Since capability outsourcing is new territory for many procurement organizations, the CPOs we surveyed reported difficulty in developing the skills and experience required for this sort of sourcing. Because of its long-term implications, capability sourcing involves a more holistic business perspective when evaluating and selecting vendors. With outsourcing, for example, procurement must carefully assess a potential partner's overall business health and marketplace longevity before entering what are typically multiyear agreements.

As capability sourcing expands, procurement organizations must become more adept at forecasting the future – weighing a supplier's future capability, not simply what it offers today. Procurement needs to understand and compare strategies, discovering new areas where a strategic supplier can add value and become more integral to the company's operations. Equally important, it becomes procurement's responsibility to foresee conflicts of interest that might push the parties in different directions and derail long-term agreements.

CPO PERSPECTIVES ON PROCUREMENT OUTSOURCING

With their most familiar capability being procurement, CPO attitudes toward outsourcing vary by process area (see Figure 4). To date, indirect materials, procurement technology and accounts payable have been the most common outsourcing candidates. However, many companies continue to view direct materials sourcing as core to their businesses and, consequently, choose to retain that function in-house.

Figure 4. Status of procurement outsourcing.

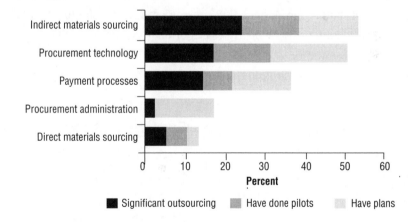

Source: IBM Institute for Business Value Chief Procurement Officer Study.

Make suppliers part of your team: The best value chain wins

During our interviews, CPOs spoke of continued supply-base consolidation, leading to fewer, deeper supplier relationships focused on long-
term value creation. The emphasis on value creation is key. In today's
business environment, suppliers do not just "supply" – they are participating in the full product lifecycle, moving upstream into product development and downstream all the way to disposal. Suppliers are becoming
tightly integrated into the company's value chain.

*"Our strategy for complex, high-tech items is
clear: long-term relationships and partnerships
with a small number of suppliers."*
– Industrial products CPO

The expanding influence of suppliers makes strategic supplier management even more critical. The CPOs interviewed agree – TCO and
management of preferred suppliers were considered to be the top two
drivers for supplier value creation (see Figure 5). Acknowledging the
upstream progression, CPOs viewed product development collaboration
with suppliers to be nearly as important to value creation as supply chain
collaboration.

Figure 5. Key drivers for value creation with suppliers.

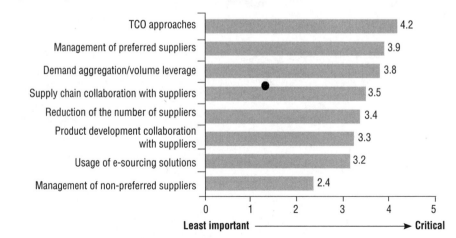

Source: IBM Institute for Business Value Chief Procurement Officer Study.

Despite the perceived importance of strategic supplier management, 41 percent of those surveyed were actively managing less than half of their direct materials supplier base; management reporting associated with indirect materials suppliers was even less common (see Figure 6). Faced with complex relationships and sophisticated contracts, procurement organizations often find that they lack the skills needed to manage supplier performance.

"Purchasing is not strong on supplier management and contract performance; we tend to be reactive not proactive."
– *Financial services CPO*

Figure 6. Percentage of supply base covered by regular performance reporting.

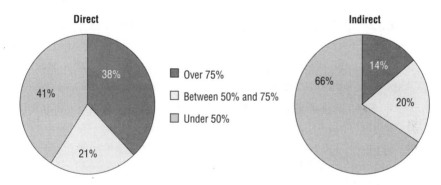

Source: IBM Institute for Business Value Chief Procurement Officer Study.

Pursue low-cost sourcing: A world worth exploring

With technology bridging borders and enabling global commerce, the choice of suppliers today truly is worldwide. CPOs are taking advantage, seeking out viable suppliers in low-cost jurisdictions that can offer comparable quality and better price points. According to our survey results, finding better-value suppliers globally was the number three strategic goal for CPOs (just behind the mainstays of cost and quality). And China was their top destination (see Figure 7).

Figure 7. Percentage planning to increase procurement volumes and upgrade sourcing capabilities in specific regions.

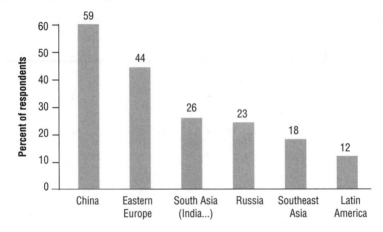

Source: IBM Institute for Business Value Chief Procurement Officer Study.

With its financial potential, procuring globally also brings challenges and risk. Even if a company can overcome the language and cultural obstacles, the average procurement organization typically lacks the expertise required to establish and manage contracts in different countries – particularly in emerging markets. CPOs recognize these shortcomings; while just over half believe their organizations have the right knowledge and skills to address sourcing in Eastern Europe, their shaky confidence dwindles even further when considering Southeast Asia or Russia (see Figure 8).

Figure 8. Percentage currently equipped with the right knowledge and skills for procurement regions.

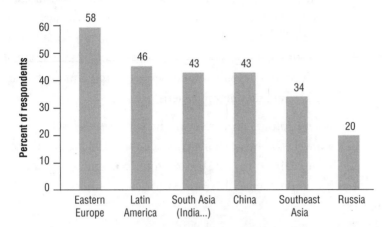

Source: IBM Institute for Business Value Chief Procurement Officer Study.

Although CPOs' concern with skills is justified, based on our experience with clients, a general, paralyzing fear of global sourcing is unfounded. In most geographies, pioneers have already tackled many of the anticipated issues, and effective risk mitigation and management approaches exist. For instance, because of their small size and relative obscurity in Asia, many Western companies are adjusting their procurement approaches. Without the purchasing volume or reputation to command deep discounts individually, they are pooling their leverage and sourcing jointly. With such great potential for cost savings, CPOs owe it to their businesses to evaluate sourcing options outside of their traditional purview.

"We need to find and integrate new personnel with fresh views and different backgrounds...rotation of our procurement staff into other departments is also in our plan."

– Consumer goods CPO

Conduct the ultimate talent search

While conducting interviews for this study, a persistent theme came across in almost every discussion: a fundamental need for new skills and expertise. Virtually all avenues that CPOs are counting on to boost procurement performance – greater use of outsourcing, more strategic supplier relationships and expanded sourcing in emerging markets – are pushing their personnel into unfamiliar territory.

With the corporate role of procurement changing so radically and so quickly, CPOs are scrambling to build enhanced skills and change habits across their organizations. In fact, the top three performance improvement strategies among the CPOs surveyed were people-related (see Figure 9).

Figure 9. Top strategies for procurement performance improvement over the next three years.

Source: IBM Institute for Business Value Chief Procurement Officer Study.

In the end, transforming procurement into a competitive advantage depends on winning the battle for talent. With the marketplace's shallow talent pool and internal financial constraints, companies cannot depend on hiring to fill all of the gaps; businesses have to develop expertise among their existing staff. In addition, with today's economic and competitive pressures, companies do not have time for traditional staff development approaches. The transformation of procurement personnel must happen in months, not years.

BP: BUILDING CAPABILITIES FOR COMPLEXITY

As part of BP's transition from inorganic to organic growth, procurement was identified as a key value lever in delivering the business strategies. To capture this value, BP has focused on taking procurement from a somewhat reactive, internally facing service function to a proactive, market-facing business capability. As the organization and accountabilities have progressively moved toward market-facing lines, attention has shifted toward building the capabilities necessary to capture and deliver the increasingly complex sources of value.

The first priority was to build category strategies in support of the business strategies. These were developed in 2004 in consultation with stakeholders using a common framework. Performance management within the function is progressively shifting toward category lines as these strategies become operational.

The next priority was to build both the skills (e.g., leadership, strategic, financial, program management, technical and communication) and the knowledge (e.g., business strategies and supply markets) within the organization necessary to capture complex sources of value. BP is using recruitment and coaching to achieve this objective.

Recruitment covers sourcing commercial talent from within BP, expanding its graduate programs and finding experienced professionals from outside BP who can fill key gaps (e.g., market knowledge/experience or strategic process expertise). Coaching helps develop the key talent already existing within the organization.

BP has taken an innovative, programmatic approach to capability development that it calls the "Capability Accelerator." The approach is designed to compress three years of development into six months through expert on-the-job coaching. Individuals are independently assessed against "role model" job profiles and receive a tailored, blended learning plan that covers the full set of skills required – not just technical ones.

The program is being delivered in waves to key members of BP's global procurement community. Program management is being driven internally by BP, with expert coaches coming from both internal (such as BP finance) and external sources (such as IBM), depending on the module. The program's impact has been encouraging so far, and many of its features, including blended learning and expert coaches, are likely to form part of BP's ongoing learning program beyond this "Accelerator" phase.

As they reflect on current capabilities and the challenges ahead, CPOs have to ask themselves whether their procurement organization will bask – or bake – in the spotlight of increased corporate attention. Undoubtedly, procurement performance can have a significant impact on a company's bottom line and strategic positioning in the marketplace. Therefore, as an organization, procurement must master each of the dimensions of change we have discussed here – not just excel in one or two areas.

KEY CHANGES AHEAD – SPEED IS CRITICAL

- ***Become business partners, not just buyers.*** Focus on business value contribution by enhancing customer service capabilities and category management skills and establishing measurements that track procurement efficiency and effectiveness.

- ***Explore new value frontiers: It's not just about price.*** Explore additional capability sourcing options and develop the expertise to evaluate suppliers in a broader, future-state context.

- ***Make suppliers part of your team: The best value chain wins.*** Nurture supplier relationships to more actively manage supplier performance, and seek broader value contributions from key suppliers.

- ***Pursue low-cost sources: A world worth exploring.*** Gain the expertise required to evaluate sourcing options, establish agreements and manage contracts in different geographies, and use co-sourcing (using multiple suppliers for the same product) or similar arrangements to reduce risk and increase buying power.

- ***Conduct the ultimate talent search.*** Equip the procurement organization with the new capabilities needed to achieve all of the above.

- ***Accelerate the development of more sophisticated procurement capabilities.*** This is the final and most important step:

  - ***Establish an education program.*** Develop a formal program to provide tailored education, training, coaching and knowledge transfer activities to staff and drive projects through a structured schedule.

  - ***Leverage specialized external expertise.*** Draw on the strengths and experience of external partners to help the organization reach the desired level of performance more quickly.

  - ***Integrate the portfolio of capabilities.*** Combine in-house and external capabilities to establish a procurement organization that differentiates your company in the market.

  - ***Capture value from the strategy.*** Realize business value from procurement strategy, strategic sourcing and supplier management through the introduction of processes, tools, techniques and best practices that translate performance into financial results.

CONCLUSION

In companies where procurement offers a true competitive edge, we expect to find CPOs who have won the talent contest, who have turned buyers into business partners, who consider capability sourcing to be routine, who take suppliers deep inside their operations and who constantly explore low-cost sourcing options wherever they emerge. And those CPOs in the spotlight deserve to take a bow.

Low-cost sourcing in emerging markets can benefit a company's bottom line

By Frank Crnic, Udo Kleemann, Christian Seider

Revenue growth is the number one priority for four out of five CEOs according to the IBM Global CEO Study 2006.[38] CEOs seeking revenue growth often must reduce costs to maintain or expand profit margins. Both tasks are made more challenging when customer demand changes on a whim, supply chains are interrupted, costs for materials increase unexpectedly and the competitive landscape morphs apparently inexplicably. So what can companies do?

LOW-COST COUNTRY SOURCING HELPS GROW REVENUE

Companies should consider sourcing materials or products to low-cost countries as a reduced-cost alternative. Companies can realize significant direct material savings – up to 40 percent in purchase price[39] – for their global factory network when they successfully use low-cost sources in emerging regions (see Figure 1).

Figure 1. Range of potential savings for selected spend categories when using low-cost sources in emerging regions.

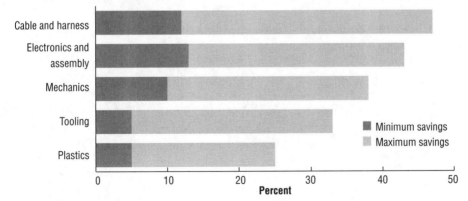

Source: IBM Integrated Supply Chain analysis, 2006.

Implementing sourcing programs in economically emerging regions like Asia-Pacific, Eastern Europe and Latin America can help a company compete more effectively. The following countries are typically considered to be emerging markets that offer a low-cost environment:

- China
- Thailand
- Vietnam
- India
- Ukraine
- Romania
- Bulgaria
- Mexico
- Brazil.

Savings generally result from low labor and infrastructure costs in these regions. These savings present compelling reasons for companies to migrate manufacturing operations to low-cost areas. Figure 2 illustrates the dramatic differences in labor costs between regions. The hourly costs for labor in China and Mexico, for example, are substantially lower than in North America and Western Europe.

Figure 2. Sample average hourly compensation costs of manufacturing workers in selected economies and regions.[40]

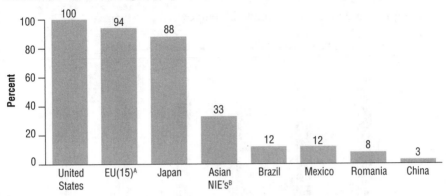

[A] EU(15) are the European Union member countries prior to the expansion to 25 countries on May 1, 2004.
[B] Asian NIE's are the newly industrialized economies of Hong Kong, Korea, Singapore, and Taiwan.
Source: Bureau of Labor Statistics, "International comparisons of hourly compensation costs for production workers in manufacturing, 1975–2003," Nov. 18, 2004; on the Internet at http://www.bls.gov/fls/home.htm. For China, data are from this article and not from the BLS series. The data for China refers to all employees rather than just production workers. Hourly compensation for Romania in 2002 as per Eurostat Web site: http://epp.eurostat.cec.eu.int.

Labor is only one element in the total cost of a component's price, of course. To determine the total cost, a company must include the component's manufactured price plus shipping costs, customs charges and other expenses involved with moving a component from the manufacturer to the point where it is incorporated into the final product.

If, for example, the cost basis is 100 points for a component manufactured in Germany and 70 points for the same component manufactured in China, the gross savings is 30 points. Shipping the component to Germany and customs charges may add another 10 points, bringing the component's total cost to 80 points. The net savings of 20 points may still be enough to warrant sourcing that component in China.

Procurement savings can make a direct contribution to a company's bottom line compared to other methods for improvement. As can be seen in Figure 3, for a company in the electronics industry, for example, virtually every procurement dollar saved may go directly to the company's bottom line. To otherwise achieve the same impact, the company must increase revenue 29 percent.

Figure 3. Spend and net profits as percent of revenue for selected industries.

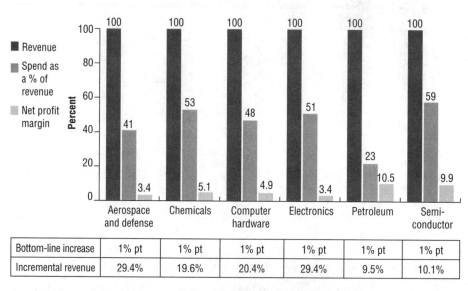

	Aerospace and defense	Chemicals	Computer hardware	Electronics	Petroleum	Semi-conductor
Bottom-line increase	1% pt	1% pt	1% pt	1% pt	1% pt	1% pt
Incremental revenue	29.4%	19.6%	20.4%	29.4%	9.5%	10.1%

Source: IBM Global Business Services analysis, 2006. Reprinted with permission from the publisher, the Institute for Supply Management(tm) and W.B. Carey School of Business at Arizona State University.

OTHER BENEFITS FROM LOW-COST COUNTRY SOURCING

Turning to sources in low-cost regions offers other benefits in addition to cost. A significant example is the competitive advantage gained against companies that don't effectively incorporate low-cost sourcing in their procurement processes. Companies can boost revenue by reinvesting procurement savings in new products. They also can establish substantial markets for themselves by extending highly competitive pricing to buyers. Companies that tap manufacturing sources in low-cost countries can further expand their business by offering goods they produce for local consumption.

Some forward-looking companies are radically restructuring their cost bases as they shift to globally integrated manufacturing and supply chains that include low-cost sourcing. Freed from managing multiple sets of supply chains, other parts of these companies are able to concentrate on customer relationships and value-added engineering. One approach to accomplishing this is moving to a shared-services model for back-office activities, often using an outsourcing provider. The shared-services model provides those companies with far greater ability to integrate acquisitions and realize value from them.

LOW-COST COUNTRY SOURCING IS INCREASING

The competitive and bottom-line benefits of low-cost country sourcing are attractive to many companies. That is why, according to the Aberdeen Group,[41] 60 percent of manufacturers now source from China as part of their low-cost sourcing strategies, and almost half of their low-cost country sourcing spending is for direct materials – chips, circuit boards, cables and other parts used in end products (see Figure 4). In fact, the average total spending for direct materials with low-cost country suppliers is projected to almost double – from 21 percent to 39 percent – through 2008 (see Figure 5).

Figure 4. Average percent of spending by category in low-cost countries.

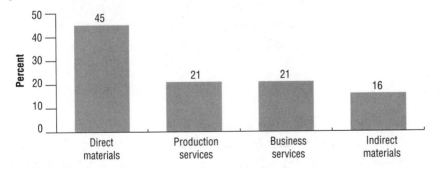

An average of 45 percent of surveyed companies'
spend in low-cost countries is for direct materials.

Figure 5. Average percent of total spending for direct materials with low-cost country suppliers.

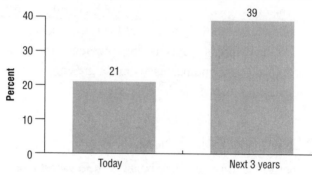

Source: Aberdeen Group, Inc. "Low-Cost Country Sourcing Success Strategies – Maximizing and Sustaining the Next Big Supply Savings Opportunity," June 2005.

Surveyed companies plan to almost double their
spend in low-cost regions.

Sourcing in low-cost countries extends beyond just individual companies. Entire industries are gaining footholds. It is not unusual for tier one and tier two manufacturers to build plants on the same property or very near to the manufacturer of the end product. Why? Low labor and land costs, increasing tax benefits, maturing manufacturing and services, improving infrastructures and stabilizing political environments all play a role.

POTENTIAL RISKS OF LOW-COST COUNTRY SOURCING

While sourcing in low-cost countries offers enticing benefits, it also presents potential pitfalls and difficulties to achieving benefits. The obvious issues are cultural and political differences. Another issue is finding capable suppliers in unfamiliar places. Then, when you find them, you must ask whether the suppliers can provide the consistent quality that you need and your customers expect. Companies seeking low-cost country sources for the first time may find that establishing and qualifying those sources and making the transition to them may take longer than expected.

Companies new to sourcing in low-cost countries should also be concerned about other issues. These issues include staff quality and technical capabilities in the region, government interference, intellectual property protection and the potential for fraud. Let's take a closer look at the specific risks, then we will discuss how to address the risks of sourcing in low-cost countries.

Operational risks
Working in a low-cost country often adds complexity to a company's operations. Operational risks include:

- Inflexible customs practices
- Intellectual property protection
- Foreign exchange controls
- Business licensing limitations
- Political or joint-venture partner interference
- Project management challenges associated with migrating manufacturing operations effectively.

Technical risks
Technical issues related to manufacturing and shipping the product can arise. Technical risks include:

- Poor product quality
- Low-tech and labor-intensive production
- Infrastructure weakness
- Distant client markets.

Staffing risks

Good staff can be difficult to find and retain, and other related issues can also arise. Staffing risks include:

• Poor-quality staff

• High turnover or even poaching of effective employees

• Lack of experience

• Fraud

• Ineffective use of expatriate staff.

Supply chain risks

Establishing a new manufacturing source brings change, which affects the supply chain – especially early in the process. Supply chain risks include:

• Difficulties in communicating with staff and vendors

• Availability of accurate baseline data

• Underestimating the time required to complete transitions to low-cost country sources

• Sustaining savings after the initial benefit.

Now let's look at ways to address and overcome these risks.

OVERCOMING RISKS OF LOW-COST COUNTRY SOURCING

Companies can overcome the risks involved in sourcing in low-cost countries. As for overcoming operational risks, forming deep, key relationships at critical points along the supply chain's inflection points helps reduce potentially rigid customs practices or foreign exchange restrictions. A considered approach and developing deep, lasting relationships with vendors help ensure intellectual property. Because business license and value-added tax fraud can be commonplace, companies should perform comprehensive documentation checks to help ensure that licenses are proper and taxes have been paid. More and more, as countries derive the economic benefits from companies relying on low-cost manufacturing sources, political or joint-venture partner interference is diminishing. Finally, as with virtually any change in manufacturing operations, good project management is critical.

Overcoming the technical risks involved in sourcing in low-cost countries is also possible. Suppliers with the latest high-tech equipment and the ability to solve problems onsite rapidly can help achieve the product quality that companies have come to expect from mature market suppliers. And suppliers with shorter tooling development cycles tend to offset increased shipping distances. If necessary, companies must monitor constrained air freight capacity to support timely shipping of products. In the end, technical issues are often no worse than in virtually any other supply market, and high quality local resources can be deployed to manage them.

Actively recruiting and developing quality staff are the most effective ways to overcome staffing risks. This includes concentrating on training and developing staff, and hiring good local managers to help retain good employees. At the same time, companies should provide appropriate performance-related compensation and incentives. Also, to prevent procurement fraud, it is important to develop strategic missions locally. That activity includes implementing tight process controls and executive-level vendor relationships. Building a capable local organization that uses mature processes is a prerequisite for success in a low-cost region.

To reduce or eliminate supply chain risks, companies should establish a rigorous product development process, making a significant initial effort to expose the full, comparable costs of sourcing. Also, the procurement department and suppliers must be involved early in the product development process. Developing and acting on a detailed project plan – including risk management – throughout the enterprise and with contract manufacturers is essential to move manufacturing successfully to a low-cost country.

QUESTIONS CPOS CONSIDERING LOW-COST SOURCING IN EMERGING COUNTRIES MUST ASK

Despite the risks that companies face when doing business in an emerging region, they are driven to do so by competitive pressures and the desire to expand to new markets. Hence, CPOs must do their homework first to help smooth the way.

Say that all of the direct materials that Acme Company uses in the manu-facturing process come from high-cost regions, and the company is losing competitive ground. To reduce costs across the company, Acme's CPO decides to move 30 percent of the company's current spending for direct materials to low-cost country sources. As the CPO ponders the necessary steps to meet the CEO's requirement, many questions come to mind.

First, the CPO must determine which components should be sourced in low-cost regions. Components with low complexity and high labor costs usually present the best opportunity for savings in low-cost countries.

After identifying which components to manufacture in low-cost countries, the CPO must determine where the best suppliers are. To find the best supplier or suppliers for the company, the CPO must ask questions such as:

- Who are the right suppliers?
- What are the strengths and weaknesses in commodity coverage in a supplier's country or region?
- How can I help ensure savings considering total cost of ownership?

- How can I build a business case?
- How can I maintain product quality?
- How can I most effectively manage the extended supply chain?
- How can I help ensure competitive lead times?
- How are contracts set up?
- What are the legal requirements?
- What are the benefits or pitfalls regarding local taxation?
- How can I manage the local language and cultural challenges?

Answers to these questions will help the CPO narrow the list of potential suppliers. Then the CPO must be assured that the company's intellectual property is protected. Questions to ask include:

- Does the supplier work for the competition?
- Does the supplier demonstrate business ethics that are in line with expectations?
- Is the supplier's country known for corruption?
- Has the supplier indicated a reticence to sign a nondisclosure agreement?
- Does the supplier have a proven track record of treating intellectual property confidentially?
- Have there been any negative news or rumors about the supplier not acting in an appropriate manner?
- Does the contract include significant penalties for intellectual property violations?
- Is the supplier willing to provide customer references?

These questions are unlikely to reveal complete answers. However, the answers will provide initial direction for the CPO and the CPO's company to take in building valuable, viable manufacturing sources in low-cost regions.

LOW-COST COUNTRY SOURCING CAN DELIVER TANGIBLE RESULTS TO THE BOTTOM LINE

Companies can potentially realize significant direct material savings using low-cost sources in emerging regions. But companies must have strategic sourcing experience and skills to attain those savings at a manageable level of risk.

To help with what can be a daunting task, companies and CPOs should consider working with a third party with relevant experience as a consultant. Working with a third party may help reduce up-front capital investment, help reduce risk and, combined with a holistic approach to procurement transformation, can help expedite achieving the desired savings.

Executive interview

Christine Breves, Chief Procurement Officer, Alcoa Inc.

Alcoa Inc., with 2005 sales of over US$26 billion, is the world's largest producer of primary and fabricated aluminum. The company also serves the aerospace, automotive, packaging, construction and industrial markets as well as making and marketing a number of consumer brands.[1]

Christine Breves is the Chief Procurement Officer for Alcoa where she is responsible for Alcoa's purchases of goods and services globally which includes primary raw materials, resins, non-smelter energy, transportation, commercial metals and indirect materials and services. During this interview, Christine discusses how Alcoa is addressing global sourcing and their ongoing procurement transformation.

IBM: *Sourcing from low-cost jurisdictions certainly offers attractive savings in purchase price but with attendant issues, both real and perceived, that must be addressed. Are you currently taking advantage of low-cost jurisdictions for sourcing?*

Christine Breves: Yes, we are. We currently have an IPO (International Procurement Organization) in Asia. That's our biggest group and the biggest area where we're sourcing from low-cost regions to supply higher cost regions. But we also have a smaller team in Eastern Europe and small teams in Mexico and Brazil.

So we definitely think that this is important for the future, because in our commodities, it's important to have some competition to the traditional suppliers from these lower cost sources. But you have to be really careful to make sure that you end up with a landed cost that is actually lower.

[1] http://www.alcoa.com

IBM: *That's a very good point, especially when you consider all the risk factors and logistics. In addition to that landed cost, what are the key issues that you see? And how is Alcoa addressing those issues?*

Christine Breves: With non-traditional suppliers, you're taking a lot more risk. So you have to have a lot more contingency planning in place. You've got to really work with the supplier to help ensure consistent quality. You've got to work with the supplier to know that you can count on them when they get another, better offer – that they'll honor their contract.

For example, when you have an extended supply chain, you have to think about if you're going to carry more inventory. If you're going to keep your inventory level the same, then obviously there's more risk if the supply chain is longer and from a place farther away and also where the infrastructure can't be counted on as much. So there are a lot of things that you have to think about in your contingency planning to help ensure that you're going to have continuity of supply.

IBM: *Are these formalized contingency plans that you create? And how often do you create or update those plans?*

Christine Breves: We do it on a case-by-case basis. It's a commodity manager's responsibility to constantly assess the situation. At this point in time, they would probably look at it on a yearly basis, but we haven't really formalized that it has to be updated on a certain frequency.

IBM: *So for example, if there were political issues in a geographic area – that might cause you to update the plans or at least review those plans?*

Christine Breves: Yes, the whole idea about contingency planning is that you've tried to think through all the possible scenarios, issues like political risks or undependable transportation systems in the country.

"If you're going to keep your inventory level the same, then obviously there's more risk if the supply chain is longer and from a place farther away and also where the infrastructure can't be counted on as much."

All those kinds of issues are built into the plan – you're trying to anticipate all the possible things that could happen and line up plans while you have time to think about it and develop alternatives.

IBM: *Are there risks that you addressed that might not be intuitively obvious to a lot of our readers?*

Christine Breves: I think a lot of people understand the risks with non-traditional suppliers. Because I think a lot of people have heard all the stories about issues with low-cost suppliers. You hear stories of inconsistent quality, of people not honoring the contracts when the price goes up. You hear stories of intellectual property that ends up in the hands of suppliers other than just the supplier you're working with – out in the market. So I think a lot of the risks are pretty well known.

IBM: *Procurement has taken on greater responsibility in the last 5 to 10 years. And there's been more emphasis on sourcing and comparatively less emphasis on the actual transaction processing. How has this changed the mix of skills and capabilities Alcoa needs in your procurement organization, and how are you acquiring and developing those skills?*

Christine Breves: I think the skill mix for procurement professionals is definitely changing. We have a very deliberate focus to shift the resource focus in our organization to a higher percentage of strategic value-added activities and away from transactional processing. We think in order to do that you have to have a transaction strategy so that you can reduce the number of resources tied up in transactions.

We have a lot of emphasis on both sides right now, because we want to spend more of our resources on the strategic side. In the past we've had far too high a percentage of our resources tied up on the transactional support side.

That's one of the reasons why we're undergoing the current transformation that is underway – because we believe that we can have a much higher value organization at a lower cost by reorganizing into a global best practice model and making sure that we're putting technology in place. We are consolidating into transaction centers, we're doing a lot more hands-free transactions – all of those things – so that we can free up the resource costs in the transaction area to invest in people that have the new strategic sourcing and commodity management skill sets that can really drive more bottom-line and top-line impact.

IBM: *Could you elaborate for a minute on your global center and the best practices?*

Christine Breves: We're in the process of developing the transaction centers. We have two low-cost centers right now. One is insourced and is located in Hungary, and the other one is outsourced and is located in India. We are shifting a lot of our transactional work to those centers. Currently we have accounts payable there, but also we're pulling a lot of the procurement transactions, purchase order processing for example, into the transaction centers. We also have a North America center right now, but, long-term, at least parts of that will move to a low-cost region.

IBM: *Do you both insource and outsource as a way of managing your risk, or is that a transitional position?*

Christine Breves: We actually do both. We have found that it's more effective in Hungary to insource, and in India it's more effective to outsource. One center can be the backup for the other center is also part of the thought. We're just starting to form a center in Brazil because we have a major facility there. That will probably be a combination of insourcing and outsourcing.

"That's one of the reasons why we're undergoing the current transformation that is underway – because we believe that we can have a much higher value organization at a lower cost by reorganizing into a global best practice model and making sure that we're putting technology in place."

But the real story is about the value side. We have the transaction strategy so that we can free up resources – not necessarily all of the same people because a lot of times it is a different skill mix. We want to take the cost of procurement and make sure that the majority of the resource cost is invested in strategic activities. Specifically, we're putting a lot of new emphasis on commodity management and also what we call the "Procurement Center of Excellence," which is a group that supports people, processes and technology for the procurement organization.

IBM: *And your Procurement Center of Excellence does that globally?*

Christine Breves: Yes. We are driving global processes, and the commodity management organization is global as well. We support our local plants with the part of the organization that we call "Procurement Operations." We felt that Procurement Operations needed to be regional so that we would really understand the needs of the specific region.

IBM: *So from a tactical perspective, it's more of a regional focus but retaining the global strategic focus overall.*

Christine Breves: Right. Procurement Operations keeps the plants supplied. They are the customer interface, making sure that the commodity management organization and the whole procurement organization is delivering what the business needs from Procurement. The sourcing activity sits in the commodity management organization.

IBM: *That leads us to our next question. As commodity management and sourcing has become a key element of strategic procurement focus, how are you coordinating and orchestrating those processes and technologies globally?*

Christine Breves: Commodity management is about both technology and process and having the right people and the right skill sets. We are organized into commodity councils in Alcoa. All of our spend has been broken into nine councils, based on the nature of the spend. We have an executive-level sponsor – a business sponsor. Usually they are the key consumer of what's being bought by that council or at least one of the major consumers of what's being bought in that council.

An important part of the council structure is to have the executive sponsorship to make sure that you really can reduce the total cost of ownership. The councils take a long-term approach, making sure we are making the right strategic decisions. And if investment is required, that executive sponsorship is essential as well as support for rationalizing specifications and making other changes. That kind of business support and alignment is critical. You need to have that level of support within the business.

The commodity management structure is made up of the councils, and the council acts as the steering group for the commodities in the council. In the council structure, you have specific commodity teams. The specific strategic sourcing initiatives are executed in the specific teams.

IBM: *And those are done, as we talked about, on a global perspective – with the execution of the procurement transactions a responsibility of the specific regions.*

Christine Breves: Exactly. The commodity management structure is global. It's a global leveraging of the buy under a global strategy. We have regional representation so that we'll really understand the regions' specific needs. But after specific agreements are in place, the execution and implementation of those agreements are done by the Procurement Operations organization.

"An important part of the council structure is to have the executive sponsorship to make sure that you really can reduce the total cost of ownership."

IBM: *So if I could paraphrase, you're flowing requirements up to your councils. Then the sourcing is done, and then the execution is back at that regional level.*

Christine Breves: Right, we have a total global view of the spend. That allows global spend management of each category.

IBM: *Now, as we've talked, I've heard two key metrics described: One is the degree to which your team is focusing on strategic activities as opposed to tactical and, also, the total cost of ownership. Are those the primary metrics that you use, or are there others?*

Christine Breves: We use a lot of different measurements to track our progress. We track leveraged agreement compliance. We track working capital contribution. We also track process metrics to identify improvement opportunities.

IBM: *As we conclude the interview, I'd like to ask you to share with our readers any advice or lessons learned that you feel are important – particularly in light of the fact that we can often learn from what other industries are doing.*

Christine Breves: We're in the process of making a change – a restructuring of our global procurement organization. We are starting to see the power of the new model. It's always difficult to change and restructure an organization as large and complex as ours. But I think our businesses are starting to see the benefit of having people with focused expertise in each of the categories – deep knowledge, good financial acumen and collaboration skills. We also are going out and targeting very specific skill sets for some categories that we didn't have in-house. We are expecting great things out of the new organization.

As far as lessons learned, we are at the beginning of seeing the value of the new model. In particular, total cost of ownership will be a lot easier to go after in the new model than under our previous structure. That's because, before, the structure almost forced us to be very price focused, whereas now we can look at the whole supply chain and how to bring value at all different parts of the chain.

Executive interview

Farryn Melton, Vice President and Chief Procurement Officer of Amgen; Tyson Popp, Associate Director of Manufacturing Materials for Amgen; and Steven DeClercq, Associate Director of Fill & Finish Material and Contract Manufacturing for Amgen

Amgen is a leading human therapeutics company in the biotechnology industry with over US$12.4 billion in annual revenues. Over the last 25 years, Amgen has tapped the power of scientific discovery and innovation to dramatically improve the lives of various people. They employ over 16,500 full-time staff. The wide variety of goods and services required to support Amgen creates some interesting supply chain challenges that Farryn and her team are working to optimize.[1]

Farryn Melton is the Vice President and Chief Procurement Officer, Amgen, where she's responsible for Amgen's purchases of goods and services globally. Joining Farryn during this interview are Tyson Popp, Associate Director of Manufacturing Materials for Amgen and Steven DeClercq, Associate Director of Fill & Finish Material and Contract Manufacturing. These three executives provide thought-provoking perspectives on sourcing and procurement strategies.

[1] http://www.amgen.com

IBM: *Sourcing from low-cost jurisdictions certainly offers attractive savings in purchase price, but with the attendant issues – both real and perceived – that must be addressed. Are you taking advantage of low-cost jurisdictions for sourcing?*

Farryn Melton: Today, we don't have a strategy that includes low-cost country sourcing per se. It is not a primary driver for us right now nor is it necessarily aligned with what our business requires. Our primary concerns are effectiveness, assurance of supply and scaling for growth – these are things that will not necessarily in and of themselves drive toward low-cost countries.

However, we are looking at low-cost countries for some of our categories. For instance, in our clinical area for data analysis, if we want to have a presence in places like India, we may go into those countries from a supply base standpoint or a captured standpoint to do work. We would hope to achieve lower costs as a result, but it wouldn't be a primary driver.

IBM: *That's a good point. As you look to move into India and other areas for the items you just mentioned, what key issues do you see, and how do you intend to address those?*

Farryn Melton: It really comes back to the strategy. So in the business areas where we want to have a presence, it will be the typical things that other firms have dealt with such as, intellectual property and the overall capability of that region.

Obviously, India is growing in its capabilities, and our concern is less around capabilities for services like data analysis. We want to be careful in how we select what work we place where. It's primarily going to be driven by the capability of that supply base versus cost for us. These really are the same challenges that other companies have, but they may take a little bit of extra risk for low-cost reasons, whereas we wouldn't do that.

"But truly, assurance of supply is our biggest challenge as we've grown so quickly – not necessarily the cost of our raw materials."

The other point in Tyson and Steven's area is the cost of goods and materials in chemicals, where naturally that's where some of the supply base is going.

Tyson Popp: I think in the case of the direct materials, we will find ourselves with chemicals and commodities in low-cost countries; however, we're not going to be driven there by our own nature. We will be driven by happenings in the world market around us – things like oil price as well as regulatory concerns that influence where capacity will be built.

So if we go there directly, we'll go there with a proven supplier and make certain that we're driving to effectiveness and the right capabilities. But truly, assurance of supply is our biggest challenge as we've grown so quickly – not necessarily the cost of our raw materials.

IBM: *So you're looking more to where the capabilities reside to be the most effective than necessarily trying to generate savings from the materials that you're purchasing.*

Tyson Popp: That's correct. And on a capabilities side, it's more than just people's skills. It's also the experience that suppliers have with Western regulatory agencies, specifically FDA and European regulators.

IBM: *Aside from India, are there any other countries that jump out at you or is it too broad of a question based on everything that you buy?*

Tyson Popp: Certainly China and others. In the area of contract manufacturing, we know that South Korea is becoming a player, as is Singapore. If you really think about the direct materials with aspects of manufacturing, you start to raise the question of where are the right places to do business from a tax perspective, which is more of a corporate strategy issue.

IBM: *Interesting. When IBM was heavily into PC manufacturing, our tax strategies leveraging Singapore were a big part of our supply chain success.*

Farryn Melton: As we answer these questions, keep in mind the business that we are in is different than pharma. It's about biotech and pioneering in this area. We're really growing a new business. Therefore we have different business drivers than a lot of companies might.

IBM: *Procurement has taken on greater responsibilities in the last 5 to 10 years, with more emphasis on sourcing and comparatively less emphasis on the actual transaction processing. How has this changed the mix of skills and capabilities that you need within your procurement organization, and how are you acquiring and developing those skills?*

Farryn Melton: Our mix is changing in concert with any organization that's going through a transformation to strategic sourcing. So one of the things that Amgen, as well as other companies, is doing is leveraging systems to allow us to automate and eliminate non-value added process and make the remaining processes more effective and more efficient. One of the things that we're doing is implementing an ERP system.

"We have sourcing people in research all the way through to manufacturing and distribution – all along the line."

The way to eliminate those non-value-added activities and change the mix of skill sets has everything to do with not spending time and energy on the transactional activity but finding ways to streamline and automate. What we have been doing is implementing strategic sourcing skill sets over the last year or so with an emphasis during the last six to nine months on bringing in "category management" capability. That is the backbone of our strategic sourcing and our vision and strategy. It has to do with thinking about sourcing in a different way, not as a transaction and not as a deal but managing the category spend and coming up with a strategy at the material or service category level.

If you think about the sourcing group, and the value that it can bring, transaction is really not the top value proposition. It's a means to an end, as is the contract itself. So we're trying to emphasize building the strategy that gets you there and also managing that marketplace and supply base on a continual basis. Sourcing is one of the most unique organizations that has touch points throughout the value chains. We have sourcing people in research all the way through to manufacturing and distribution – all along the line.

If we can find a way to harness that value and tap into it and leverage it, it's just that much more powerful. Our skill set mix is changing dramatically in that regard, where our focus is more on category management and category managers and leaders like Steven and Tyson. These people are helping drive strategies for the business. Therefore that is where our focus is and where our future lies.

IBM: *That's a great point. And we mentioned in the last question how different the biotech supply chain is. What would be the top one or two categories that you're faced with and challenged with when you look for the expertise that we just talked about in category management?*

Tyson Popp: I think the key differences are that although we look like pharma, and we have a common supply base with pharma, our leverage comes in different places. So the key categories are those that support cell culture – how we make our biotech products. The key challenge is that our growth has been dramatic and, in some cases, has been tough to forecast. The same growth stress is placed upon our suppliers and they must try to keep pace with us. And more importantly, the suppliers must anticipate how our growth is going to occur over time.

It's a real challenge. We've gone from US$3 billion to north of US$12 billion in sales in a few short years – this has had a real impact on the unique supply base that's supporting biotechnology. That's the key challenge and probably the most significant one.

Farryn Melton: One of the things that comes to mind is one of the strategies and one of the areas that Steven is focused on: contract manufacturing.

Steven DeClercq: This refers back to the primary question, where the skill sets and innovations typically found in the supply base aren't that prevalent in the area of biologics manufacturing services. Therefore, we are trying to extract the most value from our top-tier suppliers and really leverage their knowledge as opposed to just optimizing the tactical supply of goods and services, if you will.

Another area that we are focusing on is closely collaborating with our suppliers to spur more innovation. This takes a different set of skills than the traditional category management has required. This means that we need to bring in people that have dealt with some of these development areas so we can extract that value from our supply chain going forward.

"...we are trying to extract the most value from our top-tier suppliers and really leverage their knowledge as opposed to just optimizing the tactical supply of goods and services, if you will."

IBM: *Great point. It amazes me how many people think that the bigger you are, the heavier your hammer is, the easier it is to do supply chain management. And the challenges you just articulated make for some creative strategies.*

Farryn Melton: Our leaders and teams understand the business, and they need to understand the impact of what we're doing in order to be effective. You can walk into a contract manufacturing negotiation with a real strategy on how to deliver the most value. That's worth a lot more than just saving a dollar or two per hour on a rate.

There are a couple more things we all collectively want to say about that point. One is that category management is a process that provides a strategic way of looking at your supply base and your supply. Currently, Amgen is driving approximately US$13 billion in revenue with almost US$4 billion in spend. So if you think about how much we spend to create US$13 billion in revenue, there needs to be nearly as much strategy in the supply side as there is in generating that revenue.

That's where we think category management is powerful and we've taken a lot of time and effort to train our people in category management strategies. Everyone who has anything to do with sourcing has been trained for four full days and also receives coaching and on-the-job training. During this training they are learning about strategic category management, how to develop a category strategy and how to execute against it. In addition to training staff, we are bringing on talent that has the category management skill set. We have a good mix of functional expertise as well as process expertise which is how we've been developing the organization.

IBM: *That point actually ties right into the next question about how you leverage technology to help sustain those benefits and realize them. Aside from the ERP project that you mentioned, are there any other pieces of technology that you're leveraging to, again, help you realize and sustain those savings that the category teams are coming up with?*

Farryn Melton: In order to spend more time on doing strategic work, we need to spend less time on transactional and tactical work. One way to accomplish this goal is to minimize non-value-added activities which we accomplish by eliminating them, automating them or streamlining them. Consequently, everybody's objectives are to analyze their area of responsibility, evaluate their non-value-added activities and develop a plan to eliminate, automate, outsource or a combination thereof.

We're bringing all that together and starting to evaluate our roles and responsibilities. We are now looking at the things we do from a new perspective, i.e. what can we do to bring more value? One area we are examining is how we currently automate our operations. Our technology is the ERP program and implementing an end-to-end integrated system which will provide better data in real-time allows us to do our category management in a more effective way than manually pulling data.

We did an opportunity analysis a few months ago. It took us weeks to pull the data because we had to do it from multiple systems and manually had to create Excel spreadsheets. What we want from the ERP system is to help us do data gathering through a central "business warehouse" with effective reporting tools.

But we also want improved compliance tools. Once the strategic sourcing is done, how do we know we're actually utilizing those leveraged strategies? Steven or Tyson, is there anything that you want to add?

"What we want from the ERP system is to help
us do data gathering through a central 'business
warehouse' with effective reporting tools."

Steven DeClercq: The other variable is, when you implement these systems, to ensure that you are adopting new and improved processes as well. So to ensure that you actually gain sustainable savings, one way, like you said, is measuring or ensuring compliance.

The other way is ensuring that your system reflects the true sourcing processes that you want to instill throughout the organization versus an implementation of processes that focus on one-time savings or that don't reflect the desired outcome, which would drive people to revert back to their old habits and implement the systems inconsistently. So I think that's an element to consider as well when implementing systems.

IBM: *With this change in focus to category management and leveraging the systems to take out a lot of the transactional day-to-day tasks, how have you dealt with the changes in skill sets within your organization, and how have you brought people along? Or have you found that you've needed to reshuffle the deck and move people on?*

Farryn Melton: We have taken action in both ways and it goes back to category management training. It's establishing a new vision and a new way of working and clearly articulating that message over and over again to the whole organization. We're a fairly large organization and we're spread out around the world. To address our depth and breadth, we developed a vision and a mission focused on business partnering and category management which drives everything we do.

Any change effort takes time to implement, and when you first change your way of doing business dramatically, you need on-the-job training. You don't just go through four days of Six Sigma training and then call yourself a "black belt". You can't just go do category management. So we've enlisted external support. The individuals who have helped us do the training are now sitting with people on these projects doing on-the-job training and working with them so that they're really embedding the process into our actions.

IBM: *That's a good point. It should be one of the more rewarding scenarios – getting people to go from the day-to-day firefighting to actually appreciating what it's like to add that value.*

Farryn Melton: Absolutely. And the people can begin to see it and feel it. One of the bigger challenges is how do we flip the paradigm so that we can be more strategic because we're so day-to-day focused. That's the challenge that we're facing, that everybody faces. That's why we're getting rid of the non-value-added activities and becoming laser focused.

Tyson Popp: The key question that we keep coming back to answer, is this activity really helping Amgen to succeed? Is this furthering Amgen's business strategy? And to the extent that it's not, we try to step back and think about how SS&P (strategic sourcing & procurement) should be engaged. Like many firms, we have more to do than we have people to do it. We resultantly have to make some tough choices and make certain that we don't leave the high-value opportunities on the table.

IBM: *As organizations rely even more on extended supply chains, there becomes an increasing emphasis on complete, accurate and timely information.*

Tyson Popp: We understand that more extended supply chains will be a focus for our business and that we'll be maturing many of our supplier relationships in the next few years in order to get and stay ahead in this

"Supplier relationship management is increasingly critical for us and the success in how we're going to grow in this area of extended supply chain."

area. Supplier relationship management is increasingly critical for us and the success in how we're going to grow in this area of extended supply chain. We do not have nearly the integration with our supply base that we could have.

IBM: *As supply chains become longer and more complex, the enterprise encounters new risks, including hazardous materials, geopolitics, even weather. Even more traditional risks such as buyer versus supplier power, the ability of substitutes and barriers to market entry take on new dimensions. To manage these risks, how do you evaluate your business environment, learn from industry innovators and share that information across your extended enterprise?*

Tyson Popp: I think the first thing is that we're at a point in our growth where the "traditional risks" should be factored into our strategic plans. We evaluate traditional risks of supplier versus buyer power and question if we are properly positioned with our supply base. This is part of category management. We need to look out to the market and make certain that we're properly positioned to really have the developmental opportunity that Amgen requires. We have to be careful not to be taken advantage of, exploited or treated like a small company coming along into pharma.

If you step beyond the traditional, we have some interesting regulatory concerns in biotech, things like animal-derived materials, things that could be disruptive to to the biologics market overall.

The third aspect of risk is vulnerabilities from environmental concerns. It's not the environmental risk of Hurricane Katrina or those things hitting our business – and certainly, we have that risk. The risk that concerns me is with our tier two suppliers where we have unique materials and where we may not have as much visibility. We have had some experiences with this risk and we deal with that every day.

IBM: *What supply chain lessons, both positive and negative, have you learned from other industries that you've been successful at applying here?*

Steven DeClercq: One of the aspects we talked about before was vertical integration and really looking at how can we strike value. And one of the areas we're trying to get at is what extra value or additional value of services can these providers bring to the table that we're not extracting today.

The second element is business development. A lot of the suppliers in our base are developing along with us. So what role can we play as a developed and established biotech company to develop the suppliers out there? And I think all of the automotive or some of the engineering firms have vertically integrated to the extent of even parts or component suppliers developing their skills sets and capabilities – we need to extract some of that value as well. So not only extracting it but also educating and developing our suppliers is a two-way street that we could learn more about from the other industries.

IBM: *As we conclude the interview, I'd like to ask each of you to share with our readers any advice or lessons learned that you think would be particularly appropriate for your peer group.*

Farryn Melton: My mantra is always about making sure that what you're doing is aligned with the business strategy and that it is adding real value. You need to constantly look at yourself objectively and critically to make sure you're doing the right things, and that you're focused on the right things. And not just staying relevant, but really being ahead of the curve. That's my best advice to anybody.

"We have a role to bring back some of the innovations or lessons learned from others and to collaborate with our internal stakeholders to bring these opportunities to the forefront and really derive value out of these relationships."

Tyson Popp: I think the key aspect for me is recognizing that as you do more and more strategic sourcing, the aspects of value become clearer. Clearly, it's more than price, and it really comes back to truly driving the business strategies. We need to stop and almost forget what we know about what procurement is and transition to approach our work from a different perspective, asking: How do I help the business strategy? And finally, drive at what's going to make the firm successful and what's in the best interests of our patients.

Steven DeClercq: I think the nature of this job is such that you interact with many third parties, suppliers and industry peers, that we are a conduit to the outside world. We have a role to bring back some of the innovations or lessons learned from others and to collaborate with our internal stakeholders to bring these opportunities to the forefront and really derive value out of these relationships. I think we forget this at times and we should take advantage of this unique vantage point as a lot of other business functions tend to be really internally focused.

Executive interview

Ron Schnur, Vice President of Strategic Sourcing, Coors Brewing Company

> With annual sales exceeding 32 million barrels, Coors Brewing Company remains at the forefront of the brewing industry. Its heritage is exemplified by the commitment made by Adolph Coors in 1873: to brew the finest-quality beers using the highest-quality ingredients available.[1]
>
> Ron Schnur, Vice President of Strategic Sourcing for the Coors Brewing Company, shares his insights on procurement from a wide range of topics including low-cost sourcing and the procurement profession itself.

IBM: *The first question is around sourcing from low-cost jurisdictions. Certainly, it offers potentially attractive savings in purchase price, but there are a lot of attendant issues – either real or perceived – such as time zone, intellectual property, logistics, etc. that must be addressed. Are you currently taking advantage of low-cost jurisdictions for sourcing? Do you plan to in the future, and, if so, what are the key issues you see? How do you intend to address them?*

Ron Schnur: The answer is yes we are today buying some products from what we would all probably refer to as low-cost countries, emerging countries. Not a great extent to compare what we buy to heavy manufacturing or diversified manufacturers or automotive; we're nowhere near on the glide path of moving significant portions of our spend to lower-cost developing countries because, quite frankly, a lot of our spend doesn't lend itself to take advantage of one of the key benefits, which is the lower-cost labor. And many of our products don't lend themselves to efficiencies around transportation or logistics costs.

---

[1] http://www.coors.com

"Purchase price or product piece prices is just one element of what it is we need to be about in terms of managing our spend and managing the dollars as though they were our own."

But to the extent that we are continually looking to evaluate low-cost suppliers in low-cost countries, the one thing that I try to reinforce with my team here is a total cost look at the picture. Purchase price or product piece prices is just one element of what it is we need to be about in terms of managing our spend and managing the dollars as though they were our own.

I'll give you a case in point. We buy cooler bags from China. We started to buy cooler bags from China in the last couple years. Let's say that the total cost of the cooler bag is US$3 a bag, and over 50 percent of that cost is transportation and the requisite logistics costs, duties, taxes, freight forwarding – all the easily recognizable costs that go into the movement of the product. So when you're looking to source cooler bags if you only get zeroed in on the product cost, you are missing a significant cost element of what it would take to bring that stuff in from China.

I will say the other thing that we've seen in the recent past is that, as an example, as China has continued to grow and become more capitalistic in the way that they are approaching business and the marketplace, we've seen a significant increase in their labor costs. Five years ago when I was spending a lot more time over in China, we were seeing manufacturing rates at about US$100 per month for an FTE (Full-time Equivalent) labor cost. Today that cost in many cases is US$250 a month. Now it isn't that much, and it isn't that significant a cost compared to what we would pay for similar labor over here in the U.S., but it's an increase nonetheless.

And then when you start looking at the cost of professional talent, the support talent, once again, five years ago I could hire a supplier quality specialist with multiple degrees, great experience, and they were costing me US$10,000 or US$12,000 a year. Today those people in significant demand, surprisingly, might be pushing US$100,000 a year.

So we've actually seen from a lean perspective that Mexico, as an example, is becoming more and more attractive as a low-cost provider of goods and services. That's because of what we've seen inflation in China, and we've seen the inflation in logistics and transportation costs with everything that's going on with freight and capacity constraints in the ocean shipping and/or truckload or less than truckload or inter-modal type of moves coming from the ports in, let's say, Long Beach, for instance.

So while we continue to look at low-cost country suppliers and we have some suppliers in Eastern Europe and China specifically, it's not to the greatest extent that you might see in other heavy industrial manufacturing companies. But, quite frankly, as we continue to evaluate total cost, we're actually seeing things turn somewhat more favorable back into Mexico and Latin American types of markets.

IBM: *That's a great point. And your experience five years ago, was that with another company?*

Ron Schnur: Yes it was. That was with Eaton Corporation, which is where I was prior to coming to Coors.

IBM: *Great, thank you. Next question, procurement's taken on greater responsibility in the last 5 to 10 years with a lot more emphasis on sourcing and, it would seem, comparatively less emphasis on the actual transaction processing. How has this changed the mix of skills and capabilities you need in your procurement organization, and how are you acquiring and developing those skills? Additionally, how are you eliminating or minimizing those non-value-added tasks to allow time for the more strategic activities?*

"So while we continue to look at low-cost country suppliers and we have some suppliers in Eastern Europe and China specifically, it's not to the greatest extent that you might see in other heavy industrial manufacturing companies."

Ron Schnur: More and more, even today, it's surprising if you ask some people if procurement and supply management is a profession, you still get a variety of responses. While we've made a lot of progress in the professional field, it's still an emerging field I think.

I'm still shocked today when I ask that question to people, how many blank stares I get back. You know, surprisingly, no one will question that sales is a profession, or engineering is a profession, or finance is a profession, but there is still some gap, at least in my experience in the consumer packaged goods industry, of viewing procurement and supply management as a profession that people such as myself go and get advanced degrees in and get certifications in. Manufacturing again, and automotive, and probably even technology companies – I don't see that much of a gap in those industries as I do in my travels in the last three years.

But even in consumer packaged goods companies, that is becoming less and less of an issue. You know we've spent a lot of time during my time here at Coors at trying to develop and capture what we call leadership and technical success factors for professional procurement and strategic sourcing organizations. And they're not dissimilar to what you see in other professional activities.

For instance, to come into Coors as a strategic sourcing or supply management professional, our evaluation and our interviewing process is much more rigorous around these types of skills: getting results, strategic thinking, talent management, interpersonal effectiveness, leadership maturity, and then what we'll call stakeholder and/or customer focus. When you think about those types of skill sets and competencies, more and more it's about being good business people. It's about being deep and broad in your understanding of what drives businesses, how businesses make money, how we grow and develop and nurture talent.

I think 10 years ago in Coors Brewing Company, we wouldn't even be talking about that kind of stuff. We'd be talking about the ability to write purchase orders and the ability to expedite parts and the ability to maybe manage people but not so much lead and grow people.

One thing that I'm a real stickler on here as a measure internally for strategic sourcing – a measure of are we making progress – is what I call the exporting and importing of talent. I want strategic sourcing to be a place where people want to come into, recognize it as being a fertile ground for skill development and business growth and impact on the business. And then for some people who don't want to be professional supply chain people, they go on to other things in other departments – finance, marketing, program management, what have you.

The bottom line in the second half of your question, around transaction processing to the extent that we can outsource and download that type of activity to third parties, to incorporate technology that manages that at the source – we are absolutely on a glide path doing more and more of that, be it managing our storerooms, be it managing our temporary labor, be it managing our procurement of some promotional items. We're absolutely doing that to a significant extent.

And once again, five years ago we would never have made an investment in an e-procurement tool to facilitate and enable transaction processing, contract management, spend analytics. And we're 30 to 40 days away from going live with our e-procurement technology solution.

"I want strategic sourcing to be a place where people want to come into, recognize it as being a fertile ground for skill development and business growth and impact on the business."

IBM: *The import/export of people throughout the Coors organization definitely speaks well of what you've been able to do in the company for the last few years.*

Ron Schnur: Yes, I think that's a tremendous win. I want more of that to happen, for people to see this as a place that you can come and add value, grow your own skills and get great coaching and mentoring. And if you so desire to stay in the organization – great, if not, then we have built a credible organization that other departments want to come in and, quite frankly, poach our people.

IBM: *The next question we have is around commodity management and sourcing and how they really are key elements of the strategic procurement focus. Effective commodity management requires the orchestration of process and technology. How are you leveraging the capabilities of your enterprise both within and outside procurement to achieve those objectives? You touched a little bit on the technology play a minute ago. Do you want to elaborate or expand on that?*

Ron Schnur: Well let me start with the process piece because I think the process piece is very important. You know you don't want to digitize or implement a technology solution on top of bad process. I came here three years ago, and we've spent the first two years really working on, as I talked earlier, laying out success factors, laying out revised job descriptions and role responsibilities and what those critical success factors look like.

We spent some time really getting our arms around what does a good strategic sourcing process look like and what are those inputs and what are those outputs and what are those deliverables? And there's – call it what you will – the 5-step process, 7-step process, 15-step process, it's all the same. But we really spent a lot of time around introducing what that good process looks like, what good spend analytics look like, what good supply market analysis looks like, what a good deliverable looks like and then educating our people around those key process steps and key process deliverables.

And then right on top of that, as I said earlier, we're going to launch our e-procurement tool that is going to address the workflow, the content, the catalog pieces of some of our high-volume, low-spend, perhaps low-impact spending areas. So some of these people that we have brought into the organization and that we have educated and that we have really attracted with great strategic sourcing or supply management experience, we unchain them from the desk of pushing paper to really now do leading practice or good practice strategic sourcing.

This is an exciting time for us because people see the roadmap, and they now see it starting to really take hold. Up until the last six months or so, doing strategic sourcing here, it was hard to get at the spend analytics, it was hard to understand by category what we're spending our money on. It's been very frustrating for some of our folks, and I can understand that. So now with the launching of the technology on top of a lot of good work that's gone on in the process side, there's a lot of excitement here.

That's then on top of the profile of the person that we've been hiring that can help us still manage the change and help us collectively with the transformation. I've posed a question of my peers at times: People first or process first? You need both, but what have you done at other companies?

"So we really have focused on people and the skill development, the process, and now we're going to start applying some leading or at least current technology tools that will only enhance our strategic sourcing activity."

Surprisingly, and not so surprisingly, great people can work around bad process and help you create the "to be" process that you aspire to execute. So we really have focused on people and the skill development, the process, and now we're going to start applying some leading or at least current technology tools that will only enhance our strategic sourcing activity.

IBM: *That's a good point, especially when you're trying to sustain the savings that your teams have been able to identify through the sourcing efforts. Next question: As organizations rely even more on their extended supply chain, there is increasing emphasis on complete, accurate and timely information. Transparency is necessary for meeting not only manufacturing and logistics requirements but also regulatory requirements and effective sourcing. How are you optimizing your organization, systems and tools to enable this transparency? I think we've touched on a couple of those points with your process standardization earlier.*

Ron Schnur: Yes. The one thing I have found in coming to Coors compared to my heavy manufacturing-automotive background is there's much more dedicated effort and focus on the limited resources and the limited capital dollars that we have to spend on tools and technology. Clearly, that's going to the customer-facing activities first and foremost.

So, in some regards, we will never be at the leading edge of what I would call back office, downstream supply chain tools and technology just because with every extra free dollar that we have, we're going to probably put that on our customer-facing roadmap – how we interact with point-of-sale data with our retailers or our distributors, or how our distributors order their materials, and how we're able to track that throughout the manufacturing, distribution, customer service piece of the supply chain.

It's changing a little bit. I think of the incoming supply piece – suppliers self-scheduling, suppliers self-releasing, and suppliers self-policing their ASNs (advanced shipping notices), quite frankly going into our portal and any portal and being able to see their up-to-date, time-sensitive performance for on-time delivery or quality or defects. We're several years and probably several generations of technology behind automotive and some of those other industries.

So what our e-procurement platform is going to provide us, at least at a very basic level, will be a supplier portal for some insight into our release schedule and our production schedule that we don't have today. It will help us take our supplier rating system and our capturing of the incoming delivery and incoming quality defect rates and will be an incremental improvement over what we have today. It's still three or four generations, probably, behind automotive and some of the other companies but an improvement nonetheless.

So are we where best-in-class is? No. Will we ever be? Probably we can be best-in-class in some procurement activities but most likely not in technology. But I think we've gotten to a place internally where we all agree now that there's a baseline level of capability and capacity and competency that we need to be at in order to adequately support and sustain this extended supply chain of plan, source, make and deliver.

A key input into that is, obviously, incoming material, quality and delivery, and cost. Up to this point we've been doing a lot of things by Excel spreadsheets, e-mails and faxes, and to a significant extent that's going to go by the way of the horse and buggy whip here in the next 3, 6, 12 months.

"...I think we've gotten to a place internally where we all agree now that there's a baseline level of capability and capacity and competency that we need to be at in order to adequately support and sustain this extended supply chain of plan, source, make and deliver."

IBM: *What supply chain lessons, both positive and negative, have you learned from other industries, and are there things that you're going to avoid trying to implement where you're at and things that you're going to try to emphasize in an industry that may not have embraced those previously?*

Ron Schnur: I think the one of the more significant philosophical thoughts that I've tried to bring to Coors and that I've been continuously pushing and advocating is that we clearly are not as big as our primary competitors in the North America market, SABMiller, Interbrew and Anheuser-Busch. But we can be as good as, if not better than, them in how we add value in procurement and supplier management.

As I told our CEO when I interviewed here three years ago, we don't outspend those companies, we don't out-asset those companies, we don't out-capitalize those companies, we don't out-resource those companies, so we have to do things differently. We have to be focused on finding and identifying those key categories and those key business relationships that we need to nurture and harvest and grow and, at the same time, demand and expect great performance.

So that's quite a shock to a traditional purchasing person who may be all about hammering the supplier or threatening the supplier or using the power of the buyer over the supplier. And so we have to be really smart and innovative and creative and, quite frankly, perhaps more interested in listening and finding ways to create win-wins for our key suppliers because we can't do it the more traditional way of just flowing more and more volume through their business.

We do have some suppliers here that have been suppliers for a long time. Some perhaps less on merit than others and, in those cases, we've been very direct and transparent with those suppliers on what we need them to be doing. As I frequently say, if we ship bad beer to distributors and consumers at a 90 percent quality level or on-time level, they don't pay me for that. Why would I accept anything less from the supplier base? And what and how do we need to connect our two teams to make sure we both win?

I'm a firm believer that if you can't find ways for suppliers to make fair and reasonable margins that they can, in turn, reinvest into their business and reinvest into innovation that they want to bring to you, you have an unsustainable supply chain. So while we want a fair price and we want a market-competitive price, we clearly are about understanding cost for what it is, what goods or service it is we buy. We also want our suppliers to make some money so that they are here next year and the year after and the year after that. And more importantly, they want to do business with us, and they want to bring innovative ideas to us, and they know that we won't violate intellectual property or shop their designs haphazardly.

So I think I'm touching on the back half of that question, around positive and negative lessons learned. I don't want to give you any sense that we're naïve, or soft, or Pollyanna-ish in our approach, but we clearly recognize that we're an 11 percent player in the U.S. market, not a 25 or 48 percent player. So we have to do things a little bit more creatively and engage our internal people as well as our external supplier base in a different way and in a more collaborative way than perhaps they might see elsewhere.

"...we have to be really smart and innovative and creative and, quite frankly, perhaps more interested in listening and finding ways to create win-wins for our key suppliers because we can't do it the more traditional way of just flowing more and more volume through their business."

IBM: *That actually makes for a more interesting environment for you and your team. I mean, there's only one 800-pound gorilla in every industry. There are a lot of supply chain professionals out there who are facing, in various industries, the same challenges you are. As we wrap up this interview, are there one or two nuggets you can give them from an advice standpoint of things to look out for when you're not able to use just a leverage play – either lessons learned or key things to help them become successful when they are the underdog in the supplier scenario?*

Ron Schnur: Yes. Integrity and authenticity are something that a lot of people talk about these days, and I think the authentic leader makes social and corporate responsibility part of the company's plan. I believe that there are still some integrity issues around, and there are a lot of challenges in working with suppliers across the supply chain.

When we have a supplier that's having a problem with throughput or whatever, and I say let's parachute in a black belt to help them uncover and eradicate some waste, I'm always shocked to hear someone be against it.

But I sit there and say waste is waste. Somewhere, somehow we're all paying a part of that waste. Isn't it better for us to come in, maybe show them or help them or teach them how to identify and correct issues within their plant that they can, either with our ongoing help or of their own volition, transfer across their organization so we can benefit on an ongoing basis for a better, more robust, healthier, more efficient and effective supplier?

I'm a firm believer that, in the long haul, we'll get our fair share of that supplier's cost structure, of their intellectual capacity, and of their support and their creativity. We may not scoop it up this week, or this month, or next month, but building a healthier supply chain, making a bad supplier better, even though it might look like it's directly impacting a competitor's line or what have you, I think the benefits are there.

I continue to always harp on my folks, waste is waste, and we need to be better tomorrow than we were today. There's a great quote that I keep near and dear to my heart talking about six months from now, you will not be in the same place – you will either be better or you'll be worse than you are today, but you will not stay the same.

If you internalize that and really believe that and really predicate everything that you do around that hypothesis, then I think in the long run you'll have a sustainable, healthy, productive business.

Executive interview

Mark McDaniel, Vice President, Procurement and Logistics for Supply Chain Management, Halliburton's Energy Services Group

Halliburton, with 2005 revenue of approximately US$21 billion, is one of the world's largest providers of products and services to the oil and gas industries. Revenues are almost evenly split between the Energy Services Group and KBR. Over 70 percent of Halliburton's 2005 revenue was generated internationally. Halliburton employs more than 100,000 people in over 100 countries. Mark's organization itself is responsible for approximately US$5 billion of spend with 1,100 employees.[1]

Mark McDaniel is the Vice President of Procurement and Logistics for Supply Chain Management for Halliburton's Energy Services Group, where he's responsible for purchases of goods and services globally, including both direct and indirect goods and services. During this interview, Mark provides his insights on several key topics, such as procurement strategy, supplier collaboration and risk mitigation.

IBM: *Sourcing from low cost jurisdictions certainly offers attractive savings in purchase price, but there are attendant issues, both real and perceived, that must be addressed. Are you currently taking advantage of low cost jurisdictions for sourcing?*

Mark McDaniel: We are. When we launched into the effort more actively, we analyzed our spend and found we were actually buying and purchasing more from the low cost countries than we initially thought.

---

[1] http://www.haliburton.com

But it's obvious it's not enough in the current environment to help us generate the extra capacity that we need. We also realized that we need to do more to make us more cost advantaged and to position us for growth in the eastern hemisphere.

So we are aggressively doing that. First, we are getting our spend data together, which we now have a better handle on. We now understand the strategies of our product service lines so that we can deliver the products that they need. And finally, we're focusing on building, what we call, local "boots on the ground" resources in both India and China.

IBM: *What are the key issues you see, both in your last 18 months of more aggressive efforts and in your previous experience? And how do you intend to address them?*

Mark McDaniel: You must understand the business volume and the business needs in other markets. We've learned it is very critical to understand that we're in a technology business with some complex products; procurement cannot just go out and start buying things differently from a different place. You have to build a concerted and coordinated effort with engineering, technology, and quality programs. The learning curve that we're on now is to make sure that we have alignment, we get resources identified and we establish processes to make this more of a core competency.

IBM: *It sounds like that integration and alignment is really perhaps more of a key factor than the transactional sourcing itself.*

Mark McDaniel: If we wanted to dramatically increase the volumes that we were purchasing in low cost sources, then we had to get our processes aligned. We're also finding that we're developing the culture of how you manage new supplier development, how you must support them in their first article builds and you must devote the quality and technology resources to support them as they start. And we know that you have to do that locally. The resources that we're placing in country have been valuable in the communication and exchange of information as well as reducing the time it takes to generate first articles.

We've learned it is very critical to understand that we're in a technology business with some complex products; procurement cannot just go out and start buying things differently from a different place. You have to build a concerted and coordinated effort with engineering, technology, and quality programs.

IBM: *And how are these resources coordinated? With activities in 100 countries worldwide, Halliburton has a presence in many of the countries that you're sourcing from.*

Mark McDaniel: At this point, our focus has been on India and China. So that's where we're focusing our hiring at this point. It doesn't mean that we won't focus on other regions at a later time. Our business needs will dictate where we add local resources.

IBM: *Procurement has taken on greater responsibility in the last five to 10 years. And as you've just pointed out, with increasing emphasis on sourcing and, I would suggest, comparatively less emphasis on the actual transaction processing. How has this changed the mix of skills and capabilities Halliburton needs in its procurement organization? And how are you acquiring and developing those skills?*

Mark McDaniel: You can't neglect the transactional part of the business. We have taken a balanced approach on that philosophy. We have focused on trying to eliminate the low value added processes that procurement has been encumbered with over the course of time. The field is reacting to very high workloads with processes that can be more efficient.

Last year we made multiple process changes to eliminate low value added work for our field employees that are in the transactional part of the business. We're trying to give field employees the tools and processes to streamline their work.

We've learned that handling the transactional part of the business really gets you to the table with the operations piece of the business and it makes you a valuable partner in the battlefield as you're handling transactions and helping them execute their daily business.

It's very important to do the tactical well and do it right. But now we have added a strategic component to our procurement organization through category management, strategic sourcing, the development of Supplier Relationship Management (SRM) tools, and process improvements. We brought in employees from the outside that had the strategic sourcing and analytical skills needed to move the organization forward.

IBM: *And are there specific initiatives that you have completed or are in the process of completing that allow you to focus on the responsive execution of those transactions, but – at the same time – minimize some of the less important or non-value added tasks?*

Mark McDaniel: Yes, we've just implemented a contract management solution as part of our SRM overall delivery. We've created an electronic repository system and are currently loading contracts into that system. We've trained hundreds of our field people to utilize that system. So it's very exciting for our field employees who manage contracts on a daily basis to have the capability to manage them more efficiently.

We've also implemented a logistics platform that ties into our manufacturing facilities and can improve the shipping and the optimization of our packaging and consolidation. The platform has added some visibility into our logistics shipments.

We've also increased our bidding limits to try to get away from the three bids and a buy and the amount of low value activity. These two things will impact the field as much as anything at this point.

But now we have added a strategic component to our procurement organization through category management, strategic sourcing, the development of Supplier Relationship Management (SRM) tools, and process improvements.

IBM: *Commodity management and sourcing is a key element of a strategic procurement focus. You've pointed out some of what's been done from a commodity management perspective and it certainly requires your orchestration of processes and technologies. Can you expand a bit on how you are leveraging the capabilities of your enterprise, both with in and outside procurement, to achieve those sourcing objectives?*

Mark McDaniel: First of all, we've identified the key commodities and created category areas within the company. We have 13 category managers that are managing the critical spend – which is not necessarily just the highest spend categories. We're supporting our manufacturing group's most critical categories with category managers organized around their key raw materials, machining and freight and logistics. We've created and matured 'category councils' within the key businesses to ensure that our strategies are aligned and that we're meeting their customer needs for maintaining continuity of supply. We're also monitoring the leading indicators around the supply chain markets.

Within the Halliburton organization, we are applying Design for Lean Six Sigma into our processes and the product design technology to bring a complete supply chain view to product design.

IBM: *Is there a structured process for commodity managers to interact with other organizations, for example manufacturing? Or is that done within their day to day activity?*

Mark McDaniel: It's done within their day to day business activity. In Energy Services though, procurement and manufacturing all report into a Senior VP of Supply Chain. So we don't consider ourselves procurement and manufacturing, we consider ourselves all part of the Halliburton Supply Chain. It makes it very easy for us to work together and support each other. Our category managers typically come from an operating business background so they have established internal networks and product knowledge. We teach them best practices and category management skills.

IBM: *Mark, as organizations rely even more on their extended supply chain, there is increasing emphasis on complete, accurate and timely information. Transparency is necessary for meeting not only manufacturing logistics requirements, but also regulatory requirements and effective sourcing. How are you optimizing your organization systems and tools to enable this transparency?*

Mark McDaniel: One benefit is that we utilize SAP throughout all of Halliburton's Energy Services Group. So the data, the spend analysis, is much simpler to extract – although it requires what I call scrubbing of the initial data out of SAP. But the single SAP system allows us to achieve more transparency and faster analysis of the spend. We probably spend less time at Halliburton scrubbing data than I have in other organizations where spend data comes from several different systems.

Logistics is one area where we really needed to improve the transparency of our data. Because of this need, we launched a logistics platform last year to create visibility. We've discovered that on the logistics side, for example, our internal customers don't necessarily require exact supply chain event management, just the basic visibility of data that allows them to manage their business more effectively. The platform can provide 80 percent of what they need.

"So we don't consider ourselves procurement and manufacturing, we consider ourselves all part of the Halliburton Supply Chain. It makes it very easy for us to work together and support each other.

Now on the regulatory side, we're working to revalidate all of our classifications and ensure country of origin issues are avoided. We are leading the initiative to improve material master data as well.

We also have one of the best collaborative relationships between our IT organization and supply chain organization that I've seen or observed. It's a very supportive environment and the IT employees know our business very well. We get a great deal of support from them.

IBM: *That type of collaborative relationship is one that, frankly, a lot of organizations would be envious of. Have there been specific activities or initiatives that led to that collaboration? Or is that a function of the culture at Halliburton? Or a combination of the two?*

Mark McDaniel: I don't have a long history at Halliburton, so I don't know for sure. The relationships were established when I came into the organization. We have an IT director in place that had worked in supply chain and had been in an IT organization within supply chain. Having that individual in place has made the collaboration possible. It is a function of the people that we employ along with the corporate culture.

IBM: *That will certainly help. Because what we're finding is that as supply chains become longer and more complex, the enterprise encounters new risks. These may include hazardous materials, geopolitics, which you certainly must be familiar, and even weather. Even the more traditional risks such as buyer versus supplier power and availability of substitutes and barriers to market entry are taking on new dimensions.*

To manage these risks, how does Halliburton evaluate the business environment from the supply chain perspective, learn from industry innovators, both with in and outside the enterprise, and share that information across the enterprise?

Mark McDaniel: Those issues are certainly real, particularly in today's market with tight commodities and services. There's an element of risk in the countries in which we operate. We understand and are used to the geopolitical risk, so it doesn't frighten us. Weather, we can't control, but we learned so much from the hurricanes in 2005. For example, when the hurricanes damaged the chemical capacity in the Gulf Coast, our category managers quickly reacted. They worked with suppliers and restored our supply of critical chemicals and found alternate supplies, as well.

So in tight markets, we've encouraged product substitutions, identified new suppliers, tapped into additional capacity of sole suppliers, and added additional capacity as needed. So I think for the most part, our category managers have played a key role in mitigating those risks.

IBM: *That's an impressive organization response to a difficult situation. As we conclude the interview, I'd like to ask you to share with our readers any advice or lessons learned that you think would be particularly appropriate for your peers.*

Mark McDaniel: When implementing a strategic component to the organization, it is critical to include everyone in the process. Many times the field employees will feel left out of the transformation and won't understand it. I've spent a great deal of time communicating our vision to the field and showing them what we're building and how it will benefit them and their daily work.

In general, transformations tend to bypass the tactical procurement organizations so they may feel like it was done because they weren't performing. While that may or may not be true, all employees need to buy in to the change and understand why it is occurring.

"So in tight markets, we've encouraged product substitutions, identified new suppliers, tapped into additional capacity of sole suppliers, and added additional capacity as needed."

Be realistic about the timing and impact of the change; particularly in a global organization. Leadership will always start with the highest impact locations and spend. Therefore, it is critical to let the other 20 percent know how long it will take before they feel the change. You must communicate early and often to each and every stakeholder in the process.

We learned that if you focus just on communicating monetary savings, that's what the organization is going to use to measure your progress. If you do things correctly, then you're not only saving dollars, but you're also delivering value beyond savings. Organizations need to move quickly from a cost reduction style of communication to a value delivery communication for the stakeholders.

IBM: *Communications has been a central theme. Are there particular techniques that you use for communicating? What techniques did you use that might be above and beyond the ordinary?*

Mark McDaniel: I'm not a communication or change management expert, by any means and admit we could have done things better. However, I spent a great deal of my time traveling to our international locations to address the product line leaders and our procurement organization to explain our vision, the changes we were making and the role they would have in that change, then I focused on the rest of our procurement managers that run the global organization. I brought them to headquarters and trained them on the transformation and the role they would play in the process. The face to face interaction and the open feedback seemed to be very effective.

But you get the most effective communication when category managers travel to meet with the stakeholders and demonstrate how they are specifically helping that region or country and providing value to the product service lines. When you achieve buy in at that level, you really see things take off.

We also learned to communicate in sound bites. Communications don't have to be long, formal, and written by experts. Blackberry friendly emails easily communicate the value we provide to the rest of the organization and are time and cost effective. One thing that I have not witnessed is an effective change management program. I've never seen anyone who has cornered the market on that; I certainly didn't see it here, but I don't think we're that unusual.

IBM: *It appears that the key is execution – and steady process in communication. And perhaps a lot of listening, as well.*

Mark McDaniel: Yes, listening is key. But you have to have the executive level support; which we had. The support has actually strengthened over the last year at the executive level now that they've seen the value delivery. We aligned ourselves with the financial organization in the early savings delivery and we won't quote numbers if the financial organization or the stakeholders won't buy into those numbers. So that was one of the enablers.

Another enabler in the change has been the high quality of skills and talent we have hired into this organization. These strategic analysts go into a business and start tearing down the spend analysis and building cost models. That quickly drove credibility and an understanding of, "Wow, this is different." It also helped with the change management when our stakeholders saw a differentiating skill set and a talent base.

4

Perspectives on global logistics

Introduction

By Colin Taylor

Fifty years ago the imagination and foresight of Malcolm McClean led to the historic sailing of a converted tanker named Ideal X from Port Newark. Bound for Houston, Texas, the Ideal X had 58 metal boxes – very similar to the ubiquitous 40-foot containers we have today – lashed to the deck. Thus started the container shipping industry. McClean's innovative solution to loading and unloading ocean cargo caught on, and the industry and ships grew quickly. By 1980, the largest container ships carried over 2,700 twenty-foot equivalent unit (TEU) containers; today's ships carry over 8,500 TEUs. The largest ships currently in construction will carry 10,000 TEUs and, like most things today, they are being made in Asia.

So has global logistics become bigger, faster and cheaper?

It's true that vessel sizes keep growing. Increases in shipping capacity track the soaring demand driven by the global sourcing strategies of retailers and manufacturers as well as federal government initiatives that utilize commercial shipping capacity to reduce costs and extend reach. Also, transit times have been reduced, with some of the fastest ocean services between Hong Kong and the West Coast taking only around 11 days. But whether or not global logistics is cheaper depends on when and what you measure.

With deregulation in the ocean industry, competition has helped control rates but rates still fluctuate with the season, fuel prices, labor shortages, and congestion charges and other additional fees. While the industry remains fragmented, recent acquisitions and mergers have some shippers wondering if the emerging "mega-carriers" will take advantage of their size to pass on the cost reductions or whether they will hold onto the extra profit. Or perhaps they will use their newly combined weights to transform the industry with new services such as near-realtime visibility and tracking.

Many retailers and manufacturers of goods with shorter or fashion-sensitive shelf-life depend on more expensive air freight to be first to market. But just as many shippers use air freight to expedite a shipment because their product development, sourcing, and logistics processes and systems do not integrate or synchronize, resulting in less than predictable delivery schedules.

One thing is certain: Whether you are moving manufacturing offshore or looking to suppliers in Asia, South America and Eastern Europe for lower cost goods, the global logistics cost components of landed costs are increasing. Never before has it been so critical to have import logistics information integrated with other supply chain functions to form a seamless, flexible, predictable and responsive inbound supply chain. And never before has that been such a complex feat to achieve.

Traditionally, supply chain and logistics executives have been unanimous in voicing the difficulties they have encountered trying to elevate their logistics initiatives to the executive suite. Despite Chief Executive Officer (CEO) directives to "Go global" or "Increase global sourcing by 50 percent next year", there was not as much inertia behind transforming logistics operations. However, the tides are turning as the real impact of global sourcing strategies is starting to put a visible strain on corporate performance.

CEOs and Chief Financial Officers (CFOs) are getting wake-up calls due to increased inventory, higher levels of working capital, increased out-of-stock positions and glitches in manufacturing performance. Forward-thinking companies are now realizing that logistics holds a key to competitive advantage and is a key enabler in today's global, end-to-end, demand-driven supply chain. As a result, logistics is moving from the "basement to the boardroom" and – with focused efforts in improvement – delivering tangible, differentiated results to corporations.

Chapter 4 looks at global logistics from both a shipper's perspective and that of a logistics service provider. We explore why global logistics is on the agenda of CEOs in retail and manufacturing and the subject of massive investment by logistics service providers. We also look at RFID as an enabler to visibility; RFID has become one of the key capabilities that industry and government agencies pursue to reduce surplus inventory and optimize the rapid availability of required goods. Finally, we look at logistics as a vital component within the broader "sense-and-respond" value net of the military.

We hope the perspectives in this section not only stimulate thought among logistics managers but raise awareness among business leaders as well. With products being sourced around the globe, logistics is no longer a back-burner issue but a key strategy for a company's survival and competitive advantage.

Why global logistics is rising from the basement to the boardroom and five steps for transforming logistics

By Colin Taylor

Traditionally, global logistics has been almost an afterthought when it comes to corporate strategic planning. Because it is an unavoidable cost, logistics has been seen as a complex detail that can be attended to in the margins of the business. But this is no longer the case.

We will explore why global logistics has become so strategically important and recommend steps a company can take to transform logistics operations to meet global challenges. IBM's own experience in transforming its logistics operations serves as a case study to offer insight into the performance benefits gained from a strategic focus on logistics.

REASONS GLOBAL LOGISTICS IS RISING FROM THE BASEMENT TO THE BOARDROOM

With the rising strategic importance of global sourcing, logistics planning is becoming the focal point for supply chain managers. You source globally to keep costs down, and it doesn't make sense to let the rising costs, longer transit times and complexities associated with global logistics erode those savings. It's no longer possible to make a decision about where to obtain parts, locate a manufacturing facility or open a retail outlet without first understanding the impact on global logistics. Chief Executive Officers (CEOs) and Chief Financial Officers (CFOs) are increasingly alarmed by rising inventory, higher levels of working capital, missed deliveries and glitches in the lean manufacturing performance, all of which can result from poor global sourcing strategies. So, as the strategic dimension of logistics planning becomes more apparent, senior management is looking for ways to get the most value and competitive advantage out of this business function.

Managing rising logistics costs

The biggest reason global logistics is now getting C-level attention can be summed up in one word: cost. Logistics costs now consume more than ten percent of sales revenues for most companies.[42] Consequently, logistics costs are beginning to erode or at least counter-balance many of the economic advantages of global sourcing.

These costs are driven by both internal and external factors. Internally, the increasing tendency toward global sourcing has resulted in a great deal of network complexity. The extremely rapid nature of this transition has forced logistics networks and distribution centers to assimilate loads and variables that they were not designed to manage. Additionally, most global companies are dealing with a legacy of fragmented internal logistics structures that are siloed by brand or department, which makes it difficult to apply consistent management processes and tools. This fragmentation also makes it hard to leverage cost savings across divisions and brands – and leads to suboptimal container-utilization levels.

External costs are also continuing to rise. Inputs such as fuel, labor and real estate show no signs of falling in price. Supply and demand curves, tight schedules and capacity levels for ocean shipping place upward pressure on costs – especially in trans-Pacific trade lanes. Additionally, some recent merger and acquisition activity in the carrier market is creating the potential for greater price control for the tier one carriers. Finally, there are the costs and complexities related to compliance with government global trade regulations.

Managing customs declarations and other documentation, not to mention the varying fees and tariffs involved, has driven up logistics costs. Given the impact of these internal and external factors, an overall strategic approach is needed to leverage economies of scale, improve import decision support and increase lane densities.

Lean manufacturing

The advent of lean manufacturing and lean supply chain initiatives has meant that logistics must also support these goals. The lean approach helps companies move toward demand-based product flow from the point of origin to the consumer or end-customer. It has inspired global businesses to focus on reducing waste and lowering inventory.

However, while lean initiatives have reduced inventories in warehouses, the greater distances and transit times involved in global sourcing have led to longer inbound supply cycles. These longer cycles create pressure to build up stock against potential shortages, undercutting the goals of lean manufacturing. Meanwhile, shortening the supply cycle means integrating inbound and outbound sides of the supply chain. Therefore, logistics planning and execution now need to be integrated with sourcing and materials procurement – yet another reason why C-level executives are turning their attention toward enterprisewide logistics management and organizational integration.

Operating as an on demand business

In line with the move toward lean manufacturing, many companies are transforming in order to support on demand business operations. This often requires a makeover of the company's logistics operations, too.

IBM defines an on demand business as an enterprise whose business processes – integrated end-to-end across the company and with key partners, suppliers and customers – can respond with speed to virtually any customer demand, market opportunity or external threat. To stay competitive in the era of on demand business, companies need to be responsive to changing market conditions, aware of variables in their cost structures, focused on core competencies and resilient in the face of disruptions or setbacks.

For example, logistics costs need to fluctuate in relation to business revenue, as illustrated in Figure 1. Companies also need to examine how the ownership of assets, such as warehouses, truck fleets and the resources to operate them, affects their ability to respond quickly to new market pressures. To create a global logistics infrastructure that supports the goals of on demand business requires top-down planning and coordination. The good news: A business that is flexible enough to vary its logistics costs in line with revenue is well-positioned to react to unexpected changes that are geopolitical in nature and beyond the control of the enterprise.

Figure 1. IBM global logistics costs for hardware business – varying with IBM hardware revenue.

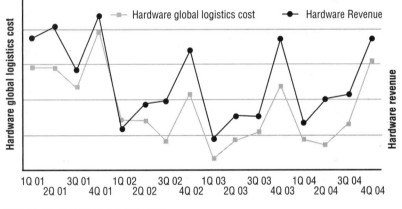

Source: IBM Global Business Services analysis, 2006.

Cross-functional sourcing decisions

The dramatic increase in global sourcing has changed the process for strategic decision-making in areas like offshore manufacturing locations, private label growth and vendor selection. To make these decisions in today's world, operations specialists from all functions within the supply chain need access to detailed logistics information.

If you want to change a vendor or manufacturing location, you need to understand how that move will affect your logistics costs. In addition, new opportunities need to be taken into account. For example, you may want to change your distribution patterns by setting up manufacturing closer to your markets to offset logistics costs. You will want to know where your liabilities and your opportunities lie, so you'll need to assess which sourcing locations best balance factors related to cost, customer service, working capital and risk. Cross-function processes must now provide what-if analyses of sourcing information based on robust information about direct and indirect logistics costs. Again, that means direct involvement of C-level executives to enable the organizational transformation and the waterfall of business objectives required to set goals and constraints.

Supply chain management

Because logistics has such an enormous impact on supply chain management, global logistics information is now essential for supporting enterprise decision-making, including forecasting and demand planning. To make good decisions, line-of-business managers and executives need to understand optimized logistics costs by both origin and destination. They also need predictable delivery dates, clear visibility into import logistics events and automated alerts when plans change or a shipment is off schedule. Automated transactions and analytics are important to help manage the growing volumes of imports – for example, to enable the automatic optimizing of carrier allocations according to predefined business rules, carrier performance and contract commitments.

Companies should closely examine their shipping options. Air freight, in particular, may harbor hidden costs, even though it is commonly perceived as the better option for moving goods overseas quickly. Companies may assume that faster shipping times justify the higher prices they pay compared to ocean shipping. However, delays in customs or other areas can wreak havoc with your inventory, negating many of the benefits of faster transit times. It is important to use a model that accounts for all aspects of the journey so you can make appropriate decisions regarding which forms of transportation to use. A framework that enables better forecasting and supports collaboration with suppliers – while managing carriers – can help you align your shipping mode with your profit goals (see Figure 2).

Figure 2. Supply chain management decision support.

Enterprise decisions...	require...	robust logistics information.
Sourcing / Landed cost and profit		Access to optimized logistics costs by origin and destination
Forecasting / Demand planning		
LEAN manufacturing / Scheduling		Predictable delivery dates
Delivery dates / Customer service		Visibility and advance warning of exceptions to plan
Inventory / Distribution optimization		Quantitative carrier performance
Managing risk / Business continuity		Reliable event visibility
Improving process productivity		Automated standard data transaction and analytics
Managing financial performance		

Source: IBM Global Business Services analysis, 2006.

Clearly, global logistics is now a critical-path operation. Regardless of your objective – to protect the economic value of global sourcing, adhere to lean manufacturing or on demand business objectives, or make better decisions regarding sourcing or the enterprise as a whole – you need to be able to track your materials and manufactured goods at all times and know what it is costing you to get them to where they need to go. Optimizing costs and business decisions usually means transforming your logistic operations to support your overall business goals. Luckily, the transformation path has been well-mapped for global companies. Let's take a look at that path.

FIVE STEPS TO GLOBAL LOGISTICS TRANSFORMATION

Take a phased approach

A comprehensive transformation of your entire global logistics operation can't be accomplished in a single project. It is a phased process, comprising multiple projects that need to be prioritized according to your most pressing business needs. And to be successful, the entire process needs to fully leverage existing investments in your logistics infrastructure.

A global logistics transformation has two main phases, although individual companies may want to create additional stages within each phase based on their needs. The stages within Phase 1 involve identifying your transformation strategy, designing your new infrastructure and beginning to deploy it. This phase is based on a number of strategic imperatives, such as organizational strength, leadership and execution, compliance, convergence and simplification, performance measurement, outsourcing and network optimization. In other words, activities in logistics should be directly related to delivering improvements in one or more of these areas. Virtually any other activities need to be redirected or eliminated during the transformation period.

In Phase 1, the lines-of-business (LOBs) must buy into the transformation. Clear business metrics need to be established so the LOBs can understand what they will gain by participating. The more buy-in you get from the LOBs, the further you can progress in your network optimization, and, in turn, the better the results you can deliver. Virtually all of the LOBs should see better reliability and responsiveness in shipping as a result of their participation in the transformation process.

During Phase 1, you create the overall roadmap of your transformation by analyzing all your business and IT processes related to logistics in terms of their components and identifying the gaps between where you are today and where you want to go. Once you understand the dependencies among the various projects that will take you there, you can create a timeline and map your projects against it.

In Phase 2, you deploy and optimize your new systems. Many companies move toward more outsourcing of logistics operations to establish a system where global logistics costs can vary on a transactional basis. This adds a great deal more flexibility to the company's business operations. Ongoing centralization – consolidation and simplification – of logistics operations and management can move your organization from an asset-based, fixed-cost organization to one that is more fully leveraged with a flexible and variable cost structure. Automated processes and reporting can help you improve efficiency and support ongoing monitoring and performance management.

Establish partner connectivity

As import volumes increase, a strategic approach to connectivity becomes essential to allow for automated event management and the ability to use other planning, optimization and execution systems. The sheer number of parties and documents involved in a single ocean shipment exposes you to a multitude of risks and liabilities in terms of regulatory compliance, delivery schedules, errors and, ultimately, customer satisfaction. For example, for one container shipment, data transactions can touch an average of 27 parties and require 40 original documents and 360 copies – *for each container*.[43]

A data services gateway can serve as an information broker between you and your supply chain partners by linking partners, applications, carriers, customs agencies and banks. Standardized interfaces can allow partners and customers to interact at virtually any time from virtually any point on the globe. Such a gateway can lower entry and exit costs, decrease interface setup times, reduce transaction time and decrease business risk. It replaces the multiple systems you would otherwise need to use to link multiple divisions with multiple partners.

As an add-on to a connectivity gateway, companies can develop an e-customs infrastructure that can serve as a convergence point for brokers and supply sources. A centralized global product database can help organize the classification function and the usage of preferential trade programs to align the entire enterprise with a standard product structure and additional capabilities that allow for paperless processing, transaction testing and easy access to shipping procedural instructions. Benefits include reduced and more variable costs, increased reliability, the ability to change suppliers as business needs change, adherence to global standards without losing local flexibility and enhanced compliance.

Know your industry

Many companies opt to bring in what Forrester Research has called a "global trade orchestrator"[44] to help them redesign and manage their logistics systems. Such a partner would need a detailed understanding of the systems, processes, data and constraints affecting all the service providers involved in moving a container from one point to another. But whether you are outsourcing this orchestration capacity or establishing it in-house, experience with integrating logistics *and business functions* is critical. The ideal skill-set base would include direct knowledge of import scope, sourcing, procurement, global logistics planning and execution, trade and customs regulations, and financial invoicing and credit checks.

Build an integrated import processes and systems framework

Creating an import framework that helps you view import logistics across all of your business functions is another essential step (see Figure 3). The single view that results from such a framework enables you to make more informed business decisions and support rapid volume growth. In this view, logistics is considered to be a horizontal business function alongside other key areas of your business, such as product development, global sourcing, procurement and finance. These functions are supported by integrated processes that include product data manage-ment, vendor selection and management, quality control, import trans-portation and compliance. Virtually all of the integrated data can then be viewed through a planning and operations dashboard, which has the ability to generate management reports. The whole thing links to your enterprise resource planning (ERP) software for comprehensive integra-tion of your business.

Figure 3. An integrated framework for import logistics can support your overall business goals.

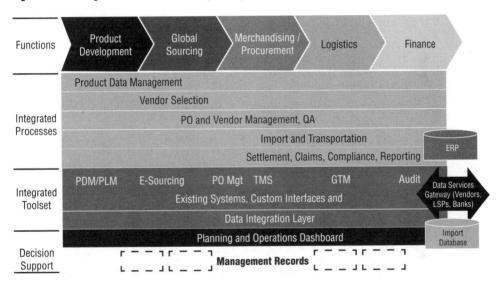

Source: IBM Global Business Services analysis, 2006.

Implement an international transportation resource planning framework

To integrate the fragmented, manual and siloed processes of global logistics, organizations are increasingly thinking in terms of parallels to ERP frameworks. An international transportation resource planning (TRP) framework can help make container shipments more predictable, visible across the organization – as well as across partnerships – and easier to manage. A TRP framework has four main components:

- *Strategic processes* – Forecasting and planning
- *Tactical processes* – Mapping forecasts and purchase orders to container utilization plan, selecting and booking carriers, managing compliance
- *Process control* – Conducting data analysis, assessing carrier contract compliance, rating performance, managing carrier relationships
- *Integration* – Integrating these processes with enterprise applications and supply chain management.

Used to continuously improve decision-making and service levels, TRP data can deliver shareholder value by helping reduce the contingency charges of inventory that typically get added to account for the variability of ocean shipping. By lowering inventory, a TRP framework can help reduce costs and promote better alignment with lean manufacturing and on demand business goals.

REDUCING LOGISTICS COSTS AT IBM[45]

In response to the changing global marketplace, IBM transformed its own global logistics operations. Our phased approach had three main segments and took ten years to complete – a timeframe that could now be condensed due to the experience gained.

In Phase 1, which began in 1995, our goal was to improve efficiencies at the organizational and tactical levels. At that time, our product lines were autonomous in virtually every sense, with each line operating its own logistics system. By focusing on project management discipline, working to build a global team ethos, understanding our client requirements, leveraging volumes and creating a logistics-focused line of business, we were able to save millions in the first phase.

In Phase 2, which began in 1996, we developed an overarching strategy for our logistics transformation process based on the seven strategic imperatives of organizational strength: leadership, execution, compliance, convergence and simplification, performance measurement, outsourcing and network optimization. We wanted to leverage the promise of our brand – that is, we set out to make sure that we achieved ideal shipping rates across our entire brand so we could access economies of scale rather than taking a piecemeal approach, with each product line trying to drive its own bargain. We optimized our internal networks, built a performance-based culture supported by metrics and ultimately saved millions in this phase, as well.

In 1997, we launched Phase 3, which is still in effect today. We now outsource over 90 percent of our logistics operations to significantly decrease the complexity of those operations. We also reduced the number of suppliers we worked with, the number of contracts involved, our logistics cycle times, the number of legacy systems we had to integrate and the number of field locations. In the end, this convergence and consolidation accounts for savings in excess of US$1 billion. Our logistics cost-to-revenue ratio has dropped by 25 percent. We trimmed our legacy applications from 350 to 60, and our client satisfaction rates have risen continuously since 1999.

As a result of our transformation, we've moved from a fragmented, asset-based fixed-cost system with limited ability to respond to market pressures to a standardized, fully leveraged and outsourced model with a variable cost structure. Our logistics operations fully support our ability to operate in the marketplace as an on demand business.

REALIZING COMPETITIVE ADVANTAGE FROM LOGISTICS TRANSFORMATION

An enterprise-wide transformation of your logistics operations can yield significant business benefits for your organization. By helping you attain better landed-cost calculations and make better sourcing decisions, it can help you increase overall profitability. Such a transformation can also help you bring your products to market faster by smoothing both sourcing and import operations and helping to ensure that product information is easily accessible across the enterprise. You can reduce your need for working capital by increasing the opportunity for collaboration with carriers and by improving your shipment forecasts. Some of the benefits IBM clients have experienced include:

- A 40 percent savings from improvements in lane density and container utilization[46]

- A 14 percent savings in total international transportation costs by mixing ocean and air shipping[47]

- Reduction in transit times by about five days

- Cost recovery of 2-10 percent, due to comprehensive invoice auditing[48]

- Increased productivity due to automated processes and tools.

By leveraging the expertise already available in the marketplace, you can follow a well-mapped path to your logistics transformation, reducing the costs and time involved in the journey. Ultimately, you will be acting to protect the economic benefits you gain from global sourcing against erosion caused by the rising costs and complexities associated with global logistics management. The benefits of such a strategy can include a significant increase in shareholder value.

Building value in logistics outsourcing: The future of the logistics provider industry

By Karen Butner and Derek Moore

Customers of logistics services – whether they are across the globe or on one subcontinent – are seeking greater reliability at lower total cost. But as higher performance due to greater end-to-end integration and better visibility tools becomes more attainable, logistics services providers' approaches are diverging.

More customers are recognizing that to realize the full value of the potential tradeoffs from outsourcing, they need to broaden their span. They need to move from purchasing many piecemeal transportation and warehousing services to purchasing fewer and bigger contracts with much wider scope. In response, the logistics provider industry has been evolving to offer greater scope and more complex solutions. However, for the more demanding customer segments – those seeking greater integration and higher degrees of process conformance – there often is a gap between buyer needs and provider capabilities.

Often, providers market and represent capabilities that they have not yet implemented, so they over-promise and under-deliver. Unfortunately, the business model of most providers traps them because of their inability to scale offerings. Thus, they fail to meet the expectations of high process conformance buyers. High process conformance, in this context, is the ability to deliver end-to-end supply chain integration and synchronization repeatedly for many customers, establishing *de facto* process & technology standards.

We will discuss how to build value in logistics outsourcing and the future of the logistics provider industry in greater detail. Specifically, we will look at:

- Why the needs of buyers are diverging
- What is shaping the future industry structure
- The journey to value and how to facilitate value creation.

EVOLVING CUSTOMER NEEDS

As higher performance of more complex logistics services is being achieved, the needs of customers of logistics service providers are growing. We can map these needs to four diverging customer segments (see Figure 1).

Figure 1. Future customer segments.

Customer segments	Service requirements	Key features	Commercials and pricing
Wider service outsourcers Planning and control, execution and technology	• **High** process conformance • Planning and control to reduce complexity and optimize better • "One throat to squeeze"	• Want economies of scale and scope in addition to all the other features	• Shared risk and reward
High process conformance outsourcers	• **High** process conformance • Remove data complexity of using multiple providers • Extended range of services • Continuous improvement	• Want services requiring additional capabilities (e.g., retail preparation, reverse logistics) and efficiency improvements each year • Execution focus • Some specify the operating model, types of people (skills) and systems	• Fixed and variable with gain share measures to reward continuous improvement • Fixed and variable
Commodity outsourcers	• **Good** level of operational efficiency and process conformance	• Tactical outsourcing of basic services: transport, warehouse and freight forwarding	• Transactional
Insourcers	• Established internally		

Increasing scope and integration required →

Incremental requirements and features sought →

Source: *IBM Global Business Services analysis, 2006.*

In order of their increasing demands, the four logistics customer segments are:

1. *Insourcers* – These customers manage and operate most of their own logistics activities in-house. Some companies operate in-house either by accident or design. That is, some of them insource because they think of these activities as "back-office" functions without recognizing that there is high leverage potential through a more strategic, corporate focus.

2. *Commodity outsourcers* – These customers focus on the tactical outsourcing of non-core activities: transport, warehousing and freight forwarding. They expect a *good* level of operational efficiency. They call for more innovation but are not prepared to pay for it. They have a large number of providers serving niche needs primarily based on cost of service and are willing to switch providers more readily for lower prices.

3. *High process conformance outsourcers* – These customers operate in a framework where processes are clearly defined, and conformance is tightly measured. They want a demonstrably greater depth of people with very high process and target conformance and consistency. They seek a wider range of services, such as special packaging configuration, shelf stacking and reverse logistics. Within this segment are buyers who dictate the operating model and often require use of systems that they have selected. There are also buyers who demand not only a very high level of operational effectiveness but also demonstrable efficiency improvements virtually every year. This segment expects the provider to specify much more of operating model and systems. It tends to be more open to share financial results to reward continuous improvement.

4. *Wider service outsourcers of process, planning and control, execution and technology* – These buyers have concluded that to realize the full scope of the potential tradeoffs (among transport, storage, inventory and service levels), they need to move to fewer, bigger contracts allowing for more scale economies. This is combined with process improvement and better process interfaces to reduce complexity (via fewer providers) and focus on process simplification and standardization. These buyers are looking for evidence of effective end-to-end integration and more tightly engineered synchronization and optimization as well as the "traditional" qualification of industry specialization. This segment will outsource complete processes (physical and technology) embracing planning, control and execution. This implies moving the boundaries of outsourcing beyond tactical execution into strategic planning and control. Above all, these buyers want a single point-of-control. Since these buyers have a good handle on where their logistics operations fit inside their entire enterprise value chain, they appreciate the competitive advantage that can be achieved by carefully selecting a sophisticated partner to drive their integrated processes.

THE LOGISTICS PROVIDER INDUSTRY

With customer needs increasing, the logistics provider industry is evolving to offer greater scope and more complex solutions. Logistics providers also have a decision to make. They need to choose between serving a large commodity customer segment or the more demanding, yet faster growing, high process conformance customer segment. The payoff for providers that choose the high process conformance customer segment is tighter integration with customers along the supply chain, delivering greater value and increased "lock-in." Increased complexity offers more opportunities to sustain higher margins. Success will be measured by customers in terms of how well providers increase reliability and overall service performance at a reduced total cost.

In keeping with the expanding customer needs, the logistics provider business model has evolved to offer greater scope and deeper integration (see Figure 2). Over the past 30 years, the industry has expanded its scope and grown in stature. It has moved from providing low-complexity, basic foundational services (such as trucking and warehousing) to core services that combine different execution capabilities to extended services that support a wider range of capabilities. This tactical, execution-focused outsourcing typically reduces the buyer's logistics costs by 10 percent.[49]

Figure 2. Evolution of logistics provider business model.

Service offerings	Outsourcing models	Relationship	Pricing
Synchronized supply chains	• Synchronized provider • Supply chain integrator • Lead logistics manager • Global trade orchestrator	• Collaborative more than contractual partnership	• Shared risk and reward
Lead logistics	• Lead logistics provider (LLP) • Big brand(s)	• Contractual	• Fixed variable with some risk sharing
Core and extended services	• Inbound centric third-party logistics provider (3PL) • Freight forwarder • Outbound centric 3PL	• Contractual • Contractual • Contractual	• Fixed and variable • Transactional • Fixed and variable
Foundation services	• Transport, warehousing, customs broking	• Contractual and/or spot	• Transactional

Increasing scope and integration

Source: IBM Global Business Services analysis, 2006.

As customers seeking wider services have emerged, Lead Logistics Providers and, more recently, one or two "Big Brands," have developed to serve them. Big Brands are defined as very large global logistics groups (with less than a 10 percent share of the customer segments they serve) with the capability to execute all of the activities within their own organization.

Despite the emergence of Lead Logistics Providers and Big Brands, most organizations today still procure logistics services on a piecemeal basis. In doing so, they may forego the benefits of reducing inventory carrying costs, which can be realized by end-to-end management of the supply and transport chain. These costs are on the order of US$750 billion globally, equivalent to over 25 percent of total freight logistics costs.[50]

Financial returns in the logistics provider industry are typically rather poor and make it relatively hard to attract capital (see Figure 3). Very few companies in this industry reach returns on capital above approximately 11 percent and operating margins above 8 percent (see the shaded box in Figure 3).[51]

Figure 3. Financial returns in the logistics provider industry.

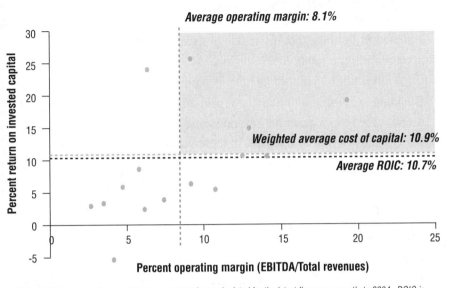

Average operating margin: 8.1%

Weighted average cost of capital: 10.9%

Average ROIC: 10.7%

Percent return on invested capital

Percent operating margin (EBITDA/Total revenues)

Notes: ROIC and operating margins are average values calculated for the latest five years, mostly to 2004. ROIC is defined as net income/total capital. Averages are the simple averages of all players plotted on the graph. Weighted average cost of capital is based on U.S. industry average.
Source: IBM Global Business Services analysis, Thomson Financial for financial data, WACC data from Ibbotson & Associates, 2006.

Historically, 50 percent of the valuation of shares is typically associated with a provider's growth.[52] A credible growth rate backed by attractive returns (such as twice the weighted average cost of capital) allows leaders to fund growth and innovation more readily than their competitors.

Margins among providers vary, but the highest rewards for market share gains tend to lie in activities driven by scale economies. If the economics of an activity are scale-driven (for example, parcel carrier, shared user third-party logistics (3PL), full truck load), then relative market share growth can be rewarded by higher profit margins.

EXAMPLE OF SCALE-DRIVEN ACTIVITY

As the density of stops per on road day increases, the inter-drop distance decreases, allowing a single vehicle to make more stops. This increasing productivity can help optimize margins.

Conversely, where activities are primarily driven by economies of scope, growth can generate more revenue and an increase in net profit, but typically at similar margins. In these cases, such as warehousing and dedicated user 3PL, there is very limited margin gain from growth in volumes.

FIVE DRIVERS OF CHANGE

The logistics provider industry is evolving quickly. This evolution is being driven by five drivers of change: customers' increasing and diverging demands, growth in global trade, continued outsourcing, technology and further industry consolidation. The logistics provider industry is also expanding due to recognition of the supply chain as a driver of enterprise-wide performance improvements and greater competitive advantage. Now let's take a closer look at the five drivers of change.

Customers have more demanding and diverging requirements

What buyers of logistics services expect will vary depending on their industry, organizational maturity, business model and preferred operating style. Looking across all buyer types, the key buying criteria are, in order of greatest importance:

- Greater reliability
- Lower total costs
- End-to-end integration and visibility globally
- Speed through more tightly engineered synchronization
- Flexibility
- Consistent capability globally

- Industry specialization
- Optimization and data warehousing
- Deep integration with buyers and partners.

LOGISTICS OUTSOURCING KEY BUYING CRITERIA

Greater reliability. Buyers want greater reliability of service (delivery to promise), which allows them to reduce inventories and provide greater service levels to their customers.

Lower total costs. Customers traditionally focus on individual logistics transactions; as a result, costs become optimized in silos but can end up being higher holistically.

End-to-end integration and visibility globally. Achieving effective end-to-end integration is another enabler of greater reliability. Automated visibility, coupled with work flow, allows exception reporting and alerts management when intervention is needed on a key-event basis.

Speed through more tightly engineered synchronization. Good data integration and automated sensing can enable process synchronization and automated responses. This entails massive orchestration by the logistics service provider to simultaneously manage volumes of informational and physical logistics transactions within a diverse global network. The end result can include improved speed and efficiency of the physical and financial flows, while performance criteria for time, delivery and cost are met.

Flexibility. Flexibility is needed to respond seamlessly to changes in demand and changes in sources of supply

Consistent capability globally. This is an enabler of greater reliability. The growth model of providers has largely been via acquisition. The post acquisition integration challenges of processes and systems seem minor compared to the organizational and cultural adjustments. The organizational alignment needs to tolerate high degrees of freedom and diversity in terms of delivery performance, processes, business rules and systems. More demanding buyers want process conformance.

Industry specialization. Customers increasingly put a premium on this knowledge.

Optimization and data warehousing. Even with a good degree of synchronization, there typically is room to optimize further. Data warehousing capabilities can enable regular and *ad hoc* root cause and performance analyses to drill down much more effectively.

Deep integration with buyers and partners. To access logistics data and information, customers want deep, but straightforward, integration with the service provider and expect that the provider's transportation partners will be similarly connected.

Global sourcing is here to stay – but it is more challenging

Public policy is generally encouraging freer trade. The attractions include differential wage rates, skill availability and favorable taxation. However, longer transport routes are harder to manage; infrastructure capacity lags changes in demand, causing bottlenecks; and capabilities and standards are less consistent. These challenges can drive up inventory costs and dramatically shift the overall sourcing economics. Global sourcing typically leads to more frequent switching of source locations. Uninterrupted supply requirements place greater demands on process standardization to allow seamless switching. This also puts more pressure on the speed and accuracy of providing landed cost information. In turn, this requires access to dynamic rate tables and transit times from carriers.

The outsourcing envelope is finally widening...slowly

The boundaries of the opportunity space for outsourcing in logistics have slowly widened in recent years but not as fast as investors have been promised (see Figure 4). Until recently, manufacturers and retailers have done limited outsourcing for "non-core" execution processes (transport, consolidation, warehousing, freight forwarding) on a tactical basis.

Figure 4. The boundaries of the opportunity space are widening... slowly.

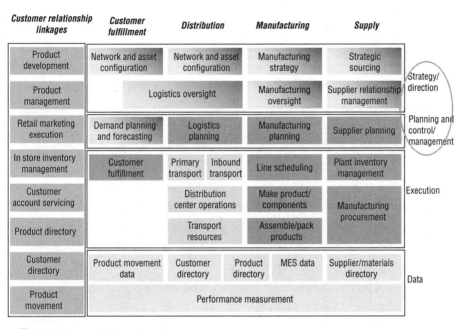

Retained core: Not for outsourcing

Traditionally core: Candidates for outsourcing extend scope of outsourcing to transform?
Either multi-source teams (in and out service) or total outsource

Non-core: Probably already outsourced

Source: IBM Global Business Services analysis, 2006.

Two forces are operating. First, the drive to achieve lower costs is leading buyers to rethink some of their assumptions. The innate conservatism of many buyers is being challenged. Labor practices made it easier to consider outsourcing physical execution, but most draw the line at outsourcing the more managerial planning and coordination activities. This is beginning to change.

Second, lowest unit costs will not automatically deliver lowest total costs. The latter requires proactive tradeoffs among transport, warehousing and inventory. Piecemeal outsourcing offers less opportunity to realize those tradeoffs. Many firms are not truly capable of bringing the parties together across different internal functional areas to examine the full potential value of business tradeoffs and to focus beyond price. In other words, they lack the sophistication needed to make highly complex integration analyses and "make versus buy" decisions. The challenge is for providers to grow their capabilities as fast as "the doors open."

THE ROLE OF ELECTRONICS, AUTOMOTIVE AND APPAREL IN WIDENING THE ENVELOPE

The electronics, automotive and apparel industries have been trendsetters in widening the envelope. Contract manufacturers in the electronics segment and procurement specialists in the apparel segment, already used to working with demand data and balancing supply, may become the new sources of convergence in the supply chain. The automotive industry has pioneered extension of the Manufacturing Resource Planning (MRP II) line of sight beyond tier-one suppliers. These leading global industries are now more willing to outsource some of the planning and control activities.

The synchronized, demand-driven supply chain requires standardization and pervasive technology

Three related sets of challenges in supply chain strategy demand seamless interfaces, fast responses and complex tradeoffs. They are:

- Tight coupling of the major supply chain functions – plan, source, make, deliver and repair/return.
- The ability to respond faster as companies focus on being driven by actual demand rather than forecast demand (the plan).
- The pressure to meet service objectives leads customers to operate multiple supply chains. Cost reduction, however, pushes them to share assets – implying some tradeoffs among the service objectives.

SYNCHRONIZATION AND VISIBILITY CHALLENGES

- Planning is challenged with fragmented information, making it difficult to synchronize supply and demand efficiently.
- Buying is complicated by lack of visibility of a product in the pipeline globally, all the way to the first line supplier. Often, a lack of integration with the manufacturer's systems makes it nearly impossible to receive in-transit order status information (once a product is moved or shipped).
- Sales teams are hampered from optimizing sales (cross-selling, up-selling, suggested selling based upon supply) by lack of product availability information.

Consolidation and convergence will increase... but so will the challenge to integrate effectively

Publicly quoted providers have to communicate a "growth story" to drive their share price up. Doing "more of the same," meaning doing more globally, meets part of this need. Convergence among inbound and outbound logistics by combining services such as transportation, consolidation, warehousing and freight forwarding is another element – but still low margin. Adding capabilities up the value chain to planning and control activities is expected to increase customer lock-in and margins.

In terms of their asset profile and core competency, the four traditional provider activities are very different (see Figure 5). They require different management priorities and styles. Hence, managing such a portfolio for consistent profitability is a challenge, as is agreeing on common standards for key interfaces of customer solutions.

Figure 5. Key characteristics of logistics provider segments.

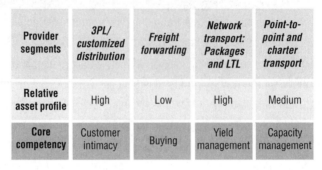

Provider segments	3PL/ customized distribution	Freight forwarding	Network transport: Packages and LTL	Point-to-point and charter transport
Relative asset profile	High	Low	High	Medium
Core competency	Customer intimacy	Buying	Yield management	Capacity management

Source: IBM Global Business Services analysis, 2006.

FUTURE TRENDS

In the following we discuss how we believe the market segments will evolve in the years up to 2015. We also discuss our view of the potential market share of each of these segments.

Market segments

In the future, we believe that the relative size of the market segments will change in favor of the more strategic buyers. Specifically, we believe that a fifth customer segment – "Strategic Outsourcers" – is likely to evolve in addition to the four segments described earlier (see Figure 6). Let's take a closer look at each of these segments.

Figure 6. Future customer segments.

		Service requirements	Key features	Commercials and pricing	Indicative outsourced market share 2015
Emerging	**Strategic outsourcers**	• Plan and deliver inventory requirements • Shared formulation of supply chain strategy • End to end scope	• Strategic relationship with "shared direction"	• Shared risk and reward	5-10%
Today's customer segments	**Wider service outsourcers**	• High process conformance • Planning and control, execution and technology • Reduced complexity – "one throat to squeeze"	• Want economies of scale and scope in addition to all the other features	• Shared risk and reward	**20-25%**
	High process conformance outsourcers	• High process conformance • Remove data complexity of using multiple providers • Wider range or services • Continuous improvement	• Want services requiring additional capabilities (e.g., retail preparation, reverse logistics) and efficiency improvements each year • Executional focus • Some specify the operating model, types of people (skills) and systems	• Fixed and variable with some risk sharing • Fixed and variable	**30%**
	Commodity outsourcers	• High level of operational efficiency; adequate process conformance	• Tactical outsourcing of foundation services: transport, warehouse and freight forwarding	• Transactional	**40%**
	Insourcers	• Established internally			

Source: IBM Institute for Business Value analysis, 2006.

1. *Insourcers* – Companies in virtually all industries and sizes will be outsourcing more and more of their logistics functions.

2. *Commodity outsourcers* – This segment will broadly behave much as it does today. The less efficient commodity outsourcers will employ 3PLs and freight forwarders but will be ready to switch for lower prices. Those with greater competencies, including a good understanding of pipeline visibility and provider capabilities, are likely to bypass the 3PLs in favor of direct use of foundation service providers. They will likely implement a control tower solution to manage their providers. In either case, brands will not matter. We expect this segment to represent approximately 40 percent of total volume.

3. *High process conformance outsourcers* – We expect this segment will continue much as today. Many buyers will adopt more widespread use of reward mechanisms for continuous improvement. This segment could represent 30 percent of market volume.

4. *Wider service outsourcers: Process, planning and control, execution and technology* – This group of customers is expected to widen. It will comprise large, often global, enterprises renowned for supply chain management excellence. For these buyers, the brand matters. They could represent up to 20 percent of market volume.

5. *Strategic outsourcers: Buyers looking for a strategic relationship with "shared direction"* – These buyers are ready to trust the partner to plan and deliver inventory availability for one or more of their supply chains. The scope will include shared formulation of the supply chain strategy with extensive outsourcing of planning, control and execution of their total supply chain. Execution will include virtually all logistics and could include specific procurement responsibility and manufacturing. The scope will be end-to-end and include demand and supply balancing, embracing the range of physical and technology dimensions of the supply chain. This segment will be limited to organizations with central-

ized supply chain management. They will require above average flexibility ("plug and play") to accommodate the variability in their business portfolio and demand fluctuations; this flexibility will be accomplished by an on demand business structure. These buyers typically will be either large global enterprises whose strategy is to only engage directly in design and marketing or significant enterprises that are not in the upper quartile of performers and find it hard to attract the best talent. This group could represent up to 5 to 10 percent of market volume.

The battle will be for the middle ground: High process conformance buyers

The business models and organizational values required to address these market segments are very different. In the period to 2015, the logistics provider industry will likely consolidate into five provider types:

- *Foundation Providers* – This large group of operators should continue to thrive. Traditionally mostly small scale, we expect that very large-scale enterprises will emerge, especially in transport, as new ways of achieving scale economies are identified. There will be very little product differentiation, although highly specialized niche-market providers will exist. Geographic reach will be mostly, but not exclusively, national.

- *Core Service Providers* – This group will comprise inbound logistics-centric 3PLs, freight forwarders and outbound logistics-centric 3PLs focused on commodity buyers. These providers will focus on and excel at specific but fewer capabilities.

- *Extended Service Providers* – This group will comprise inbound logistics-centric 3PLs, freight forwarders and outbound logistics-centric 3PLs focused on high process conformance customers. These providers will seek to provide a wider range of services – such as special packaging configuration, shelf stacking and reverse logistics – and will acquire additional capabilities. They will "deliver what they advertise," likely with higher quality execution than Core Service Providers.

- *Lead Logistics Providers and Big Brands* – These providers will focus on the wider service outsourcers – process, planning and control, execution and technology – segment. But critically, they will need a significant share of the two largely tactical, high process conformance buyer segments to attain sufficient scale advantage. They will drive more industry consolidation and be good at acquiring scale and scope in emerging parts of the world. They will aspire to provide a globally integrated offering with seamless physical and information services, which is hard to replicate. With a "global control tower" in place, they will provide supply chain performance metrics, key event status and alerts to customers on a global basis. These providers will need to be good at continuous improvement. Unless they get much better at integrating with customer processes and systems, they will experience competition from the foundation and value-added service providers. They will aim to "mass customize" logistics.

- *Synchronized Providers* – A small number of Synchronized Providers who are capable of becoming supply chain managers is likely to emerge. They will serve buyers looking for a strategic relationship with shared direction. They will aim to manage inventory availability, balancing demand and supply end-to-end. The Synchronized Providers will deliver end-to-end supply chain integration, visibility, synchronization and broad-based business process capabilities for global customers. They will do this repeatedly for several customers, establishing *de facto* process and technology standards or reinforcing acceptance of existing ones. Processes could include supplier management, procurement, contract manufacturing, logistics services, global trade financial and tax management, performance management and customer service. Service offerings will be standardized, provide ease of integration and provide flexibility in customization. The solutions will be scalable with componentized processes, enabling customers to "plug and play" responses to growth opportunities or changes. This category of provider will also exhibit an internal culture that seeks and rewards ongoing innovation, and it will need to have a wealth of existing intellectual property that it can leverage as part of solutions for its customers.

SYNCHRONIZED PROVIDER UNCERTAINTIES

- *How Synchronized Providers will emerge is less certain.* The future Synchronized Providers are likely to emerge from Lead Logistics Providers or the "Big Brands", probably as a result of progressive "reinventions" of a few leading providers. They likely will need to team with banks for trade and project finance, process improvement firms and global technology companies to reinforce their capabilities.
- *The emergence of Synchronized Providers has been hampered by buyers and providers each doubting the other.* More buyers would migrate toward centralized supply chains if they believed that providers with matching capabilities existed. Conversely, providers have been reluctant to invest in the capabilities due to lack of evidence of a market. The emergence of the Big Brands is likely to break this log-jam.

Each provider is likely to specialize in one buyer segment. However, players from virtually all segments are likely to seek high process confor- mance customers. Their specifications will be consistent with the tactical elements of the Lead Logistics Providers, Big Brands and Synchronized Providers, who in turn will need a share of their volume to achieve scale economies. Core Providers will seek a share, too, for the higher margins – and become "market spoilers." The Extended, Lead Logistics, Big Brand and Synchronized Providers therefore have a vested interest in clearer marketing messaging and positioning.

JOURNEY TO VALUE

There is more than one way to make money in logistics services. So, whichever core buyer segment(s) logistics service providers choose to focus on, how they develop and execute these capabilities will shape their competitiveness and ultimately determine how much value they create for shareholders.

The journey toward future success for providers that are focused on more strategic and high process conformance customers typically involves an overlapping sequence of activities to develop enhanced capabilities (see Figure 7). These activities include:

- Driving the standardization and integration of processes and systems to reduce costs and provide a platform to achieve scale economies

- Componentizing the service portfolio, giving providers the means to deliver customized solutions at higher margins

- Supplementing country governance with global governance processes, allowing providers to relate to their large global customers on an equal footing

- Making an ongoing investment in service innovation, which will be essential to sustaining leadership

- Developing effective teaming capabilities (applies to the few aspiring to become Synchronized Providers).

Figure 7. The journey to value.

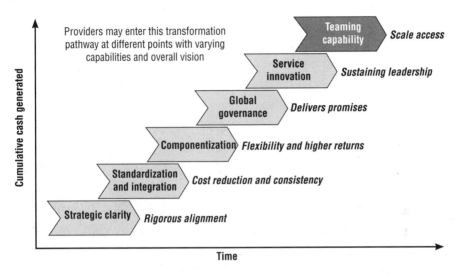

Source: IBM Global Business Services analysis, 2006.

JOURNEY TO VALUE

The journey to value starts with having strategic clarity about the market segments in which to participate. Then it involves an overlapping sequence of activities to develop enhanced provider capabilities. These steps include:

- *Strategic clarity* – Rigorously align target market segments and value propositions with organizational culture, business model, core competencies, asset planning and performance measures.

- *Standardization and integration* – Proactively sell the value of standardized and integrated global processes and shared user services – internally and externally. These processes and services will help ensure commonality of data definitions and service performance indicators.

- *Componentization* – Provide customized solutions from a set of standardized – but configurable – process, information, work flow and value-added components. These solutions will harvest knowledge and make the data readily accessible across the organization.

- *Global governance* – Improve global deal consistency by moving such contracts to global Profit and Loss statements (P&Ls) and reserving traditional country P&Ls for narrow scope activities.
- *Service innovation* – Invest in new capabilities (such as visibility, supply planning and control; dynamic synchronization and optimization of business processes; a virtual supply chain information platform). They will need to enhance existing capabilities in transport planning and control and extend into more areas of procurement. This will necessitate deep integration with customers to provide end-to-end supply chain capabilities and visibility.
- *Teaming capability for emerging "Synchronized Providers"* – These providers will need to invest in teaming skills in the new era of "co-opetition," where the value and breadth of services offered to customers will amplify as the service provider's network of partners grows.

No provider today can complete this transformation as a "single project." It is a strategic journey. The journey will need to be broken into manageable chunks of initiatives that can be realized in well-defined timelines and at relatively low risk. Where a provider should begin the journey will depend on that provider's own business goals, the market pressures and the maturity of existing capabilities.

Providers who can draw on the standardization capabilities of sister package divisions (such as DHL and UPS) should find it easier and faster to create value if they foster a culture of shared learning. Drawing on the proof points of the package experience, growth rates and scalable economics should enable providers to win over any change resistors more easily.

IN THE VALUE JOURNEY SEQUENCE...

- Strategic goals will lead to different priorities and investments.
- Standardization and integration come before componentization because the latter economically depends on standardization having been achieved.
- Componentization comes before global governance because setting up a global governance structure is a daunting task that includes overcoming corporate culture issues to achieve cooperative efforts. While global governance needs to be addressed, we believe that accomplishing componentization first is likely to free up cash flow faster.
- Service innovation is investing for leadership. The investments are likely to deliver lower returns if done right away than if a foundation of standardization, integration and componentization has been laid first.

The future logistics provider industry will be more global, more concentrated, more segmented around customer types and better at execution. Business processes will be standardized, and systems will be integrated. There will be better visibility of end-to-end supply chain information and integration with partners and customers. The industry will have effective, shared metrics to continuously measure performance and handle exception management more easily through event monitoring linked to business rules. And, at long last, providers will have a single view of their larger global customers.

EPC: A shared vision for transforming business processes

By Sean Campbell and Sachin Shah

Electronic product code (EPC) adoption is still taking shape. Leading companies are actively piloting and deploying EPC initiatives, yet EPC adoption is very much a work-in-progress. While significant advances in understanding how EPC can be used to drive anticipated benefits have been made, there is still much to learn. Therefore, Global Commerce Initiative (GCI) commissioned IBM to share the recent lessons learned and perspectives of leading EPC adopters with the rest of the industry and the market at large.

The discussion presented here is based on a joint assessment by GCI members, including representatives from both the manufacturer and retailer communities. Our goal is to provide senior industry leaders with pragmatic insights on how RFID and EPC technology can help drive major changes in the supply chain that ultimately benefit all participants.[53]

A SHARED EPC VISION

Leading retailers and manufacturers share the ultimate vision of an EPC-enabled supply chain that brings significant service and efficiency benefits to shoppers, end consumers and businesses. The EPC-enabled supply chain will enable trading partners to meet shopper and consumer needs in ways far superior to what is possible today.

EPC is a global standards-based implementation of RFID technology that is supported by the use of standards-based tags, readers, tag content and information flows. It can be viewed as a continuation of the journey that began approximately 25 years ago with the introduction of barcode scanning, although EPC makes a significant step forward with the ability to support mass serialized identification. While barcode implementation has delivered significant benefits to both the shopping experience and industry supply chain efficiency, great opportunities remain for further innovation and improvement in both areas.

Successful implementation of the technical capabilities introduced by EPC makes it possible for companies to have broad, relevant and realtime information about product movement across the supply chain, from upstream suppliers through manufacturers, third-party logistics (3PL) and distributors, to the retail store. In the near and medium term, case-and pallet-level tagging has the potential to significantly improve supply chain visibility, which will lead to increased collaboration and operating efficiency for supply networks based on both distribution centers and direct store delivery. These capabilities are expected to deliver significant benefits to shoppers, end consumers and industry adopters in the following areas:

- Store operations and replenishment
- Distribution center operations
- Logistics asset control
- Total inventory management
- Track and trace
- Shelf replenishment/shelf availability
- Goods transfer
- Promotion/event execution
- Shrink management.

Also, when item-level tagging becomes feasible in a given product category, shoppers will benefit from an enhanced shopping experience with even better on-shelf availability, fresher products, more efficient checkout, and improved service and information delivery.

RFID technology and, in particular, the standardized EPC and its associated information flow via the EPC global network are poised to enable the next wave of evolution in the way that manufacturers, retailers and their business partners share information and work together to satisfy consumer demand. EPC can be thought of as an extended barcode containing a serialized item key that enables individual products to be uniquely identified. Unlike existing barcode technology, EPC systems, based on the use of radio frequencies, do not require line-of-sight scanning. This fundamental change improves the speed and potential accuracy of data collection and provides the following new capabilities:

- Faster scanning and product handling with the capability to support hundreds of tag "reads" per second (versus one-at-a-time as with barcodes) and to conduct automated scanning with limited manual intervention
- New opportunities to collect inventory information and "see" the flow of products, potentially in real time and in locations not previously feasible across the supply chain and in the store
- Automated "triggering" of appropriate actions (e.g., replenishment orders, stock alerts) with less manual intervention
- Identification of discrete items – for example, by flagging duplicate or invalid codes, thus enhancing the execution of promotions, track and trace, product authentication and other activities.

These new capabilities will become fully realized as EPC technology matures. Today, however, many pilots have encountered technological challenges with:

- Tag quality (significant percentage of defects)
- Inconsistent read rates (due to issues with tag placement, the physics of the product or environment, and the compatibility of tags and readers)
- Tag application equipment (inability to operate at sufficient speed and volume with consistent quality).

Through current testing and initial deployment efforts, technology vendors and users are working to overcome these challenges and make effective use of the current level of performance. At this time, for example, the read rates differ when reading all cases on a pallet compared to reading individual cases on a conveyor system. While, in some pilots, 100 percent read rates are being achieved, results vary greatly depending on product characteristics and environmental conditions.

Nonetheless, over time, EPC has the potential to bring fundamental change to many areas of the marketplace, from the supply chain to store operations to consumer interactions. The nature of EPC adoption will evolve as new systems and standards are developed, technology costs come down and new insights are developed on how it can add value.

THREE STAGES OF EPC ADOPTION

The likely evolution of EPC adoption is illustrated in Figure 1. The three stages of adoption are: supply chain execution and collaboration, enhanced store experience and transformed consumer experience.

Figure 1. Envisioned evolution of EPC adoption.

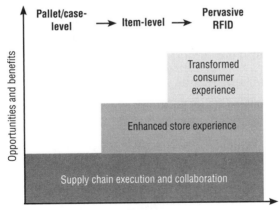

Source: IBM Institute for Business Value analysis, 2006.

Today, most companies are focused on implementing EPC in the supply chain at a pallet and case level to improve operational efficiency and trading partner collaboration. The ultimate goal is to provide consumers with greater value and a better shopping experience through fewer out-of-stocks, fresher products and better service in the store. Going forward, we envision that companies will use EPC tags at the item level and the point of sale to enhance the store experience. Ultimately, consumers may benefit from EPC-enabled capabilities throughout a transformed consumer experience. In fact, a few companies are already exploring stages 2 and 3 today. In addition, for bulk products such as pet food or electronics, "case-level tagging" could encompass the consumer saleable unit.

Now let's take a closer look at the three stages of EPC adoption.

Supply chain execution and collaboration

The focus for most companies and in most product categories today is on pallet- and case-level tagging. Even at this level, EPC adoption can lead to a better consumer shopping experience by enabling companies to improve supply chain execution and collaboration. (Note, however, that some companies are also actively exploring inner-pack and item-level tagging of products such as medicines, cosmetics, consumer electronics, CDs/DVDs and apparel to address category or brand-specific business needs and because benefits can be delivered quickly.)

To help frame the breadth of potential EPC applications, we have classified the major EPC opportunity areas within the supply chain into the following six categories:

1. Store operations
2. Distribution operations
3. Direct store delivery
4. Promotion/Event execution
5. Total inventory management
6. Shrink management.

Industry leaders have identified further opportunities to enhance supply chain execution and collaboration through EPC adoption. However, more work is required to understand the potential applications and benefits in these areas. For example, EPC holds promise in a range of "track and trace" activities, such as:

- Anti-counterfeiting
- Product diversion
- Recalls/Reverse logistics[54]
- Fresh/Code-dated product management
- Temperature/Cold chain monitoring[55]
- Legal compliance.

In addition, three major areas of EPC supply chain opportunities remain largely unexplored in the consumer products/retailing industry. They are:

- *Manufacturing operations* – While some companies have already achieved significant improvements in this area through barcode-based systems, further EPC-enabled benefits may be possible. For example, manufacturers could use the better demand signal visibility enabled by EPC to improve capacity planning and production efficiency for themselves as well as key subcontractors and co-packing partners. EPC could also help manufacturers improve tracking and management of work-in-process inventory; maintenance, repair and operating (MRO) supplies; and spare parts.

- *Upstream supplier management* – EPC may also help improve replenishment and inventory management further up the supply chain, specifically with raw materials and packaging suppliers. Track and trace initiatives have the potential to support "recipe management" and lot-tracking activities, where inbound materials are tracked through the manufacturing process and linked to production orders and finished goods.

- *Transportation and logistics* – RFID tagging of shipping units (such as trucks, containers, railcars) could help improve transportation management. As one example, the fast-track tagging of "known trucks" (with contents notified in advance) reduces the need for de-briefs and gatehouse personnel. Waiting times at the ramp decrease due to quicker unloading processes and better scheduling of arrivals. Knowing where shipping units are located at virtually any time provides for better asset utilization, leading to benefits in 3PL and indirect benefits throughout the supply chain.

Enhanced store experience[56]

Looking further out, the broader vision for EPC is to tag individual products at the item level. While technology costs remain too high to make this feasible in the near term for most product categories, these costs will inevitably come down as EPC adoption scales across various industries including consumer products/retail. As this occurs, consumers will likely see increased value and noticeable enhancements to the shopping experience, enabled by new supply chain and store management practices. For example:

- Product out-of-stocks would become rare as "intelligent," EPC-capable store fixtures provide retailers and manufacturers with stock visibility all the way to the shelf and enable more dynamic restocking procedures.

- The assortment and presentation of products would be more aligned with consumer shopping preferences as EPC data is used to improve category management, and automated shelf-level monitoring helps ensure compliance with plan-o-grams.

- Shoppers would only see "fresh" products available for purchase as item-level stock monitoring helps retail employees quickly and efficiently identify aging or obsolete products that should be removed from the sales floor.

- Store employees, with access to item-level product inventory information, could quickly help a customer find a specific size, color or model anywhere in the store or throughout the retail chain.

- Consumers could obtain valuable information that helps them make better shopping decisions (for example, product features, usage instructions and promotions on complementary products) through digital displays or information kiosks that interact with EPC-tagged products.

- The checkout process would no longer be a primary source of consumer pain as EPC-tagged products make rapid, automated tallying of purchases possible.

Transformed consumer experience

EPC might ultimately become pervasive throughout the consumer environment as a wide range of consumer devices become capable of interacting with tagged products. Glimpses of potential future applications can be seen today in other markets, such as RFID-based toll collection systems for automobiles and identification systems for pets. As successive generations of EPC technology are developed and deployed, they will likely become the basis of as-yet unimagined shopping experiences and product/service offerings. While it is difficult to predict with certainty what new applications and services will emerge, the successful ones will surely be those that respond best to consumers' needs.

LEARNING FROM THE PAST: THE BARCODE EXPERIENCE

To better understand the long-term context for EPC, the industry can review lessons learned in the adoption of the barcode. Four key aspects of this experience can help us understand the likely road ahead for EPC, as discussed below.

Standards are critical to drive widespread adoption. By accepting common standards, such as product code specifications and the graphic design of the barcode itself, companies were able to invest in the required new technologies with confidence that their barcoded products and scanning systems could be used with virtually any trading partner in the industry. Technology vendors could focus on application and function-ality innovation knowing they had chosen the right platform on which to build. While there were some local variations, this was not a major issue at a time when trade was more "local" than "global." The EPC initiative has the opportunity to avoid this shortcoming by moving to one global set of standards from the start.

Collective industry action is key to achieving critical mass and speeding realization of benefits. Supply chain technologies inherently face implementation challenges because they typically involve high initial costs and long-term, gradual benefits. Companies prefer to have assurances that a large percentage of their trading partners are going to adopt compatible systems and business processes before committing to large-scale deployments.

In an industry environment more fragmented than today, the barcode initiative faced several daunting challenges. Three things had to occur simultaneously:

- Persuading manufacturers that enough retailers would adopt scanning technology to make their investments worthwhile
- Assuring retailers that sufficient numbers of suppliers would source-mark their products with barcodes
- Convincing technology vendors that adequate industry demand would materialize to justify their R&D investments.[57]

The group of industry executives that advocated barcode adoption focused heavily on this critical mass problem and personally worked to build support across the industry. However, it wasn't until the vast majority of products were barcoded that a significant number of retailers adopted scanning systems. In today's more consolidated competitive environment, a comparatively smaller number of retailers should be sufficient to achieve a critical mass of EPC-enabled product flow.

Full realization of benefits requires open information sharing and sustained change in business practices and processes. Companies achieve benefits not simply by deploying new technology, be it data processing, the Internet, or RFID, but by implementing changes across and within business processes to exploit the new capabilities available. In many areas, including those targeted by EPC, this requires coordinated change on the part of multiple trading partners and participants in the industry value chain.

The historical experience related to barcodes illustrates this critical point. Many of the expected benefits were based on the premise that manufacturers and retailers would cooperate and share point-of-sale (POS) data to better manage cross-company activities like replenishment, inventory management and shrink control. Some of these opportunities were partially, but not fully, achieved, and others remain completely untapped.[58]

Forecasting benefits and costs is difficult. At an early stage in the adoption of virtually any technology, quantification of benefits and costs is subject to many uncertainties. That is the case today with EPC. In such an environment, companies may be conservative in their estimates. Focusing on tangible costs and benefits, initial business cases may underestimate the technology's full impact.

The barcode experience provides a clear case in point. Startling results came from a comparison of the original business case for barcode adoption in the U.S. grocery industry with estimates of the actual impact over 20 years later (see Figure 2). Two key conclusions stand out.

First, the originally projected costs of adoption were twice as much as the actual costs, as technology prices dropped more quickly than anticipated. As can be seen in the evolution and introduction of many technology-based goods (think DVDs and mobile phones versus televisions or VCRs), price/performance improvements are accelerating and adoption cycles compressing.

Figure 2. Estimated barcode scanning benefits, 1975 versus 1997.

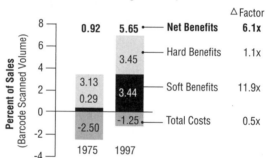

Note: "Hard benefits" refers to measurable cost reductions in areas such as checkout and price-marking labor, checkout losses and bookkeeping. "Soft benefits" refers to gains in areas such as inventory reduction, shrink control, sales lift and improved warehouse operations.
Source: IBM Institute for Business Value analysis, 2006.

Time will tell whether EPC adoption patterns will mimic those of the barcode, but the lessons learned should be heeded as we tackle the new opportunities enabled by EPC.

In particular, the industry's historical experience with barcodes illustrates the importance of:

• Developing and adopting truly global standards
• Open sharing of information among trading partners

- Active collaboration on required business process changes
- Continued monitoring of actual versus forecasted costs and benefits to update business case projections.

EXPLOITING EPC'S FULL POTENTIAL: SCENARIOS FOR TRANSFORMATION

The full impact of EPC will not be achieved simply by deploying technology in today's supply chain processes. While some product categories appear to have characteristics that afford a clear path to economic returns, the full scope of benefits may not be as obvious or as fast as in other categories. Therefore, to achieve EPC's full potential, manufacturers and retailers need to understand what it will take to achieve currently identified benefits and to explore ways of further exploiting EPC-generated data to expand the benefit potential and improve the long-term return on investment (ROI).

Leading companies are actively investigating these opportunities across the industry supply chain, all of which will require companies to "rewire" their existing processes, systems and business practices. To share and deepen knowledge across the industry and to focus attention on the most important opportunities and issues, we will explore six scenarios for EPC-enabled transformation based on case- and pallet-level tagging (see Figure 3). We will discuss the following for each:

- *Where the pain is* – Identification of today's business practices and problems
- *What's possible* – A detailed description of future EPC-enabled processes
- *What the impacts are* – The anticipated economic benefits from EPC adoption in these areas

- *What needs to change and who needs to take action* – The key implementation requirements across people, processes and technology systems; areas of responsibility across different participants in the industry value chain (e.g., manufacturers, retailers, logistics providers); and the expected timeframe for implementation.

Figure 3. Major EPC supply chain opportunities across the industry value chain.

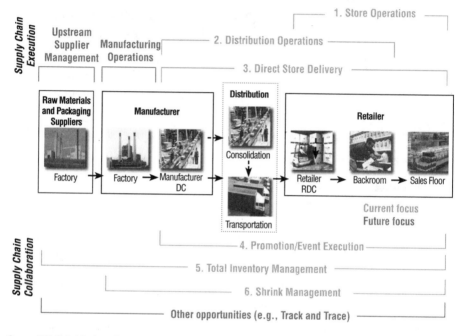

Source: *IBM Global Business Services analysis, 2006.*

While companies in the industry are also exploring ways of improving supply chain performance using existing technology (e.g., barcodes or EDI), EPC brings a new set of capabilities that can enable more effective approaches to these challenges. .

Many of the new business processes described in these scenarios require the ability to identify all cases on a pallet to enable transformational changes in accuracy and material handling. It should be noted that 100 percent read accuracy is not necessarily required to obtain some of the benefits as process workarounds can help compensate for gaps. In addition, these scenarios generally assume the following:

- The performance of the RFID technology (e.g., tag yields and read rates, tag application speed and reliability) is adequate for the applications described.
- Trading partners are using accurate, synchronized item data and sharing EPC-generated product movement information.
- The requisite standards are available and being used.

Furthermore, it is important to note that these scenarios depict fully enabled EPC processes and operations, not interim processes and solutions that companies may need to deploy to manage duplicate or hybrid processes for both tagged and non-tagged pallets and cases.

The first set of transformation scenarios focuses on improved execution of core supply chain activities through EPC enablement. Many of the capabilities developed and deployed in these areas provide the critical foundation for future benefits that could be achieved through improved supply chain collaboration.

Store operations

This scenario covers store receipt of products from retail distribution centers ("store replenishment") and the movement of products within the store itself ("shelf replenishment").

Current issues

EPC-enabled store and shelf replenishment practices can address many of the problems retailers and manufacturers face today that cause out-of-stocks[59] and limit the time store employees spend serving customers. These problems include:

- *Inaccurate receiving into the backroom* – "Blind received" deliveries provide no guarantee of receipts.
- *Poor/lengthy check-in routines* – The alternative to blind receiving is to take the time to manually check products. Store employees may spend excessive time correcting internal IDs for received products. For example, a product arrives at the store, but the GTIN is not in the system or is inaccurate (due to faulty data entry at corporate). Store operations are disrupted as the product cannot be sold until a category or store manager corrects the error.
- *Actual versus book stock inventory discrepancies.*
- *Excessive time spent on inventory counts and searching for products.*
- *Distorted and delayed store demand signals* – Unable to find a given product in cluttered backrooms, store employees may incorrectly "zero out" store stock information, leading to unnecessary orders.
- *Inflexible or arbitrary replenishment routines* – Employees work according to a fixed timetable instead of in response to actual customer demand and shelf conditions (for example, "cheeses at 10 a.m., detergents at 11 a.m.").

Process view

With EPC enablement, both retailers and manufacturers believe that store employees will have more capability to improve inventory accuracy, track product movement from the backroom to the sales floor, find products in the backroom more readily and, ultimately, better manage shelf replenishment to improve product availability. Specifically:

- *Efficient and accurate store deliveries* – When products are received at the store, an EPC-enabled process can identify case receipts and update the store inventory system. In addition, with new software functionality, receipts could be compared to expected deliveries to validate that the right goods were delivered to the right stores and identify any overages or shortages. Discrepancies would automatically generate "alert" messages to inform delivery and receiving personnel, who would also have an "override" capability to handle damages and breaches. Improved delivery accuracy is thus obtained without increasing labor requirements. In fact, turnaround times should become shorter, and deliveries should consume less driver and store staff time.

- *Segmented stock monitoring (between the backroom and sales floor)* – The store's book stock system would become significantly more accurate as inbound deliveries cause this information to be updated automatically. And with EPC readers located at the doors between the backroom and the sales floor, stock levels in each part of the store can be monitored separately. Additional EPC readers at the compactor, baler or waste area (depending on how the store handles emptied cases) help verify that cases brought to the sales floor were actually emptied, and when. It is generally believed that retailers will see improved store-level inventory accuracy, providing a better foundation for store execution processes and systems.

- *Demand driven store replenishment practices and the timing and quality of orders placed with the distribution center* – With improved accuracy and visibility, store employees would also have greater confidence when looking for a particular item and be able to locate products more quickly with the creation of new backroom management processes. Retailers could also implement a variety of alert-based practices to improve shelf replenishment. For example, they could compare existing electronic POS data with product movement to the sales floor and proactively generate alerts for employees to investigate shelves believed to be running low on stock. Emergency orders could be classified for rapid handling, enabling "fast-track" movement to the sales floor upon receipt.

With future reader technology, alerts might be directed to handheld readers that act more like locator devices to help employees locate specific EPCs and cases in the backroom. The result is proactive shelf replenishment that is more in line with consumer demand, helping to avoid intra-day or peak-hour stock-outs. Employees can then replenish a greater number of shelves in less time and focus more effort on items most in danger of being out of stock.

- *Improved administrative efficiency* – With greater visibility to stock levels into the backroom and sales floor, store employees would spend less time performing routine tasks such as product counts and rotation of fresh or code-dated products (and/or do them less frequently). EPC numbers could be linked to product expiration information at manufacturer tagging points, or even within the retail distribution process all the way up to the shelf, to help identify soon-to-expire products more efficiently.

- *Improved yard security and inbound management* – Receiving doors could be protected with EPC readers to improve management of and control over product cases and delivery assets. With future tag technology (potentially making use of "active" instead of "passive" tags), transport carriers and trailers may include identification devices that are linked to the contents of the shipment to help retailers prioritize trailer unloading.

Economic benefits

In the ways described earlier, EPC enablement can help drive revenue growth for both manufacturers and retailers and improve retailer productivity through more efficient labor utilization. The retailer could choose to refocus store staff on promotional, merchandising and other more customer-facing, revenue-generating activities. Consumers would enjoy better service from store employees and, in general, have greater assurance that the products they want to buy are in stock and "fresh."

Distribution operations

This scenario covers core supply chain activities involving the distribution centers of virtually any participant in the industry value chain, whether a manufacturer, retailer, 3PL, etc. Specifically, it includes:

- Shipment and receipt of products between trading partners (referred to as "goods transfer" below)
- The movement of goods within distribution centers
- Management of logistics assets (referred to as "asset control" below).

Current issues

Companies throughout the supply chain can use EPC to address today's distribution process bottlenecks and failures that often result from the complexity of product flow and human error. These include:

- *Complex, labor-intensive receiving processes* – Typically involve actions such as manual barcode scanning and label application; some trading partners utilize EDI ASN/DESADV receipt with SSCC.
- *Errors missed due to "single-scan" receiving* – Retailers often must choose between scanning a single case of each inbound shipment (and accepting errors) or scanning virtually every pallet/case (at high cost in labor and delays). Discrepancies lead to deductions for trading partners.
- *Labor-intensive cycle counting and physical inventory counts.*
- *Frequent human errors in marshalling products for delivery (e.g., wrong unit, wrong lane)* – Distribution centers often engage in manual checking/audits of outbound shipments to reduce likelihood of claims and shipping errors. Despite these efforts, errors still occur.
- *Assets badly organized, unreturned, misused and stolen* – Asset return schemes have largely failed due to the difficulties and costs of tracking them. Assets build up on site, disrupting operations and becoming

vulnerable to theft. As a result, required assets are not available when needed, and asset utilization is not optimized (for example, expensive roll cages are used when product warrants only less-expensive dollies).

Process view

Through EPC enablement, distribution operations could become substantially more efficient, orderly and accurate. Specifically:

- *Efficient and accurate receiving process* – As with store deliveries, any shipments received by a distribution center (e.g., from manufacturer to retailer) would be rapidly and automatically counted into the distribution center inventory system via reads of EPC tags on the shipped pallets. A "three-way match" process could check that the goods actually received match the original purchase order and the shipper's electronic shipment notification. Distribution center personnel simply have to visually check the received goods for breaches or damage, or manually override the check-in process in case of a discrepancy alert. This is of particular importance where mixed pallets are being shipped.

- *Smooth product handling* – Within the distribution center, EPC readers strategically placed around conveyor belt systems could achieve close to 100 percent read rates on cases being moved within the distribution center regardless of how the cases are placed on the belt (assuming the belts themselves are built from RFID-friendly materials). This would provide significant improvement over today's barcode-based systems, where misreads due to covered or damaged barcodes result in piles of "rejected" products that must be dealt with manually. Note, however, that the use of conveyor belts is less common in European distribution centers. In this region, goods are typically received, checked and stored on pallets. EPC-enabled forklifts or handheld readers will help companies improve the checking and storage of goods and achieve higher performance compared to today's barcode-based procedures. It will, for example, be possible to identify the location of goods while in transit from the dock doors to the warehouse storage racks.

- *Improved inventory management* – Through automated, verified stock check-ins and EPC readers strategically placed around the distribution center (e.g., in doors or on forklifts), the accuracy of location information for cases and pallets would be improved significantly. Distribution center staff could spend far less time in cycle counting and/or conducting physical inventories.

- *Increased cross-docking accuracy* – Similarly, the use of EPC readers in the cross-docking area would help ensure that the right product is moved to the right place.

- *Efficient and accurate shipping process* – Distribution center staff could use EPC readers to track cases and pallets as they are picked and packed, enabling "green light" shipping with much less manual compliance checking and processing time. Distribution center staff would thus have greater assurance that the right product was sent to the right door and, ultimately, to the right customer or store.

- *Improved RTI/asset control* – Tags on returnable transport items (RTIs) and other logistics assets (such as pallets, totes, trays, roll cages, etc.) would enable companies to better track their movement and location, providing several benefits. Asset misuse would be reduced and the opportunity for actively managing logistics assets enhanced, helping to ensure that the right assets are available when needed. Asset theft could be prevented more effectively. In addition, companies could better encourage and monitor the return of assets to their proper source.

Economic benefits

As a result of deploying EPC in their distribution centers and goods transfer processes, businesses can obtain the following benefits over time:

- Significantly improve distribution center labor productivity (and therefore lower operating expenses)
- Reduce the level of claims and deductions for manufacturers
- Reduce the amount of time spent on claims resolution for both retailers and manufacturers
- Reduce the added capital costs of "cushion" asset inventory and lost assets.

Direct store delivery

This scenario addresses some of the supply chain execution issues and opportunities specific to direct store delivery-based supply networks. (Note that collaborative opportunity areas such as promotion/event execution, total inventory management, asset control, and track and trace may also be applicable to direct store delivery.)

Current issues

EPC enablement can help direct store delivery suppliers and their retail customers address current issues such as:

- *Delivery errors* – Similar to retailer distribution centers, the direct store delivery model requires distributors to pick products at their supply depots for a wide range of customer locations and deliver the right products to the right stores on "multi-drop" delivery routes. The inherent complexity of this activity often leads to delivery errors.
- *Check-in wait and turnaround times* – Today, most retail customers require direct store delivery suppliers to replenish product during normal store delivery windows so retail staff can monitor deliveries

and verify product receipt. As retailers continue to drive efficiencies by reducing delivery windows, often the receiving process involves lengthy wait times caused by multiple deliveries arriving at the same time. These include the retailer's own delivery vehicles arriving from their own distribution centers.

- *Out-of-stocks and lost sales* – The inefficiencies in the direct store delivery supply chain described previously can lead to missed or rushed delivery stops, lower performance on shelf replenishment and merchandise presentation, and, ultimately, out-of-stocks and lost revenue.

- *Invoice discrepancies* – Delivery errors help fuel inconsistencies in delivery receipts and invoices and the need to reconcile financial records between retailers and direct store delivery suppliers.

Process view

As in traditional distribution center operations, EPC can drive improved efficiency and accuracy in shipping and receiving activities and asset control. It can also reduce back-office transaction discrepancies (i.e., invoice discrepancies). And with cooperation from retail customers, direct store delivery suppliers could achieve store-level benefits in terms of on-shelf availability and labor productivity. Specifically:

- *Improved warehouse management* – There is the potential for direct store delivery distributors to improve warehouse operations through the use of EPC/RFID in the areas of fleet management and pick-and-pack activities. The level of improvement will depend on the current degree of automation in the warehouse. Note that because most direct store delivery distributors have a large number of supply depots, the cost of EPC enablement may be much greater than that of a warehouse manufacturer or retailer.

- *Efficient store deliveries* – In an EPC-enabled model, readers at the store backroom would automatically capture the movement of direct store delivery products into the store and enable migration to a more automated check-in and delivery process. This change can reduce the wait times caused by manual check-in and may offer the opportunity for off-hour deliveries.

- *Improved store-level service* – This delivery scenario provides quicker turnaround times to direct store delivery personnel, helping to reduce the incidence of missed or rushed drops at the end of the day. In addition, personnel can spend more time at each drop reviewing merchandise presentation, product quantities and promotion execution. Replenishment and service to the store and end consumers would improve.

Economic benefits
Direct store delivery manufacturers can realize improved on-shelf availability and sales, higher labor and asset productivity, and reduced invoice discrepancies. Retail customers can benefit from reduced out-of-stocks and reduced labor requirements in the receiving process.

Promotion/Event execution
This scenario addresses some of the issues and opportunities specific to the execution of promotions, events and new product introductions. It encompasses activities from the manufacturer distribution center to the retail sales floor.

Current issues
EPC can help trading partners address the issues that arise from lack of visibility into store-level promotion execution. These issues include:

- Delayed compliance or non-compliance by stores

- Diversion of promoted products to the wrong stores

- Poor coordination with advertising programs, leading to out-of-stocks, lost sales, reduced consumer satisfaction, and excess markdowns or returns.

Process view

To help resolve these issues, trading partners can build on the EPC-enabled capabilities outlined in the Store Operations scenario discussed previously to enhance communication and collaboration among trading partners related to promotional and new product introduction activities. Specifically:

- *Improved store-level visibility* – With EPC readers located at store receiving and sales floor entry doors, realtime data would be available to help companies verify that on-promotion product and promotional materials (e.g., displays) are delivered to the store and moved onto the sales floor to coincide with specific promotional activities.

- *Actionable, more efficient compliance monitoring* – As this information is shared by retailers with their suppliers, manufacturer personnel would have greater visibility into promotion compliance at the store and may be able to reduce the number of store visits they have to make to address non-compliance issues. In addition, trading partners could proactively work together to coordinate the staging and movement of products with planned advertising and other events, improving the effectiveness of promotions in the marketplace.

Economic benefits

These changes, when coupled with EPC-enabled replenishment processes, can help drive improved on-shelf availability for promoted products and, therefore, higher consumer satisfaction and sales for both trading partners. Manufacturers can better monitor the effectiveness of their promotional spend, reduce wasted investment and decrease labor costs related to compliance management. In the future, the information provided by EPC could also be used in promotion planning and trade funds allocation discussions to better optimize spending in these areas.

Total inventory management

This scenario outlines how trading partners can exploit the broader, more granular, realtime stock visibility afforded by EPC to reduce overall inventory levels across the supply chain.

Current issues

EPC-enabled systems and processes can be harnessed to address one of the major issues that continue to plague industry supply chains: the ripple effect of excess inventory and safety stocks that manufacturers and upstream suppliers must maintain as a result of:

- *Poor downstream inventory visibility* – Manufacturers, for example, have little visibility of product flow through the retailer's supply chain. Unable to precisely monitor demand levels and forecast when new orders will be placed, they need to build up safety stocks to maintain service levels. Retailers themselves have less-than-optimal visibility into store-level inventory and demand fluctuations.

- *Disconnected forecasting and planning activities* – Demand planning throughout the value chain is largely based on historical sales patterns rather than active, realtime monitoring. Planning accuracy for manufacturers is dependent on the frequency of retailer orders and manufacturers' ability to use retail POS data, which can be problematic in terms of accessibility, reliability and ease of integration with forecasting systems. Time lags between orders and updates also help to drive up safety stock requirements.

- *"Corrupted" store demand signals* – When store employees "zero out" inventory in the store book stock system, it can lead to the placement of premature or unnecessary replenishment orders, causing a buildup of excess inventory at that store.

Process view

The EPC-based capabilities detailed in the store operations and distribution operations scenarios provide the foundation for improved supply chain collaboration on total inventory management. Specifically:

- *Improved store demand signal* – As EPC is rolled out in stores to enhance store and shelf replenishment, one of the second-order effects of increased stock information accuracy would be improvement in the demand signal. Store employees should no longer be allowed to incorrectly zero out inventory in the store book stock system simply because they cannot find the product. The replenishment orders placed would thus more accurately reflect the true level of inventory and demand at the store.

- *Improved planning and forecasting* – By sharing EPC case and pallet movement data with their suppliers, retailers would allow manufacturers to use this information to improve their planning and forecasting activities. Manufacturers would receive more granular and more frequent updates about inventory levels in the downstream supply chain, allowing them to more regularly compare actual product movements with their forecasts and to update them accordingly. Short-term planning and execution would be done in line with actual store activity and shipments versus historical sales forecast information.

- *Reduced safety stocks across the total supply chain* – With improved visibility and confidence in the stock information at their stores, retailers could reduce the levels of safety stock held at their distribution centers. For their part, as manufacturers build greater confidence in the accuracy and consistency of downstream demand signals, they could implement more dynamic replenishment processes and potentially change their inventory policies to reduce the safety stocks held at their own distribution centers.

- *Upstream supply chain benefits* – If manufacturers, in turn, shared their forecasts and production plans with their own suppliers, these inventory reduction benefits could similarly be shared with raw materials and packaging suppliers.

In the long run, some companies view EPC as an enabler to help transform the purchase order process as we know it today. As suppliers gain more visibility into store-level inventory and product movement data, they could take a more active role in managing their product inventories at the store. Suppliers could, for instance, use EPC demand signals to execute their own replenishment plans. If this process was linked with financial transactions, EPC reads could automatically trigger replenishments, transfer of ownership and underlying financial transactions between trading partners. More timely payments could offset the additional costs of managing inventory at a store level.

Economic benefits
Upstream suppliers, manufacturers and retailers that are able to collaborate with their trading partners in these ways will likely be able to free up valuable capital currently tied up in excess inventory.

Shrink management
Companies across the industry supply chain could take advantage of EPC-based product movement data to better identify and control shrink. As with the preceding scenarios, this vision is built on the EPC capabilities outlined in the store operations and distribution operations scenarios as well as direct store delivery for those types of supply networks.

Current issues
The sources and causes of shrink have been studied extensively in various industry studies (see Further reading). In general, though, they can be classified into four categories:[60]

- *External theft* – Theft from store thieves, grazing and returns fraud

- *Internal theft* – Theft by employees, contractors and collusion (at POS and receiving)

- *Process failures* – Due to incorrect deliveries, counting or pricing; out-of-date or damaged goods; markdowns

- *Inter-company fraud* – Willful mis-shipments or pricing discrepancies.

Companies across the supply chain are vulnerable to these forms of shrink largely due to poorly managed processes or controls. Some of the issues that inhibit more active and effective management of shrink include the following:

- Lack of visibility into key links in the supply chain, such as transportation between distribution centers and stores, where theft often occurs

- Lack of timely information about when and where shrink occurs, making it more difficult to trace after the fact; reactive tracking with a significant dependence on employee accuracy and honesty

- Insufficient security deterrents for own or trading partner employees.

Process view

The potential role of EPC in shrink management is straightforward. Improved shrink management would be achieved by comparing the actual EPC tag movements being captured by readers installed at receiving/shipping doors and other key locations with the movements that are planned or expected. Discrepancies could be automatically logged, highlighted or sent to relevant managers for their prompt attention.

Economic benefits

By exploiting EPC's capabilities as outlined in this section, companies can reduce the magnitude and impact of shrink, improving their bottom line.

CONCLUSIONS

EPC adoption is happening today as leading companies actively pilot and deploy EPC initiatives addressing many of the areas just discussed. It is, however, very much a work-in-progress. Significant advances in understanding how EPC can be used to drive anticipated benefits have been made, but there is still much to learn. Key conclusions based on the lessons learned and perspectives of leading EPC adopters are discussed below and summarized in Figure 4. Recommended actions are also presented.

Figure 4. Top-level conclusions of this report.

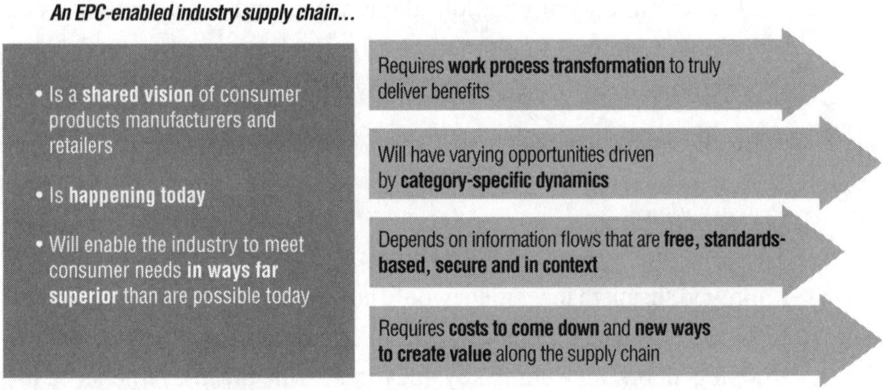

An EPC-enabled industry supply chain...

- Is a **shared vision** of consumer products manufacturers and retailers

- Is **happening today**

- Will enable the industry to meet consumer needs **in ways far superior** than are possible today

Requires **work process transformation** to truly deliver benefits

Will have varying opportunities driven by **category-specific dynamics**

Depends on information flows that are **free, standards-based, secure and in context**

Requires **costs to come down** and **new ways to create value** along the supply chain

Source: IBM Global Business Services analysis based on Global Commerce Initiative data, 2006.

Work process transformation is required for EPC to truly deliver benefits

Leading adopters generally expect four primary sources of benefit from EPC adoption in the near to medium term:

- Increased sales from improved on-shelf availability
- Reduction in inventory levels
- Improved labor productivity in stores and distribution centers
- Reduction in post-sale transaction and administrative costs (e.g., claims).

However, to fully realize these anticipated benefits from EPC adoption, trading partners must simultaneously pursue both process and technological changes. These benefits are dependent on companies making requisite changes in business practices and work processes, both internally and in collaboration with trading partners.

Category-specific dynamics drive differences in opportunity

With respect to EPC adoption, different product categories have different dynamics including cost structures, required infrastructure support, distribution models, value to the consumer and role in the retail store. Manufacturers and retailers involved in the production, sale and merchandising of many categories of consumer products recognize category dynamics as a key driver of the business opportunity in EPC adoption. They also recognize the need to "learn by doing" and to conduct pilots in categories that reflect the greatest opportunities based on mutual trading partner business cases.

Trading partner collaboration is dependent on information flows that are free, standards-based, protected and in context

Process change of any kind is difficult and even more so when it requires coordinated action across trading relationships. To enhance the likelihood of success, trading partners need to operate using the same information. Therefore, it is essential that industry participants have a fundamental willingness to collaborate and share supply chain information with trading partners. Progress must continue in establishing accepted "best practices" for the sharing of important information among trading partners for EPC to truly work and for the industry and end-consumers to benefit.

Costs must come down, and new ways to create value along the supply chain must be found

In addition to the transformation of specific work processes, a key driver of EPC's potential benefits is the value of the pallets and cases being tagged relative to the cost of the EPC tags and the RFID infrastructure. Collaboration among early adopters, industry participants, technology vendors and EPCglobal will be required to continue improving EPC's cost of implantation and overall value proposition; the ability to deliver consumer benefits ultimately depends on the reduction of these costs. Steps include the following:

- Focus by individual companies on understanding their specific business case
- Completion of meaningful pilots by trading partners
- Recognition by the industry of the key technology improvements that are needed.

Learn from the barcode experience

To better understand the long-term context for EPC and help predict its key success factors and likely challenges, the industry should review lessons learned in the adoption of the barcode, a process with many similarities. Time will tell whether EPC adoption patterns will mimic those of the barcode, but the lessons learned should be heeded as new opportunities enabled by EPC are tackled. In particular, the industry's historical experience with barcodes illustrates the importance of:

- Developing and adopting truly global standards
- Open sharing of information among trading partners
- Active collaboration on required business process changes
- Continued monitoring of actual versus forecasted costs and benefits to update business case projections.

RECOMMENDED INDUSTRY ACTIONS

Key actions that the GCI recommends for EPC adoption are presented below. The recommendations are geared toward individual companies, trading partners and the industry as a whole.

Action steps for individual companies

Actions that individual companies should take in regard to EPC adoption are:

- Understand and communicate the EPC vision within your own organization, setting up a cross-functional team and identifying an executive-level champion.
- Learn by doing. Conduct your own business case analysis, and experiment with and investigate opportunities for using EPC in your own company.
- Help ensure that your company has clean, accurate product data that is aligned with trading partners and is being shared automatically with those trading partners (through Global Data Synchronization, a recognized industry best practice).
- Participate in and support industry groups, especially EPCglobal, at local, regional or global levels to share lessons learned and engage in the standards-setting process.
- Understand and proactively address the consumer and public policy perspectives on EPC.

Action steps for improved trading partner collaboration

Actions that trading partners should take in regard to EPC adoption are:

- Embrace the exchange of supply chain information and collaboration via the EPCglobal Network as a source of business improvement versus viewing them as a threat. Establish clear information-sharing work practices with your trading partners and support the use of free, standards-based information exchange.

- Engage in meaningful pilots with trading partners, focusing on opportunities identified in mutual business cases.

- Leading adopters should share their knowledge, experience and findings more widely in industry forums, including information on pilot results and business value.

- Manufacturers and retailers should collaborate to craft a workable roadmap for EPC deployment focusing on high potential categories and the most accessible supply chain opportunities.

- Upstream suppliers and 3PL and distribution service providers should keep pace with industry adoption to avoid creating gaps in the capabilities of the end-to-end supply chain.

Action steps for the industry as a whole to address critical technology issues

Actions that the industry as a whole should take in regard to EPC adoption are:

- Industry participants should work with EPCglobal to prioritize the development of future requisite regulations and standards, such as tag classes, software interoperability and data sharing, that can be globally accepted and adopted.

- Industry participants, technology vendors and EPCglobal should work together to make required capabilities available to drive expected benefits. Focus areas should include improved tag read rates and accuracy, high-speed tag application and embedding technology, a scalable EPC information network, and a conformance and performance certification process.

In summary, EPC implementation is a substantial investment that requires in-depth, joint planning. Trading partners need to figure out the best path to an EPC-enabled value chain, working together to determine how they can deploy EPC in an economically viable way to achieve an end-state that drives lasting value.

Transforming the military through sense and respond

By Grace Y. Lin and Robert E. Luby, Jr.

Today's military and intelligence environment is fast-changing and unpredictable. Terrorist acts and other threats to the security of our nation and its citizens require the military and intelligence communities to address significant challenges. These challenges include:

- Coordinating multi-agency, multinational units so they may more effectively respond to rapidly changing situations

- Creating a logical fusion of fragmented and uncertain information gathered from the various theaters in which military or intelligence branches are engaged

- Configuring value nets intelligently and dynamically to support common goals between autonomous yet interdependent joint forces.

To face these challenges, the military and intelligence communities are turning to sense and respond – an innovative managerial approach originally developed by IBM that is designed to revolutionize organizational structure and operations.[61,62] The interpretation of sense and respond by the U.S. Department of Defense (DoD) has resulted in three major transformational efforts: Network-Centric Operations (NCO), sense-and-respond logistics and military culture change.[63,64,65]

The sense-and-respond model offers agile, adaptable, scalable and interoperable response capabilities. We have proven the capabilities and value of sense and respond to both internal IBM and commercial clients. Based on this experience, we share DoD's belief that adapting sense and respond to the nation's defense needs will provide the military and intelligence communities with many benefits during their large-scale and long-term transformation efforts.

SENSE-AND-RESPOND MANAGERIAL FRAMEWORK

The sense-and-respond managerial framework is based on the premise that changes in the business, security and technology environments are so swift that they have outstripped our ability to foresee and plan for them.[66] A successful response will come from rapidly sensing and adapting to change rather than relying on process designs, hierarchies of authority and industrial-age command-and-control action plans designed for events that are more predictable.

The sense-and-respond managerial framework is based on five core competencies: design organizations as adaptive systems, context-giving leadership, decision clock-speed, know earlier, and dispatch capabilities from the effect back (see Figure 1). While planning for operations is still needed, its nature must change dramatically. Specifically, designs for action must replace courses of action as an expression of military strategy.

Figure 1. Five key competencies for the sense-and-respond organization.

Design organizations as adaptive systems – Integrate units connected through common purposes, governing principles and shared risks, collaborating on achieving common goals.

Context-giving leadership – Train and qualify leaders as provider of the context within which subordinates can self-synchronize to achieve common goals.

Decision clock-speed – Augment human decisions with smarter and more flexible technologies and manage execution cycle through collaboration.

Know earlier – Use enhanced sensor networks for better analysis, superior pattern recognition and more comprehensive context linkage.

Dispatch capabilities from the effect back – Establish a security-enhanced collaboration mechanism for self-synchronization in a technology-enabled adaptive system based on superior knowledge of events and effects.

Source: IBM Global Business Services analysis, 2006.

SENSE-AND-RESPOND VALUE NET

The sense-and-respond value net initiated at IBM Research expands the sense-and-respond managerial framework into an integrated planning, operations, intelligence and logistics system.[67,68,69] It uses decision models and advanced technology first to monitor, detect and predict events and then to coordinate actions between networked organizations and value net partners.

Through highly adaptive, self-synchronizing and dynamic physical and functional processes, sense and respond is designed to drive shorter decision cycles and faster responses. An array of tools and technologies support the sense-and-respond value net, including agent-based distributed decision-making, dashboards, event management, intelligent analytics and business process integration and automation.

The sense-and-respond value net proactively detects events, aligns operations with strategy, integrates planning and execution, and supports sustainment. Value-net partners collaborate in decision-making, and the entire system constantly adapts to changing conditions. The value net is dynamically configured by forming and dissolving partnerships to support objectives. Value-net performance is further improved by advanced integration technologies, closed-loop feedback control and learning mechanisms. This optimization involves the sharing of information, distribution of decision rights, redistribution of work, support of sustainment, and better allocation and use of available resources (see Figure 2).

Figure 2. Sense-and-respond value net technologies.

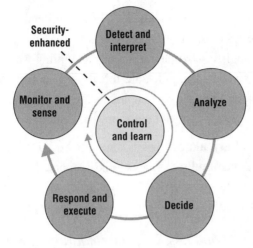

Value net support
- Collaboration support
- Impact and value analysis
- Distributed decision support

Analyze
- Realtime logistics and effect analytics
- Simulation and what-if analysis
- Risk and impact analysis
- Semantic Web
- Rulebased systems

Respond and execute
- Realtime execution support
- Autonomic computing
- Realtime infrastructure support

Monitor and sense
- Sensors and sensor networks
- Data integration technologies
- Security-enhanced communication networks

Dashboard
- Information integrator
- Situational filter based on roles
- Visualization technologies
- Portal and information push-and-pull technology

Control and learn
- Effect measurement and monitoring
- Feedback and learning technology

Detect and interpret
- Data cleansing and filtering
- Pattern and event recognition
- Knowledge mining

Decision support
- Agent framework
- Policy-driven decision-making system
- Security-enhanced collaboration support
- Distributed decision making protocols

Source: IBM Global Business Services analysis, 2006.

SENSE AND RESPOND IN THE MILITARY

To support deployed forces, the military has traditionally relied on mass-based logistics systems. This tendency is still true today, even in the era of just-in-time logistics. While traditional stockpiling was impractical for responding to sudden, unpredictable threats, just-in-time logistics – the streamlined alternative – leaves deployed forces and their support units more at risk to interruptions of their more vulnerable lean supply chains.

In an attempt to fully address these issues, the U.S. DoD Office of Force Transformation has embraced sense-and-respond logistics, a concept that has great synergy with IBM's own sense-and-respond vision. In November, 2004, DoD defined sense and respond as follows:

Sense and respond (S&R) is a foundational, managerial and leadership model for joint, networked, effect-back organizations that specifically address the behavioral imperatives of Network-Centric Operations (NCO). It empowers local commanders with information and coordination mechanisms that allow them to synchronize action with other units and make informed decisions based on realtime intelligence. It exploits adaptive technologies and behaviors to operate effectively in the rapid and unpredictable environment of asynchronous warfare.[70]

Figure 3 shows a sample sense-and-respond system that supports military operation. The sample scenario in Figure 4 illustrates how sense-and-respond value nets support logistics and battlefield operations, as well as sustainment, by observing patterns, detecting issues and performing root-cause analysis. In the scenario shown, coalition forces are deployed in support of a peacekeeping mission, and a sense-and-respond system has already been programmed with data on all rules of engagement governing coalition forces, available assets and supplies, capabilities of friendly units and suspected capabilities of the enemy.

Figure 3. Sense-and-respond value net to support military operations.

Inputs: Rules Policies Plan Command intent Desired effects	**Operational command** *Roles:* Receive mission Determine resources Determine effects desired Design plan Adapt plan	*Receivables:* Decision support Communications Data reports Availability of assets

Virtual computer
Roles:
Data integration
Commitment management
Demand/supply matching
Analysis/pattern recognition
Manage roles, responsibilities and accountability
Middleware
Modeling and simulation
Decision support

Receivables:
Information requests

Intelligence command
Roles:
Determine intelligence need
Gather data
Analyze data
Weather
Terrain
Enemy capability

Inputs:
Raw data
Filtered data
Analyzed data

Receivables:
Supply requests
Intelligence affecting supply

Logistics command
Roles:
Troop sustainment
Inventory management
Reliability management

Inputs:
Supply availability
PLM information

Source: IBM Global Business Services analysis, 2006.

Figure 4. Sample scenario: Reaction to insurgent attack – the sense-and-respond system supports a military operation.

Coalition forces are deployed in support of a peacekeeping mission. A sense-and-respond system has already been programmed with data on all rules of engagement governing coalition forces, available assets and supplies, capabilities of friendly units and suspected capabilities of the enemy.

Sense-and-respond operations: Current plans call for patrols, backed by quick reaction forces in case of contact. Sense-and-respond uses a version of the Sense, Interpret, Decide, Act Loop.

Sense-and-respond logistics: While the other activities are taking place, and the attention of commanders is focused on the combat operations, sense and respond continues to analyze all incoming data, and notices several arising support issues.

Sense: Intelligence assets receive information that several police stations and market areas will be attacked. Patrols observe and report unusually early shop closings in several market areas.
Interpret: Possible coordinated attacks at multiple locations.
Decide: Further analysis is required, possible targets are evaluated.
Act: Communication initiated with intelligence assets, troop commanders are alerted, planning begins, quick reaction troops are dispatched to possible target areas.

Sense: Patrol units were only carrying minimal food, water and ammunition loads. Several vehicles that were dispatched, or rerouted in reaction to the attacks, will drop below suggested fuel levels during the operation. The on-board prognostics of an unmanned aerial vehicle (UAV), tasked as a surveillance platform for this operation, are predicting an impending part failure.
Interpret: Sense-and-respond determines the amounts of food, fuel, etc., needed.

Sense: A patrol is attacked while approaching one of the markets. Two personnel are injured.
Two police stations (one was not originally identified as a possible target) are attacked by groups of 40-60 insurgents. Ten policemen are killed, 22 injured. Coalition teams on the ground report updated statuses of the potential targets.
Interpret: Coordinated, simultaneous insurgent attacks are underway. Other targets are still at risk.
Decide: The attacked patrol units require immediate backup. Air support and medical assistance are also required.
Act: Additional troops and medical units are sent to police stations and the market sites. Other forces and logistics units are placed on high alert. Air support is dispatched. The risks at other targets are reassessed and several teams are moved into strategic positions.

Sense: Sense-and-respond checks [available to promise] fuel (e.g., uncommitted fuel) and finds three sources. Sense-and-respond finds two sources of food and water. Sense-and-respond is unable to find available ammunition. Sense-and-respond finds a replacement part for the UAV, but it is located at the manufacturer in the U.S. and will take several days to arrive in-theater.
Interpret: Risk calculation: Based on current data, sense-and-respond determines that supply vehicles can deliver food, fuel and water. Sense-and-respond determines that lack of ammunition will become crucial if the engagement is prolonged. Sense-and-respond determines that additional units will have to be committed due to the currently engaged units' supply situation.
Decide: Presents a recommendation to the Logistics Command (LC) showing the preferred sources of supply, delivery vehicles and routes of travel. The Intelligence Command (IC) is tasked to prepare alternate surveillance assets in anticipation of a part failure on the UAV currently on-scene. Makes suggestions to the OC (operation command) on which additional units may be committed to the engagement.
All of this information is immediately displayed to the OC, LC and IC while a subset of this information is also uploaded as an input to the Sense, Interpret, Decide, Act loops of the joint forces commander.

Sense-and-respond sustainment: At the conclusion of this engagement, the sense-and-respond system sends a report regarding the parts.

Sense: This is the second instance of the same part failing well before the expected mean time to failure (MTF).
Interpret: Additional replacement parts are required, further study is also required to determine the underlying cause of failure.
Decide: The need for UAV surveillance is high, therefore a short-term increase in spare parts levels is suggested; meanwhile, reliability engineers are assigned to study the problem and recommend a long-term solution.
Act: Parts are expedited from manufacturers. Engineers begin studying the problem.

Sense: Engineers discover that current fluid screens and filtering systems are inadequate for the new operating environment.
Interpret: New filtering system must be designed; short-term fix is needed until new system is available. A combination of more frequent maintenance and improvised filters is suggested.
Decide: Manufacturing community should be informed of the problem; short-term solution will be implemented.
Act: Manufacturing community is contacted and agrees to work on a new filtering system; improvised filters are constructed (modified from helicopter filters) and a revised maintenance schedule is implemented.

Source: IBM Global Business Services analysis, 2006.

CONCLUSION

Successfully implementing sense and respond within the military and intelligence communities will not happen by chance. Rather, it will result from commitment and collaboration among stakeholders at all levels supported by changes in decision models, operations and culture. Rooted in our sense-and-respond value net framework is a paradigm shift that encompasses planning, operations, intelligence and logistics, bringing a fundamentally new perspective to our nation's 21st century defense needs.

The large-scale effort needed for transforming the military into a sense-and-respond enterprise will be more than offset by the benefits reaped from improvements in operations, logistics and intelligence and the ability to support the operations on which our national security depends.

Executive interview

Alan Estevez, Assistant Deputy Undersecretary of Defense for Supply Chain Integration, U.S. Department of Defense

The Supply Chain Integration office has primary responsibility within the Department of Defense's (DoD's) Logistics and Materiel Readiness secretariat for several initiatives including: to identify business process changes that could be enabled or strengthened through the implementation of e-business capabilities; to lead the development of modern supply chain policies in DoD, including the integration of acquisition logistics and e-commerce capabilities; and to develop and maintain DoD component implementation of supply chain management and end-to-end distribution capabilities required to meet 21st century deployment and sustainment requirements.[1]

Alan Estevez is the Assistant Deputy Undersecretary of Defense for Supply Chain Integration. Alan is responsible for developing global supply chain management and distribution policies and processes to support the war fighters' operational requirements, wherever they are in the world. This interview with Alan focuses on the DoD's use of RFID.

IBM: *I understand you assumed your current position in 2002. Can you please describe more about your role… describe a "day in the life"?*

Alan Estevez: Well, essentially, my real role is establishing policies for the way that the DoD's supply business processes work. My focus is mostly on the supply and distribution portion of the supply chain versus, say, the maintenance and transportation hierarchy.

---

[1] http://www.acq.osd.mil

"...we are supporting every type of commodity that you can imagine, from repair parts to keeping our weapons platforms operating, to food, water to keep our soldiers operating."

To give you an idea of what DoD logistics looks like, we have US$77 billion worth of inventory, we process 45,000 plus requisitions each day (from either our maintenance facilities or from forces in the field) and about 51,000 vendors that we buy materiel from. And obviously, we're supporting about US$700 billion in assets. Those are weapons platforms, 300 ships, 1,500 aircraft, 30,000 combat vehicles, just to give you an idea of what we have in the inventory. And, of course, our forces are operating worldwide, and we are at war. So they're operating, actively engaged in, combat operations in a number of locations.

The actual hands-on management and execution is done within the military services and our combatant commands and defense agencies, particularly Defense Logistics Agency. So we are supporting every type of commodity that you can imagine, from repair parts to keeping our weapons platforms operating, to food, water to keep our soldiers operating. Troop support items like body armor, chem-bio suits, desert uniforms, combat uniforms, munitions, ammo, etc. Bullets, bombs, medical devices, medical supplies, barrier equipment, Jersey walls to keep bases secure. So you think about it in the supply chain, we're managing it.

We have about five million SKUs (Stockkeeping Units) in the inventory. For us, fighting in a place like Afghanistan or Iraq, or a naval vessel on the move, a stock out can mean a multi-million dollar asset sitting stagnant because it cannot be used... best case. Worst case is a disaster, front page of the newspaper, and deaths incorporated into that.

IBM: *Yes, the criticality of it is beyond anything else, I would imagine. We've heard a lot about the military use of RFID within the supply chain. Could you talk a little bit about the program that you're responsible for in general, and how much of that is related to RFID?*

Alan Estevez: RFID is a means to an end. The end in our case is an effective supply chain. It is one of our key programs to achieve visibility of the supply chain, but you can't overlook the other facets that we're doing to enhance our forecasting capability, enhance our ability to buy materiel, and from the visibility aspect, the systems integration of our data tools in order to have actionable information.

But with regard to RFID – RFID is not new to the Department of Defense for supply chain management for tracking materiel. We started mostly in the Army playing with active RFID – high-data capacity active RFID, as a matter of fact – so that we can hold the manifest of a seavan or hold the manifest of a large air pallet on the tag itself. Started doing that post the first Gulf War, so about 1991, 1992 timeframe.

The reason we did that is when you started looking at the lessons learned from the first Gulf War, we moved a vast amount of materiels to support the 550,000 forces that we had in Saudi Arabia as we prepared to liberate Kuwait. And we moved about 40,000 seavans to that theater, and about 24,000 of those seavans had to be opened to ascertain their contents once they got there.

You look at the complexity of what we're moving and the period of time in which we're moving it. You throw in the fact that sometimes our forces out in the field do not always have the best communications in the log environment – they're able to communicate with each other, but they're not able to necessarily communicate back to the wholesale base. We viewed RFID as a tool to help us solve that problem. That is also why we went to the high-data capacity tag.

"RFID is a means to an end. The end in our case is an effective supply chain."

Now again, that was mostly in the Army, and the Army used that active RFID on-and-off over the next decade. For instance, shortly after the Black Hawk Down episode in Somalia, we put in an RFID network in Somalia. We used it again in Haiti in the mid-1994 intervention, we used it in Bosnia, we used it in Kosovo.

But what we found is it wasn't imbedded in doctrine, and it wasn't imbedded into the joint services. And every time we moved forward to go into another operation, it was really re-learn the lessons – re-learn how to set up that network again.

So as we prepared to go to war in Operation Iraqi Freedom, the folks at the United States Central Command wanted to have everything moving into their theater trackable, and asked that an RFID network be established to do that. Well, what they found was that the expertise to do that really resided in the United States European Command. So it was really find the five, six guys who have done this before and try to learn those lessons.

Well, coming out of that, on the active side, we decided we're not going to keep doing it this way, that's kind of dumb. So our policy said this is going to be our way of doing business, and we are going to use active RFID to help track our moving, large, consolidated shipments.

At the same time, we were looking at how to solidify that policy. A couple of other things were coming onboard. Obviously the work of the Auto-ID Center up at MIT, which had been put together by a commercial consortium, was coming to fruition. The DoD had been an early member of the Auto-ID Center dating back to 2000, so it's not like we just stumbled upon this. We were actually playing in it. And we also, just like my counterparts in the commercial sector, saw passive RFID – fairly cheap devices – as a tool in order to not just track our materiel in motion, but also to get a handle on where our inventory was and to do receipt processing with those tools.

I mentioned 51,000 suppliers. So we put out a requirement that our suppliers start tagging (at the) case pallet level, initially to our two largest supply depots in the Department of Defense system. And we are growing our processes from there. Simultaneously, we are working inside the Department of Defense across that global reach of our forces to start imbedding the use of passive RFID within our processes inside the DoD.

IBM: *It's certainly been quite a long trail to get where you are today.*

Alan Estevez: And it's a long trail to get to where we want to go, frankly!

IBM: *That was the next question. What are your key milestones around the program?*

Alan Estevez: Well as I said, you know, we have a requirement out now that suppliers of certain commodities, repair parts, meals ready to eat and soldier support items – that would be things like body armor and uniforms, boots, helmets, etc. – tag materiel that's going to be stored in our two key defense facilities. We're going to expand that this year to some other commodities, including barrier equipment and medical equipment to the remaining DoD supply depots in the United States. And certain of our key aerial ports, where we ship materiel moving overseas using the United States Air Force or United States Air Force-controlled aircraft.

"We probably have the most robust open-ended active RFID network..."

That will be 2006. In 2007, our plan is to expand that to all appropriate commodities and to all locations in the Department of Defense that are RFID-enabled.

And we're working through our budget process, so that we have a robust program to stand up internal DoD sites over the next five to seven years.

IBM: *A nation at war implies a lot of flexibility and rapid deployment scenarios. How does your RFID technology hold up in that sort of scenario with, presumably, the need to not only get the supplies in place, but also the technology behind the RFID and other technologies that you use?*

Alan Estevez: The reality is the Department is more focused on putting out a jammer to prevent a roadside bomb from exploding than it is in experimenting with something like RFID on the battle field.

With that said, we are doing it, in point of fact. We probably have the most robust open-ended active RFID network with that data passing up to a server so that it can be seen through some DoD systems, and folks in the field can track their supplies that are moving through that active network.

So from that standpoint, we're ensuring that they're compliant. There are issues with that, especially when you start moving to some of the more austere environments, where things are not always in the control of the Department of Defense. You put the tag that we use on a seavan that's moving over the Khyber Pass, and a third-party national driver may look at that device and not be sure what it is, so he removes it. So, you know, we are dealing with problems like that.

On the passive side, we do have a few small – really small – actions ongoing in the field. There are people out there who say, "I have a need," and frankly our best initial sites are all done by folks in the field who said, "I have a need to manage either my facility or my incoming supply chain." And those have all worked very well.

IBM: *Some of the things you're alluding to are more people and process-related than they are technology. Having the technology work is one thing, but it must be quite a change management challenge as well?*

Alan Estevez: Absolutely. I'd say the technology works. The technology not only works, it's getting better, and it's going to work even better as time goes on. So I wouldn't say the technology is a challenge at all. It's the application of the technology and how folks use it and whether they really get the focus around it is where the real challenge is. And that applies not only to forces in the field. It applies to starting up a warehouse in the United States as well. If you do it wrong, we have a tendency to blame the technology. And in point of fact, it's a bad business process, and it's a bad setup, and it's a bad application. When you do those things right, we're getting some great results.

So let me give you two great examples.

One, we have a cross dock facility in Norfolk, Virginia, which is operated by the Navy Fleet and Industrial Supply Center. They did an outstanding stand-up of an EPC application within their warehouse to the point where they're using EPC reads to document materiel being loaded into seavans. Thirty-seven percent reduction in the time it takes to manage that process. Three percent reduction in mislaid – I hesitate to use the word "lost" – materiel. But, you know, the materiel eventually gets found, it just doesn't get found in time to fulfill the order that

"Through the use of this visibility network, which RFID was a key part of, they were able to reduce the amount of materiel they were holding while at the same time increasing the supply availability of materiel and significantly decreasing the backlog of orders that they were processing from 92,000 orders to 11,000 orders."

it's being moved for. So, that's a great application. What we're doing is trying to capture what they did and ensure that we can do that on the macro scale.

Another application – and this is being done with active tags, but it could easily have been done with passive tags for part of it – is what our U.S. Marine forces did on the ground in Iraq. Now, they changed their business process which they were doing anyway, but while they were doing it, they figured out how to use the technology at the same time. They put in a data network so that they had access to the data that they need to manage this business process, incoming materiel and outgoing materiel.

Through the use of this visibility network, which RFID was a key part of, they were able to reduce the amount of materiel they were holding while at the same time increasing the supply availability of materiel and significantly decreasing the backlog of orders that they were processing from 92,000 orders to 11,000 orders. And we attribute that to the confidence that the combat Marines in the field had knowing where their supplies that were coming to support them were. So the dialogue changed – and this is a discussion I had with those Marines on the ground in Iraq. The dialogue changed, the questions coming into them from "Where's my stuff?" to "Why isn't my stuff moving?"

IBM: *Can you give us any idea of the sort of amount of data that you're collecting today and what you foresee in the future? And what you see is the next main objective around the information management?*

Alan Estevez: You know, we have a fairly robust tool for processing orders and tracking orders today. RFID will give us a more realtime and more accurate feed, and we're going to feed that data through our existing network, with some modifications, obviously, to manage that data. We also have a number of emerging, what I'll call "front ends" to those databases that give you the Google effect – pull down the data from the variety of systems that the Department of Defense has. And I won't even try to give you an idea of the complexity of the number of legacy applications, legacy systems we have out there, something like 2,000-plus logistics systems across the different services of the Department of Defense.

RFID, of course, is just going to be another feed. So the trick becomes then, what RFID data is important at the enterprise level, and what RFID data is really just important at the activity level.

When you get ready to ship something, when something moves through a cross-dock operation and the global supply chain, we want to be able to capture that at the enterprise level. So everyone who is interested in that order, can see that order moving. We need to be able to pass that data back to Boeing and Lockheed and Raytheon and Northrop Grumman and GE Aircraft and General Dynamics and AM General, etc. across our supply chain, because if you don't, you're not going to have a dynamic, flexible supply chain. I can reduce the lead times it takes to order components. Those companies can see what's moving, can see what their production is. And we can start moving toward that collaborative enterprise that the best supply chains operate under.

"RFID will give us a more realtime and more accurate feed, and we're going to feed that data through our existing network, with some modifications, obviously, to manage that data."

IBM: *Are there other tracking technologies that you're looking at?*

Alan Estevez: We today use GPS to track trucks, just like the commercial sector does, and we have different applications of that ranging from classified to just normal vehicle-tracking applications. And, obviously, we're going to continue to use other AIT-type applications like 2D data matrix scans and the like. In our maintenance area you'll see more diagnostic-prognostic-type devices built into our platforms. The goal there, of course, is to send the signal that "it is time to change the oil filter." So the oil filter is waiting for you when the plane lands or the vehicle drives up. You can tell I'm not a maintenance guy!

IBM: *What is the potential here in terms of savings for the supply chain?*

Alan Estevez: Just from RFID – RFID in use with the network – we did a very high-level of business case analysis. And we looked at it from two aspects, very conservative and our most optimistic. We looked at some commercial projections because, frankly, there's not a lot of real-world experience on anyone's part.

Our business case analysis showed a range from US$70 million savings (over a five-year period) to US$1.7 billion savings (over a five-year period) to the Department of Defense. Now what's critical in that is that those savings did not, I repeat, did not take into account any kind of savings in inventory that we could achieve related to the capture of data. And it did not, more importantly, take into account readiness savings.

If you take it to its logical end, if I have a supply chain that's functioning effectively, I can deploy less of those platforms to accomplish the same mission that I'm trying to accomplish. And, you know, there's a great spiral that goes on with that because every time I deploy one less weapons platform, not only do I not deploy the crew that has to operate that weapons platform, I can deploy less maintainers to maintain that, I'm deploying less inventory to sustain it, I'm deploying less force protection to take care of those people, and I'm deploying less food, fuel, water, etc., around that whole thing. So I get a much more agile footprint on the ground increasing the flexibility of our military forces. Doing it properly, you really get greater military capability on a smaller force.

You asked a couple of other things there about the length of time. One of the things about RFID, it's an interesting side effect, is that to really apply this – and we all have the pave-the-cow-path tendency and I hate to use these clichés – but to really apply RFID you have to look at your business process. So while you're looking at your business process to take advantage of the technology, you should be doing a value stream mapping. You should be doing a lean Six Sigma-type event around your business process. And you know what? If RFID doesn't apply, you're still ahead of the game because you've done a business process assessment that you should be doing.

So I've lumped all of these things under a continuous process improvement area of application. And continuous is obviously continuous. If you sit, you get stagnant, then you're not doing continuous process improvement, so this is really lifetime work.

Let me just throw out one other thing about working with the commercial sector. I am the DoD liaison to the EPCglobal Board of Directors. I can't overemphasize, obviously, the need for standards, which is why we're working with EPCglobal, because for me, it gives me that reach-in

"But more importantly, we decided early on that for passive RFID implementation, we were going to embrace EPC standards. And, frankly, it was a no-brainer because an EPC process is moving through an (ISO) process as well."

to the commercial sector in areas that we normally wouldn't work and gets us access to some of the lessons that I was just discussing and the sharing across the environment.

But more importantly, we decided early on that for passive RFID implementation, we were going to embrace EPC standards. And, frankly, it was a no-brainer because an EPC process is moving through an (ISO) process as well. But when you look at the Fortune 10 companies that embrace EPC, who are also suppliers to the Department of Defense, and you look at the aerospace companies who have also embraced EPC, some of them coming on the heels of us moving in that direction, some of them are because they were moving that way anyway.

The other thing that we've done is we've worked across the federal government, across federal agencies, to ensure that we all know what each of us is doing to, again, preclude a mix-up in standards, if you would. I'm using an active RFID device to track materiel. I'm intensely interested in the direction the Department of Homeland Security may go in putting out any kind of security guidance. I'm interested in what FDA is doing with regard to EPC tags on drugs because I buy drugs from the same companies. So I just thought I'd throw that in, to show the synchronization that we are working on in order to make this come out right for both us and the commercial sector.

IBM: *One last question – if there was one thing you've learned over the last four or five years that you would change if you had to go on this – or start – this journey again, what would it be?*

Alan Estevez: Boy... it's not something I'd say I'd change, but you really have to find the right change leaders. And the people who are doing, who are willing to put themselves on the line for a potential failure because things are out there – you know, you do a beta, you do a test site – you have to be willing to bump your nose and skin your knee in doing that because it's not going to work perfectly. And we come from an environment...a military culture where people don't want to fail. So sometimes they become too conservative and don't want to try because it, essentially, can mean failure. So it's finding those right people and then building that consensus across the military department, recognizing the budget issues that you have to manage. So, that's one. And I think we're actually doing OK in that regard.

The second area is, frankly, just the regulatory process across the federal government. You know, the Department of Defense cannot decide to insert a contract clause in and of itself. It has to work that through the interagency process. And in doing so, there's a lot of – in the RFID world – erroneous data floating through the Ethernet out there. So getting the people and getting them to understand what's real and what's not is a difficult challenge, especially when even the RFID trade press shoot for the "it-didn't-work" stories, not the "it-did-work." No one wants to write that, "Man Walked Dog." (They want to read) "Dog Bit Man."

So it's just getting that message out so that the whole regulatory line-up, and that goes from the U.S. Congress and other agencies in the executive branch on down, are inline to support this. And again, it's something that we've been working hard on and I wouldn't say we've done a bad job of, but we've made some missteps along the way ourselves.

Further reading

Recommended IBM Institute for Business Value reading

You can access IBM Institute for Business Value studies through:

1. The IBM Institute for Business Value external Web site: ibm.com/iibv

2. Subscribing to the IBM Global Business Services thought leadership e-newsletter IdeaWatch: ibm.com/bcs/subscribe

IBM Institute for Business Value – Supply chain management specific

- Building value in logistics outsourcing
- Follow the leaders: Scoring high on the supply chain maturity model[71]
- Energize your supply chain network – A European perspective
- Taking center stage: The IBM Chief Procurement Officer study
- The GMA 2005 Logistics Survey
- A retailer's guide to supply chain management
- Cost-effective supply chains
- Transforming the military through sense and respond
- Supply chain management on demand maturity model
- On demand supply chain transformation II
- Sense-and-respond supply chains: Enabling breakthrough strategy
- Energize your supply chain network
- Transforming your supply chain to on demand

IBM Institute for Business Value – Industry specific

- A prognostic study of on demand business in the electronics industry
- Product lifecycle management – Creating corporate assets or simply controlling engineering data
- Reinventing the electronics industry through enterprise collaboration

Other reading and specific industry sources

- "17 billion reasons to say thanks: The 25th anniversary of the U.P.C. and its impact on the grocery industry." John E. Nelson and Vineet Garg. PricewaterhouseCoopers. 1999.
- "Automatic product identification & shrinkage: Scoping the potential." Adrian Beck, University of Leicester. ECR Europe. July 2002.
- "A balanced perspective: EPC/RFID implementation in the CPG Industry." Prepared by IBM and A.T. Kearney for the Grocery Manufacturers of America. 2004.
- "ECR – Optimal shelf availability: Increasing shopper satisfaction at the moment of truth." Roland Berger Strategy Consultants and ECR Europe. 2003.
- "Full-shelf satisfaction: Reducing out of-stocks in the grocery channel: An in-depth look at DSD categories." Roland Berger Strategy Consultants and Grocery Manufacturers of America. 2002.
- "Guidelines on EPC for consumer products." EPCglobal Inc. http: // www.epcglobalinc.org/public_policy/public_policy_guidelines.html
- "Inventory record inaccuracy: An empirical analysis." Nicole DeHoratius, University of Chicago and Ananth Raman, Harvard Business School. August 2004.

- "Measuring the impact of information technology on value and productivity using a process-based approach: The case for RFID technologies." Brian Subirana, Chad Eckes, George Herman, Sanjay Sarma and Michael Barrett. MIT Sloan working paper No. 4450-03. 2003.
- "Retail out-of-stocks: A worldwide examination of extent, causes and consumer responses." Thomas W. Gruen, Daniel S. Corsten and Sundar Bharadwaj. Grocery Manufacturers of America. 2002.
- "Shrinkage in Europe 2004: A survey of stock loss in the fast moving consumer goods sector." Adrian Beck, University of Leicester. ECR Europe. July 2004.

Author biographies

Marc Bourdé is an Associate Partner in the Supply Chain Transformation practice within IBM Global Business Services providing consulting services to global and local clients across a broad range of industries, including consumer products, oil and gas, pharmaceuticals, automotive, retailing, paper, metal and industrial products. Marc is delivering value to clients by helping them to transform their global supply chains and increase their efficiency. Marc has delivered multiple global supply chain transformations projects that included strategy, organization, processes and system transformation. Marc is the former Supply Chain Management (SCM) Lead of the Institute for Business Value and one of its founding members. Prior to joining IBM Global Business Services, He was a supply chain director at PricewaterhouseCoopers in France and the United Kingdom. Marc Bourdé can be reached at marc.bourde@uk.ibm.com.

Karen Butner is an Associate Partner in the IBM Supply Chain Management practice, with a focus on Strategy and Transformation competencies. Karen serves as the Global Supply Chain Management Lead for the IBM Institute for Business Value. In this role, she is responsible for developing and presenting IBM's thought leadership and point-of-view strategies, white papers and associated collateral encompassing global supply chain management. Karen is also responsible for managing the development and deployment of the SCM Global Solutions Portfolio – a collection of leading, integrated end-to-end business, technology and organizational solutions to support IBM's broad and diversified multi-industry client base. Karen Butner can be reached at kbutner@us.ibm.com.

Sean Campbell is a Partner in the IBM Consumer Products Strategy and Change consulting practice. He has over 16 years of experience working with manufacturers and retailers to formulate new operational strategies and implement large-scale transformation initiatives. Sean has delivered a variety of business strategy, operations diagnostic and process improvement programs related to customer management and go-to-market activities and has led enterprise resource planning (ERP) and other large-scale change programs. Sean's particular areas of supply chain expertise include demand planning, supply planning, replenishment planning and order fulfillment. He recently led IBM's Radio Frequency Identification (RFID) consulting initiatives for the distribution sector and has delivered many RFID value proposition and implementation efforts. Sean Campbell can be reached at sean.campbell@ us.ibm.com.

Frank Crnic is a Program Director in the IBM Integrated Supply Chain (ISC) Business Growth Initiatives Group. In his current role, he is responsible for identifying marketable capabilities within the ISC and working with IBM's go-to-market organizations to develop commercial offerings. He has supply chain operational experience in the areas of procurement, engineering, and manufacturing, and has focused on reducing costs, and developing effective relationships with suppliers, as well as internal clients within IBM's hardware business units. He played a key role in developing IBM's Direct Procurement early involvement process, and has managed complex projects with global strategic and operational content, including outsourcing of key hardware development and manufacturing projects for IBM. Frank Crnic can be reached at crnic@us.ibm.com.

Dietmar Geuder is a Senior Consultant for Supply Chain Management with IBM Global Business Services in Germany and a member of the IBM Institute for Business Value. He has over ten years of experience, consulting major industrial clients in procurement, supply chain planning and logistics in large scale international projects. Dietmar Geuder can be reached at geuder@de.ibm.com.

Tig Gilliam is the Global Supply Chain Management Leader for IBM Global Business Services. The Supply Chain team serves clients in all industries and focuses on improving and transforming Supply Chain performance through strategic change, process improvement, enabling technology and outsourcing of supply chain processes, systems and infrastructure. From 2002 to 2004, Tig led the Consumer Products Industry Practice for IBM's Global Business Services and from 1998 to 2002, he led the Consumer Products and Retail Industry Practice for PricewaterhouseCoopers Consulting. Tig Gilliam can be reached at tig.gilliam@us.ibm.com.

Harris Goldstein is an Associate Partner with the IBM Global Business Services Supply Chain Management consulting practice. He has over 20 years of experience in automotive, electronics, aerospace, consumer foods, healthcare, government, and insurance. His expertise includes sourcing, procurement, product lifecycle management, strategic planning for information systems, and electronic commerce. His has led strategy, business transformation, process development and technology implementation projects. Harris Goldstein can be reached at hmgolds@ us.ibm.com.

Charlie Hawker is a Partner in the IBM United Kingdom Supply Chain Management practice and the Procurement Service Leader. He has 22 years of experience in management consulting, 15 of those years as a Partner with Coopers & Lybrand, PricewaterhouseCoopers and now with IBM. He led the European Supply Chain consulting practices of PricewaterhouseCoopers Consulting and IBM for 6 years from 1998 to 2004 and has also operated in other significant global leadership positions. His scope of responsibilities has covered all areas of supply chain management: supply chain strategy, planning, sourcing and procurement, logistics, product lifecycle management, physical asset management, operations improvement and supply chain ERP. Over the past 15 years he has gained extensive experience working with major clients across Europe, the United States and Asia Pacific to restructure and radically improve the performance of their global and domestic supply chains. Charlie Hawker can be reached at charlie.hawker@uk.ibm.com.

James Kalina is an Associate Partner with the IBM Global Business Services, Supply Chain and Operations Solutions consulting practice. He has over 16 years of experience in the automotive, electronics, aerospace, entertainment, life sciences, and travel and transportation industries. His functional expertise includes strategic sourcing, commodity management, organizational design, eProcurement, and business process outsourcing. His technical expertise includes project management, business process transformation, procure to pay optimization and business development. James Kalina can be reached at jim.kalina@us.ibm.com.

Udo Kleemann is a Senior Manager within the ISC Production Procurement team with over 25 years of technical leadership and managerial experience across IBM's Integrated Supply Chain (ISC) from production procurement, cost engineering, manufacturing engineering to supply chain management, materials management and logistics. The Production Procurement organization is responsible for the acquisition of over US$20 billion of goods in support of IBM's hardware storage and technology products such as IBM TotalStorage DS6000 and DS8000. Notably, Udo developed and patented a supply/demand collaboration tool, RSC@, which was utilized with 95 percent of the IBM Production Procurement supplier base from 1998 until 2005. Udo Kleemann can be reached at udo.kleemann@de.ibm.com

Peter J. Korsten is one of the two Europe, Middle East and Africa Leaders of the Strategy and Change Services practice with IBM Global Business Services and also leads the IBM Institute for Business Value in Europe, Middle East and Africa (the R&D/think tank unit of Global Business) and is one of the global Executive Directors of the Institute. He became a member of 'The IBM Global Business Services Executive Leadership Team' in 2001 (the group that heads IBM's Global Business Services in EMEA) and is a member of the IBM Global Business Services Global Senior Leadership Team. In addition to his work for IBM Global Business Services he spends a substantial part of his time as global account partner for several of IBM's global clients in the industrial sector. Peter Korsten can be reached at peter.korsten@nl.ibm.com.

Grace Lin is a Consultant in the Financial Management practice within IBM Global Business Services. Grace is certified in transportation and logistics by the American Society of Transportation and Logistics. Her knowledge includes inter-functional perspectives in the areas of end-to-end value-added supply chain management. Elements include purchasing, strategic sourcing, all modes of transportation in the selection and management, and inventory management as well as its policy and techniques. Through obtaining the information systems degree, she also gained fundamental understanding of the intertwined relationship between information technology and supply chain management and applied both in various case studies throughout her school years. Grace Lin can be reached at gracelin@us.ibm.com.

Robert Luby, Jr., is a Vice President in IBM Global Business Services. He leads the Supply Chain Management Services practice for the entire public sector. He has over 30 years of logistics, supply chain management, and project management experience. He is also a key partner on IBM's Defense Industry Team. His clients include the Defense Logistics Agency (DLA), various Defense Supply Centers, several major defense depots, public and private shipyards, aviation depots, and defense suppliers. Robert has been in the forefront of the development of supply chain strategy for many defense clients. He has also been the partner responsible for leading strategic sourcing efforts both with the Department of Defense and its suppliers. Robert Luby, Jr. can be reached at robert.e.luby@us.ibm.com.

Robert McCarthy, Jr. was an Associate Partner in the Supply Chain Strategy practice in IBM Global Business Services. He has now joined the IBM Software Group as the Industrial Sector Alliance Manager focused on extended enterprise collaboration issues. He provided consulting services to clients across a broad range of industries, including retailing, high-tech electronics, aerospace, consumer products, process and petroleum, and other industries. Robert McCarthy, Jr. can be reached at remccar@us.ibm.com.

Derek Moore is an Associate Partner in IBM Global Business Services. He is currently focused on the Freight Logistics provider industry, where he is responsible globally for the development of IBM business solutions. His interests straddle business strategy, change and supply chain strategy. His clients have included DHL Express, DHL Danzas Air & Sea, UPS, Federal Express, Parcelforce, Royal Mail, UK Ministry of Defence, Marks & Spencer and Grundfos. Derek Moore can be reached at derek.moore@uk.ibm.com.

George Pohle is the Global Leader of the IBM Institute for Business Value and a Vice President in IBM Global Business Services, with over 20 years of consulting and line management experience. The IBM Institute for Business Value is a world-wide group of consultants that creates practical thought leadership on industry-specific and cross-functional business issues for our clients' senior executives. Previously, Mr Pohle led the Communications Sector for IBM Global Business Services' Strategy Consulting practice, serving the telecommunications, media and entertainment and utilities industries. He joined IBM through its acquisition of Mainspring, a boutique strategy consulting firm. There he founded and led the Communications and Media Strategy Consulting practice, creating a vibrant practice that attracted a world-class team of consultants that rapidly built relationships with numerous Fortune 500 companies. Prior to joining Mainspring, he held key positions in strategy and business development at Lucent, and led the Americas Strategy Consulting Practice at Gemini Consulting/The MAC Group. George Pohle can be reached at pohle@us.ibm.com.

Shanker Ramamurthy is the Global Leader of IBM's Financial Services Strategy and Change consulting practice. He also is one of the lead authors of the Component Business Modelling (CBM) method and is the global leader for IBM's CBM initiative. Shanker is a qualified accountant with an undergraduate degree in mathematics, an MBA in Finance and a Masters in Information Science. He has over 20 years of consulting experience and specializes in business strategy, IT strategy and business transformation. He has consulted widely to Fortune 100 enterprises in North America, Europe and the Asia Pacific region. He is a widely quoted speaker and has authored several papers by leveraging his experience in transforming large enterprises. Shanker Ramamurthy can be reached at shanker.ramamurthy@us.ibm.com.

Christian Seider is a Business Development Manager for IBM Direct Procurement Services. He has more than 9 years of consulting experience covering a wide range of supply chain management topics with a special focus on sourcing and procurement. Christian has advised clients from automotive, electronics, aerospace and defense, finance and distribution industry and has delivered tangible benefits with true bottom-line impact. He has led many projects spanning business strategy through implementation. Today, he is part of IBM's leadership team that defines new service offerings and go-to-market strategies related to Direct Procurement. Christian Seider can be reached at christian.seider@ de.ibm.com.

Stavros Stefanis is a Partner in the IBM Supply Chain Strategy practice leading the Automotive Supply Chain Strategy team. Key areas of expertise are: product development, innovation management, service parts management, quality management, connected vehicle/embedded systems, integrated customer experience, incentives management, quality management, supply chain planning and shop floor control. Stavros has nearly 15 years of supply chain management and product development consulting experience including significant time dedicated to design-manufacture anywhere value chains. Stavros has published over 25 full length papers in many business and academic magazines and has over 30 conference presentations in large industry and academic events. He has also published a chapter entitled "Product Lifecycle Management Methods and Best Practices" on Webster's encyclopedia of electrical engineering and is currently authoring a book entitled "Automotive Transformation from Cradle to Grave." Stavros Stefanis can be reached at stefan1@us.ibm.com.

Colin Taylor is an Associate Partner in Supply Chain Management Services with IBM Global Business Services. He is a member of the senior leadership team for the Logistics Practice which provides consulting and solution integration services for logistics strategy, network design, outsourcing, warehousing, distribution and transportation. With proven leadership in developing new service model solutions, Colin draws upon 27 years of international management experience that spans import/ export logistics, outsourcing, business development, manufacturing, military logistics, software development and industrial engineering. Through senior management roles, Colin has led ocean transportation programs, information technology services and maintenance/repair initiatives to generate significant client savings and transform business performance. Colin Taylor can be reached at colintaylor@us.ibm.com.

Simon Terry is a Partner with IBM Global Business Services. He leads the Supply Chain Management practice in the United Kingdom's Distribution Sector. Simon has 17 years in Supply Chain Management working primarily with consumer products and pharmaceutical companies in Europe, North America and Asia Pacific. He has extensive experience working with major multinational companies to redesign, optimize and implement world-class supply chains. Simon Terry can be reached at simon.terry@uk.ibm.com.

Theo Theocharides is the Procurement Lead for IBM Global Business Services in the United Kingdom. Theo has worked in purchasing and supply chain management and other strategic business roles for 20 years, the last 12 years of which have been at the Director level. His previous experience has been in consulting, pharmaceutical sectors, chemical and building materials. Of particular note are Glaxo Wellcome Plc, Laporte Plc and Blue Circle Industries Plc. He has worked in a broad spectrum of strategic areas including, international logistics, global procurement, business strategy, mergers and acquisitions and total quality management. Particular skills and interests are category management, global sourcing, organizational development, procurement transformation and e-commerce. Theo is a Fellow of the Chartered Institute of Purchasing & Supply. Theo Theocharides can be reached at theotheo@uk.ibm.com

Mark Wilterding is a Partner and Global Product Lifecycle Management Leader for IBM Global Business Services. Prior to assuming this role, Mark was the IBM Global Business Services' Partner and Asia Pacific Leader for the Industrial Sector, which comprises the automotive, aerospace and defense, chemicals and petroleum, electronics industries, and industrial products clients in Japan, China, India, Southeast Asia, Korea and Australia. He is a member of the steering committees for the worldwide Industrial Sector practice, the IBM Institute for Business Value, and the Strategy and Change's IT Strategy competency offerings. He is also actively engaged with numerous key industry focus clients to provide thought leadership and direction to the industry and client relationship partners for their work with first of a kind, emerging and leading edge engagements. Mark Wilterding can be reached at mwilter@us.ibm.com.

Endnotes

[1] "Expanding the Innovation Horizon: The Global CEO Study 2006." IBM Corporation. March 2006. The largest survey ever undertaken based on in-person CEO interviews, this survey polled more than 750 top CEOs worldwide, representing all major countries and industries. The survey is intended to provide a comprehensive view of the CEO planning agenda for the next two to three years. http://www.ibm.com/BCS/ceostudy

[2] IBM Global Business Services analysis, 2006.

[3] "The specialized enterprise" study conducted by the IBM Institute for Business Value, 2004.

[4] "Expanding the Innovation Horizon: The Global CEO Study 2006." IBM Corporation. March 2006. The largest survey ever undertaken based on in-person CEO interviews, this survey polled more than 750 top CEOs worldwide, representing all major countries and industries. The survey is intended to provide a comprehensive view of the CEO planning agenda for the next two to three years. http://www.ibm.com/BCS/ceostudy

[5] "Follow the leaders: 2006 Value Chain Study." IBM Institute for Business Value. 2006.

[6] Ibid.

[7] Ibid.

[8] Ibid.

[9] Ibid.

[10] Ibid.

[11] Ibid.

[12] Ibid.

[13] Ibid.

[14] Ibid.

[15] Ibid.

[16] Ibid.

[17] Ibid.

[18] Ibid.

[19] Ibid.

[20] Ibid.

[21] All information in the sidebar is based on an IBM Global Business Services analysis, 2006.

[22] Burket, Michael of AMR. "Perfect Product Launch." *Supply Chain Management Review.* July 1, 2005.

[23] "Expanding the Innovation Horizon: The Global CEO Study 2006." IBM Corporation. March 2006. The largest survey ever undertaken based on in-person CEO interviews, this survey polled more than 750 top CEOs worldwide, representing all major countries and industries. The survey is intended to provide a comprehensive view of the CEO planning agenda for the next two to three years. http://www.ibm.com/BCS/ceostudy

[24] Ibid.

[25] Davis, Trevor. "Innovation and Growth: A Global Perspective." IBM Corporation. 2000.

[26] "Follow the leaders: 2006 Value Chain Study." IBM Institute for Business Value. 2006.

[27] "Advance monthly sales for retail and food services." U.S. Department of Commerce. March 14, 2006.

[28] Hyde, Linda. "Twenty Trends for 2010: Retailing in an Age of Uncertainty." *Retail Forward.* April 2003.

[29] Ibid.

[30] Witty, Michael, Jay Holman and Jason Spaulding. "CPG Manufacturing Industry Update, 1Q06." Manufacturing Insights, an IDC company. Document #M1201026. March 2006.

[31] Ibid.

[32] "Follow the leaders: 2006 Value Chain Study." IBM Institute for Business Value. 2006.

[33] Ibid.

[34] Ibid.

[35] Ibid.

[36] Taking Center Stage: The 2005 Chief Procurement Officer Study. IBM Global Business Services. IBM consultants spoke at length with 45 Chief Procurement Officers (CPOs) from 14 different industries about current performance and their views on critical procurement topics.

[37] These interviews are the source for the statistics, graphs and quotations featured in this paper.

[38] "Follow the leaders: 2006 Value Chain Study." IBM Institute for Business Value. 2006.

[39] "Low-Cost Country Sourcing Success Strategies – Maximizing and Sustaining the Next Big Supply Savings Opportunity." Aberdeen Group, Inc. June 2005.

[40] Banister, Judith. "Manufacturing earnings and compensation in China." Monthly Labor Review. August 2005.

[41] "Insights and Advice, Design-to-Procure." Aberdeen Group, Inc. Research Brief. May 2005.

[42] "Follow the leaders: 2006 Value Chain Study." IBM Institute for Business Value. 2006.

[43] IBM Global Business Services analysis, 2006.

[44] Tohamy, Noha. Adaptive Trading Networks." Forrester Research. April 21, 2005

[45] All information in the sidebar is based on an IBM Global Business Services analysis, 2006.

[46] IBM Global Business Services analysis, 2006.

[47] Ibid.

[48] Ibid.

[49] Ibid.

[50] Ibid.

[51] IBM Global Business Services analysis based on financial data from Thomson Financial and on WACC data from Ibbotson & Associates.

[52] IBM Global Business Services estimates this to be typically up to 50 percent.

[53] For the full report, see "EPC: A Shared Vision for Transforming Business Processes." Global Commerce Initiative and IBM, 2005.

[54] Most recycling opportunities rely on item-level tagging of large-ticket items (e.g., appliances and electronics).

[55] This type of application would require the use of tags with additional functionality for which standards have yet to be defined.

[56] The enhanced store experience and transformed customer experience sections are based, in part, on ideas presented in "METRO Group RFID Innovation Center: Key technology put to the test," METRO AG, October 2004; and "Item-level RFID technology redefines retail operations with realtime, collaborative capabilities," IBM Corporation, March 2004.

[57] "17 Billion Reasons to Say Thanks." Nelson, John E. and Vineet Garg. "The 25th Anniversary of the U.P.C. and Its Impact on the Grocery Industry." PricewaterhouseCoopers. 1999.

[58] Ibid

[59] The root causes and different levels of impact of out-of-stocks for manufacturers and retailers have been well documented in several recent industry studies.

[60] "Shrinkage: A Collaborative Approach to Reducing Stock Loss in the Supply Chain." ECR Europe. 2003.

[61] Haeckel, S. H. and A. J. Slywotsky. "The Adaptive Enterprise: Creating and Leading Sense and Respond Organizations." Harvard Business School Press. 1999.

[62] Lin, G. Y., S. Buckley, H. Cao, N. Caswell, M. Ettl, S. Kapoor, L. Koenig, K. Katircioglu, A. Nigam, B. Ramachandran, and K. Y. Wang. "The Sense and Respond Enterprise: Value Net Optimization." *ORMS Today*. April 2002.

[63] "Sense and Respond Logistics: Co-evolution of an Adaptive Capability," Office of Force Transformation. http://www.oft.osd.mil/initiatives/srl/srl.cfm. May 6, 2004.

[64] Alberts, D. S., J. J. Garstka, and F. P. Stein. "Network Centric Warfare." CCRP. May 1999.

[65] Lin, G. Y., R. Luby Jr., and K. Y. Wang. "Sense-and-Respond Military Transformation." *ORMS Today*. December 2004.

[66] Haeckel, S. H. and A. J. Slywotsky. "The Adaptive Enterprise: Creating and Leading Sense and Respond Organizations." Harvard Business School Press. 1999.

[67] Lin, G. Y., S. Buckley, H. Cao, N. Caswell, M. Ettl, S. Kapoor, L. Koenig, K. Katircioglu, A. Nigam, B. Ramachandran, and K. Y. Wang. "The Sense and Respond Enterprise: Value Net Optimization." *ORMS Today*, April 2002.

[68] Lin, G. Y., J. J. Jeng, and K. Y. Wang. "Enabling Value Net Collaboration." Evaluation of Supply Chain Management, ed. Chang, Y. S., H. C. Makatsoris, and H. S. Richards, Kluwer Academic Publishers. 417-430. 2004.

[69] Buckley, S., M. Ettl, G. Y. Lin, and K. Y. Wang. "Intelligent Business Performance Management – Sense and Respond Value Net Optimization." Advances in Supply Chain Management, ed. Fromm, H., and C. An, (ed.), Springer. 2005.

[70] "Operational Sense and Respond Logistics: Co-Evolution of an Adaptive Enterprise Capability." Office of Force. November, 2004.

[71] Available for Global, North America, Europe, ANZ, Japan, India and China.

IBM INSTITUTE FOR BUSINESS VALUE

IBM Global Business Services, through the IBM Institute for Business Value, develops fact-based strategic insights for senior business executives around critical industry-specific and cross-industry issues. This book is based on in-depth studies by the Institute's research team. It is part of an ongoing commitment by IBM Global Business Services to provide analysis and viewpoints that help companies realize business value. For more information, visit us on the Web at **ibm.com**/iibv or send an e-mail to iibv@us.ibm.com.

IBM GLOBAL BUSINESS SERVICES

With business experts in more than 160 countries, IBM Global Business Services provides clients with deep business process and industry expertise across 17 industries, using innovation to identify, create and deliver value faster – from strategy through implementation. We draw on the full breadth of IBM capabilities, helping clients implement solutions designed to deliver business outcomes with far-reaching impact and sustainable results.

IBM provides Supply Chain leadership from geographic and competency perspectives. These individuals are experts in Supply Chain Management and can offer additional insights on the topics presented in this publication.

Supply Chain Geographic Leaders

- Global and Americas – Tig Gilliam (tig.gilliam@us.ibm.com)
- Northeast Europe – Andrew Jackson (andrew.d.jackson@uk.ibm.com)
- Southwest Europe – Philippe Kagy (philippe.kagy@fr.ibm.com)
- Asia Pacific – Yeonho Yoo (yeonho.yoo@kr.ibm.com)

Supply Chain Competency Leaders

- Strategy – Michael LaRoche (mlaroche@us.ibm.com)
- Product Lifecycle Management – Mark Wilterding (mwilter@us.ibm.com)
- Planning – David Spade (david.spade@us.ibm.com)
- Procurement – Robin Tomlin (robin.tomlin@us.ibm.com)
- Logistics – Maurice Trebuchon (maurice.a.trebuchon@us.ibm.com)
- Operations and Asset Management – Joel McGlynn (jpmcgly@us.ibm.com)
- Supply Chain Optimization – Gary Cross (cross@us.ibm.com)

For more information about IBM Supply Chain Management Services, please visit www.ibm.com/bcs/supplychain or send an e-mail to scmcomm@us.ibm.com.

Index